The Gray Zone Playbook

The Gray Zone Playbook

Winning Without War in the 21st Century

By

Elvin Karadzi

Vij Books
New Delhi (India)

Published by

Vij Books
(Publishers, Distributors & Importers)
4836/24, 3rd Floor, Ansari Road
Delhi - 110 002
Phone: 91-11-43596460
Mobile: 98110 94883
e-mail: contact@vijpublishing.com
www.vijbooks.in

ISBN: 978-93-47436-98-7 (PB)

This book was developed using advanced writing tools to support the drafting and ideation process. All content has been thoughtfully curated, refined, and reviewed to ensure quality and relevance.

The Gray Zone Playbook

Winning Without War in the 21st Century

By

Elvin Karadzi

Vij Books

New Delhi (India)

Published by

Vij Books
(Publishers, Distributors & Importers)
4836/24, 3rd Floor, Ansari Road
Delhi - 110 002
Phone: 91-11-43596460
Mobile: 98110 94883
e-mail: contact@vijpublishing.com
www.vijbooks.in

ISBN: 978-93-47436-98-7 (PB)

This book was developed using advanced writing tools to support the drafting and ideation process. All content has been thoughtfully curated, refined, and reviewed to ensure quality and relevance.

Contents

Introduction

A fishing boat drifts at dawn, its hull scuffed from years of honest labour. At a distance, it looks almost picturesque: a silhouette against a rose-coloured horizon, nets coiled neatly, crew moving with the practised ease of those who measure time by tides rather than clocks. Yet the picture lies. Beneath the deck, antennae hum softly. The vessel's transponder broadcasts a forged identity. Its course, though meandering to the untrained eye, follows a precise pattern—one that traces the perimeter of contested waters. Before noon it will shadow a neighbouring patrol ship, collect signals, and quietly report its findings to a military command centre miles inland. Should it be intercepted, the crew will deny everything, scoffing at the suggestion of foreign ties. By evening, they will merge once more into the wider fleet of civilian craft, another ghost in a sea dense with ambiguity.

This is how modern conflict increasingly begins—not with grand declarations or the thunder of artillery, but with small, deliberate movements designed to pass beneath the threshold of conventional war. A server fails in a distant capital. A pipeline's pressure falters. A shipment is "delayed for routine inspection", though the routine in question appears nowhere in any regulation. A political rumour flares online, too precise to be accidental yet too slippery to trace. These events rarely make headlines at first. They look like glitches, bureaucratic hiccups, or the by-products of our complex, interdependent world. Only later does a pattern emerge: the slow tightening of a vice, one deniable pressure point at a time.

If there is a surprise in all this, it is not that states behave strategically—they always have—but that they now wield strategies capable of inflicting profound harm without ever triggering the legal or moral tripwire of "war". The battlefield, such as it is, has migrated into the shadows. Governments have learned that subtle tools—covert hacking, off-the-books militias, maritime militias masquerading as fishermen, economic blockades wrapped in administrative language—can achieve what force of arms once attempted, often with greater efficiency and far less scrutiny. A nation can now lose influence, territory, market access, or political stability without a single formal shot fired. The violence is real, yet the war is technically unreal. This paradox defines the twenty-first century's emerging strategic landscape, a landscape that demands a new vocabulary and, more importantly, a new understanding.

Grey zone conflict is not a wholly new invention. History is replete with boundary-testing statecraft, back-channel manoeuvres, and calculated ambiguities. But never before have the tools of sub-threshold coercion been so fast, so global, and so difficult to attribute. Technology has transformed the ancient art of plausible deniability into a near science. A shell company can route funds through half a dozen jurisdictions before breakfast. A cyber intrusion launched from one continent may appear, with clever obfuscation, to originate from another. A paramilitary force can be trained, deployed, resupplied, and evacuated with minimal visibility, shrouded by the fog of digital misinformation. The battlefield has dissolved into a series of contested spaces—territorial, economic, informational—where advantage is pursued through constant pressure rather than decisive blows.

For individuals and societies, this shift presents immediate stakes. We tend to imagine peace as the absence of war, yet the grey zone demonstrates how a nation may be destabilised, industries disrupted, and civil trust eroded well before any declaration of hostilities. Critical infrastructure can be sabotaged by unseen actors. Public debate can be poisoned by disinformation campaigns that appear organic. Companies can find themselves collateral in geopolitical manoeuvres, punished for their origin, their supply chains, or their perceived alliances. Citizens may wake to find their financial systems strained or their borders probed—not enough to provoke mobilisation, but enough to unsettle the ground beneath their feet. In such an environment, uncertainty becomes a weapon unto itself.

It is tempting to view these developments as anomalies: temporary distortions in a world still recovering from economic shocks, digital transformation, and shifting geopolitical balances. Yet the grey zone is not a passing phase. It is a strategic method that aligns perfectly with contemporary incentives. Open war is costly, morally fraught, and reputationally disastrous. Sub-threshold conflict, by contrast, offers states the perfect compromise: the ability to coerce without crossing the line that galvanises international backlash. It thrives precisely because it operates in the cracks of existing norms and institutions. The law, after all, struggles to regulate what it cannot clearly define. Diplomacy falters when its tools—condemnation, sanctions, negotiations—depend on establishing responsibility that remains deliberately obscure.

This book takes seriously the proposition that to understand twenty-first-century power, one must understand conflict that does not call itself conflict. It asks: what does strategy look like when the goal is to advance interests without triggering war? How do states exploit legal grey areas, digital anonymity, and global interdependence? Why do certain tools—proxies, hackers, maritime militias, financial pressure—prove so effective? And how should governments, companies, and civil society respond when threats arise from actors who insist they are doing nothing at all?

The chapters that follow explore this landscape from multiple angles, each offering a window into a domain of influence where ambiguity is not a flaw but a feature. We examine how covert militias blur the line between state and non-state violence. How cyber operations strike at critical systems while maintaining the veneer of plausible deniability. How legal institutions become battlegrounds as much as courts. How maritime spaces, long governed by customs of navigation, are reshaped by fleets that fly flags when convenient and discard them when not. How economic leverage can be exerted with extraordinary subtlety—sometimes through sanctions, sometimes through the quiet manipulation of supply chains. How information itself becomes both shield and blade, weaponised to distort public understanding or amplify division.

Running through all of this is a recurring motif: the shadow line. It is the line that separates peace from conflict, public truth from private strategy, visible events from hidden intentions. In the grey zone, this line is never stationary. It shifts as states experiment with new tactics, test the boundaries of legal interpretation, or probe their rivals' tolerance for risk. Understanding the shadow line—its movement, its logic, its emotional weight—is essential. For it is here, in the murky space between what is permitted and what is provable, that modern power resides.

The book does not treat the grey zone as a realm of mystery for its own sake. Nor does it romanticise clandestine manoeuvres. Instead, it seeks clarity in conditions that are deliberately opaque. It aims to equip readers with the ability to recognise patterns that often go unnoticed until consequences accumulate. By weaving together history, contemporary case studies, and strategic analysis, it provides a framework for thinking about conflict as a gradient rather than a switch. It challenges the assumption that peace is binary and encourages a more nuanced appreciation of how states exert pressure in ways that fall short of conventional war yet exceed normal competition.

We explore questions that resist easy answers. When does strategic ambiguity become strategic recklessness? How can a state defend itself against threats it cannot attribute with certainty? What responsibilities do private companies bear when their infrastructure becomes a target or their services exploited by hostile actors? How should democratic societies preserve transparency and trust when information itself is manipulated at scale? Can international law evolve to confront tactics designed specifically to exploit its slowness and ambiguity?

By the time readers reach the later chapters, they will see that the grey zone is not a single domain but an interconnected system. A cyber intrusion may support a legal campaign. A maritime standoff may be accompanied by an online disinformation surge. A proxy militia may be funded through economic networks engineered to evade detection. Each tactic gains potency from its entanglement with the others. The challenge for policymakers, military planners, business leaders, and citizens is to recognise these entanglements early enough to respond with agility rather than outrage.

The purpose of this book, then, is not merely to describe the grey zone but to illuminate the choices it forces upon us. Choices about resilience, accountability, and the kind of global order we wish to inhabit. In a world where confrontation rarely declares itself, preparedness must take a different form: broader awareness, sharper analysis, stronger institutions, and a willingness to adapt old doctrines to new realities. The grey zone rewards those who understand its logic and punishes those who cling too firmly to expectations shaped by earlier eras.

As you turn the pages ahead, consider the shadow line again. Consider how its shifting contours reveal not only the strategies of states but also the vulnerabilities of societies. Consider, too, the possibility that avoiding war is no guarantee of safety. Conflict has not disappeared; it has migrated, dispersed, and disguised itself. It waits in policy briefs, in server logs, in shipping lanes, in courtrooms, in financial ledgers, in the unassuming boat bobbing at dawn.

The questions this book poses will accompany you long after the introduction ends. How do we navigate a world where pressure is applied without acknowledgement? Where aggression is calibrated to remain deniable? Where the tools of coercion are mundane enough to be missed until their effects become undeniable? And most critically: how do we

ensure that defending ourselves does not erode the very principles we hope to protect?

The grey zone is already here. The task now is to understand it—not fearfully, but with clear eyes and steady judgement. With that understanding comes the possibility of resilience, prudence, and perhaps a more honest kind of peace.

Chapter 1

Understanding the Sub-Threshold Battlefield

At first glance, it seemed like nothing more than a bureaucratic hiccup: a coastal nation complaining that several of its communication relays had begun behaving oddly, dropping signals with maddening irregularity. Engineers blamed humidity, ageing equipment, or the erratic quirks of maritime weather systems. Only later did analysts uncover the truth. The failures traced back to a handful of barely detectable intrusions—subtle, coded manipulations routed through servers registered to defunct companies in jurisdictions not known for their transparency. No warplanes had taken off. No borders had been crossed. The world's media barely noticed. Yet for the state concerned, the incident was a quiet warning: someone had tested its defences without admitting to being there at all. The play was invisible, the message unmistakable.

That kind of moment captures the puzzle at the heart of modern conflict. Power is still contested, influence still jealously guarded, but the contest increasingly unfolds in ways designed to avoid triggering the thresholds that would traditionally demand retaliation. It is a strange contradiction: confrontations that feel unmistakably hostile yet refuse to declare themselves as such. A naval patrol encounters a flotilla of unmarked vessels darting with suspicious purpose. A government ministry discovers its internal documents have been siphoned into the digital ether. A political movement suddenly sprouts thousands of supporters online, all chanting in unison—but none of them appear to exist outside their screens. These are not the battles many were trained to recognise, yet they shape the strategic landscape with remarkable force.

States did not drift into these ambiguous confrontations by accident. The roots wind back through decades of experimentation and opportunism: early skirmishes in which governments learned how to bend the boundaries of acceptable conduct while avoiding the penalties attached to open aggression. Hybrid conflict began as a form of quiet ingenuity—a tactical sleight of hand that allowed weaker parties to probe stronger ones, and stronger states to impose their will without risking entanglement. By the time the late twentieth century ushered in globalised communications and transnational networks, governments had discovered a powerful truth: ambiguity, properly applied, could be more effective than firepower.

Those early incidents—border infiltrations attributed to rogue crusaders, radio jamming blamed on meteorological oddities, militias that appeared and vanished in politically convenient fashion—revealed something deeper. They filled gaps in conventional deterrence, exploiting the space between what was strategically provocative and what was legally actionable. A rival might feel harassed yet remain unable to point to the responsible hand. Outrage might build without evidence strong enough to rally allies. The provocateur, meanwhile, enjoyed the freedom to escalate or retreat at will. This flexible asymmetry proved irresistibly attractive to states seeking influence without the burdens of occupation or the stain of formal war.

To understand this evolution is to recognise the necessity of giving the grey zone a precise conceptual shape. *Coercion without war* is not mere strategic competition. It is the deliberate application of pressure—political, economic, informational, territorial—calibrated to impose costs while avoiding the legal and moral thresholds that define armed conflict. The use of force becomes ambiguous: is a cyber breach an act of war or a criminal intrusion? Is a militia a grassroots uprising or an outsourced regiment? Does a blockade disguised as "inspection reform" constitute aggression, or simply overzealous enforcement? The categories blur, not accidentally, but by design.

The ambiguity is compounded by a profound legal problem. International law, for all its sophistication, remains rooted in distinctions that rely on clarity of action and actor. Belligerents who claim they are *not* belligerents exploit this logic. They assert that without a declaration, without identifiable troops, without an overt kinetic strike, the accusation of warfare is invalid. It is a kind of strategic gaslighting: the aggressor insists that nothing is happening even as the consequences accumulate. Victims struggle to respond proportionately when their predicament is recognised only as nuisance rather than assault.

This is why attribution sits at the centre of modern strategy. The ability to identify who is responsible—to pierce the cloak of proxies, misdirection, and digital masks—determines whether states can respond coherently or remain paralysed by uncertainty. A telling example emerged when a financial authority in a mid-sized European state traced a series of escalating cyber intrusions to what appeared to be a loose criminal syndicate. When investigators began closing in, the group evaporated. Servers were wiped. Communication channels shrank to silence. And when a diplomatic envoy lodged a formal protest with the country suspected of sponsoring the activity, it simply denied involvement with serene calm. Without firm attribution, the crisis faded into the fog of unresolved suspicion. One could almost hear the quiet exhalation of relief from those who had orchestrated the operation. Confusion itself had been their shield.

Yet attribution, once established, can also be perilous. Naming and shaming may deter a cautious adversary, but it can equally provoke retaliation if misjudged. The decision to expose an aggressor is not simply technical—it is strategic theatre. The audience includes allies, rivals, markets, and domestic constituencies. To point a finger is to invite scrutiny of one's own vulnerabilities; to stay silent is to risk emboldening the aggressor. The grey zone thrives on such dilemmas.

Technology has multiplied these dynamics. Encryption, anonymising tools, offshore servers with cascading ownership, artificial intelligence capable of fabricating convincing identities—these developments grant states and their proxies extraordinary capacity for obfuscation. A hostile actor can launch, redirect, disguise, and abandon operations with breathtaking speed. The challenge for intelligence communities is not merely gathering information but discerning authenticity within a landscape engineered to mislead. The digital battlefield is awash with decoys, false flags, and artefacts planted to incriminate third parties. Analysts must sift through traces that may vanish in hours, sometimes minutes. They face opponents fully aware that the best offence is often to leave no clear evidence of having acted at all.

And yet, for all its novelty, this sub-threshold battlefield echoes older patterns. History is rich with quasi-wars—conflicts fought in the spaces between treaties, deniable raids carried out by privateers, feuds prosecuted by shadowy intermediaries so that sovereigns might maintain their dignity. The so-called Quasi-War between the United States and France in the late eighteenth century is a useful reference: naval hostilities conducted without a formal declaration, waged through seizures, tariffs, and patrols, all while diplomats insisted that peace technically prevailed. The tools were different—wooden hulls, letters of marque, coastal batteries—but the logic was remarkably familiar. Influence asserted through actions that avoided the ultimate political cost of war.

The continuity is important. It reminds us that sub-threshold conflict is not a product of the digital age but a recurring method by which states test boundaries, preserve deniability, and manage risk. What has changed is the speed, scale, and interconnectedness of the modern environment. A covert action in one domain can ripple instantly across others. A single cyber intrusion may support a territorial probe; a loosely affiliated militia may trigger legal manoeuvres in international courts; an information campaign may obscure a maritime incursion. The grey zone is not a place but a method—one that adapts its shape depending on the tools available.

This chapter is an invitation to step inside that method. It offers a guided examination of how hybrid conflicts took root, why governments continue to favour ambiguous tactics, and how the technological revolution has made these strategies more potent than their historical predecessors. Readers will encounter the intellectual puzzles of defining coercion without war, the practical challenges of attributing responsibility, and the enduring patterns that link contemporary confrontations to the covert manoeuvres of the past. These themes will recur throughout the book, shifting as our attention moves from cyber operations to maritime militias, from legal weaponisation to economic pressure.

But before turning to those more specialised domains, it is essential to understand the architecture of the sub-threshold battlefield itself. Only then can we appreciate why so much of today's geopolitical friction occurs in the shadows rather than in the open. Only then can we see how small actions accumulate into strategic advantage, or how hesitation in the face of ambiguity can embolden a rival.

The path ahead leads deeper into the machinery of influence and denial, where intentions are masked and consequences slow to reveal themselves. Understanding this terrain is not merely an academic exercise. It is the key to recognising early signals, identifying pressure points, and discerning the difference between routine manoeuvring and genuine coercion. If the grey zone is defined by ambiguity, then clarity—earned through careful analysis—becomes its most powerful antidote.

This chapter begins that work. The shadows are always more navigable once you learn where the light falls.

Origins of Hybrid Conflicts

On 30 January 1948, along a stretch of border near Kashmir, Indian officials reported a series of raids carried out by armed groups who were neither uniformed soldiers nor wholly independent militants. The attackers slipped back across the frontier before dawn, leaving behind spent cartridges of Pakistani manufacture and a diplomatic puzzle. Muhammad Ali Jinnah publicly denied that his government had authorised the incursions, insisting the fighters were "tribesmen" acting of their own volition. Yet their timing, coordination, and access to matériel hinted at something more organised. It was an early demonstration of state power exercised through a veil of deniability: a conflict swelling without the formal weight of a declaration. It happened quietly. It changed everything. Five men stood.

Hybrid conflict did not emerge fully formed in the late twentieth century. It grew out of a tension between two imperatives that states have wrestled with for centuries: the urge to influence rivals decisively, and the fear of triggering a full-scale war that they could not control. The Kashmir raids captured that tension with clinical clarity. They allowed one state to probe another's vulnerabilities, inflict real harm, and mobilise domestic sentiment, all while avoiding the costs—legal, political, reputational—of open confrontation. The raids followed a pattern visible in many theatres across the modernising world: an operation designed to *shape* the environment rather than seize it outright, to introduce pressure without offering the adversary an obvious casus belli. That pattern would become the motif of hybrid strategies to come: the *shadow line* separating action from acknowledgement.

The appeal of this method is not mysterious. Conventional deterrence, anchored in the threat of decisive retaliation, tends to operate in stark contrasts: peace or war, compliance or confrontation. It is effective when aggression is unmistakable. But when a provocation is ambiguous—when it can plausibly be explained as the work of unruly factions, fringe hackers, "overzealous" coastguards, or misunderstood regulatory shifts—the classic machinery of deterrence falters. Should a state mobilise over fugitives who might be freelancers? Should a navy confront a flotilla that might be fishing? Should diplomats escalate over a cyber intrusion routed through servers in three continents? The uncertainty gives aggressors freedom of manoeuvre. It *buys time.*

States learned this long before the digital age. In 1954, during the Geneva Conference, the Central Intelligence Agency supported Guatemalan insurgents under the banner of "Operation PBSUCCESS". Aircraft bearing no national insignia flew over Guatemala City, dropping leaflets and later bombs, while Washington denied any role. The absence of formal attribution clouded international response. By the time documentary proof emerged decades later, the strategic outcome had already been secured: the government had fallen. The entire episode demonstrated how hybrid tactics could circumvent the diplomatic scrutiny normally triggered by overt intervention. Show the capability, obscure the hand, and the adversary is left unable to calibrate an appropriate response.

Hybrid conflict also flourished because it solved a political dilemma at home. Leaders have always sought ways to advance strategic aims without alarming the public, draining treasuries, or attracting censure from allies. Mechanisms of plausible denial offered exactly that. Sponsoring a proxy group in a neighbouring region, deploying technical specialists to support sympathetic factions, or interfering subtly with trade flows created influence with limited accountability. The deniable character of these actions allowed leaders to adjust their narrative as needed: triumphs could be celebrated; missteps disowned; escalations blamed on others. A covert play could be marketed as restraint even as it applied pressure.

Yet these advantages raise an important question: when did such methods shift from ad-hoc improvisations to coherent strategy? Historians point to the nineteenth century "Great Game" between the British and Russian Empires, where both sides relied on spies, tribal alliances, manufactured uprisings, and covert mapping missions across Central Asia. Names such as Arthur Conolly and Yakov Potanin appear throughout the archival record, their movements threading through cities like Kabul, Kashgar, and Herat. States sponsored clandestine operations to test boundaries without provoking open confrontation. But the period's slower communications and limited global scrutiny meant these actions, while covert, did not yet form a systematic doctrine.

The twentieth century changed that. Two global wars exposed the catastrophic costs of escalated conflict, and the Cold War introduced a strategic stalemate that rendered full-scale war between superpowers suicidal. Hybrid conflict—special operations, covert funding, disinformation, deniable sabotage—became a structural feature of competition between the United States and the Soviet Union. In Angola in 1975, Cuba deployed soldiers at Moscow's request while the USSR framed the mission as independent revolutionary solidarity. In Iran in 1953, the overthrow of Mohammad Mossadegh was executed by operatives who cultivated the appearance of local unrest. Deniability was no longer an occasional convenience; it was a disciplined craft.

Hybrid strategies filled another gap left by traditional thinking: they addressed situations where force was too blunt but diplomacy too slow. When East Germany diverted water from the Spree River in the 1960s, affecting West Berlin's supply, the move was framed as an infrastructure decision, not coercion. When the Soviet Union jammed Radio Free Europe transmissions, it dismissed complaints as technical errors. When North Vietnam used the Ho Chi Minh Trail through Laos and Cambodia, it categorised the network as a logistical coincidence rather than an extension of the war. Each example illustrated how states exploited grey areas created by jurisdictional complexity, technical ambiguity, or bureaucratic opacity.

There were limitations, of course. Some operations collapsed under the weight of exposure or miscalculation. The Bay of Pigs in 1961 revealed the fragility of hybrid tactics when execution faltered. The fiction of deniability evaporated the moment Cuban forces captured U.S.-supplied equipment, and Washington's embarrassment became global. This counter-example did not undermine the logic of hybrid conflict, but it did highlight a structural truth: deniable operations depend on precision, timing, and political coherence. When these elements fail, the sponsor is left with little to hide behind. And yet, far from deterring future covert plays, such failures refined the craft. States learned to mask their fingerprints more thoroughly, diversify their proxies, and disperse operations across multiple domains.

The shadow line remained both the method and the metaphor. It reappeared in the Soviet Union's use of "little green men" in Crimea in February 2014—armed personnel in unmarked uniforms, conducting coordinated actions while Moscow insisted they were local volunteers. Their deployment mirrored earlier patterns: assemble pressure without triggering NATO's collective defence commitments, obscure the chain of command, and create confusion long enough to establish facts on the ground. The effectiveness of the tactic revealed how hybrid conflict thrives in environments where institutions hesitate to act without certainty, and certainty is precisely what the aggressor seeks to deny.

Technology enhanced these tendencies. Encryption allowed covert actors to coordinate rapidly. Offshore server farms created layers of intermediaries between actions and sponsors. Social media platforms enabled influence campaigns framed as genuine civic expression. Hybrid operations became faster, less costly, and harder to detect. A government could fund a militia, deploy cyber proxies, or manipulate commodity flows with unprecedented agility. The shadow line grew more porous and more tempting.

Hybrid strategies also played on the psychology of thresholds. Conventional deterrence depends on clear triggers—breaching a border, sinking a ship, downing an aircraft. Hybrid conflict avoids those triggers by design. A cyber intrusion may cause economic disruption yet fall short of the damage associated with kinetic attack. A paramilitary patrol may harass without firing. A covert operation may destabilise a region without revealing the sponsor. The ambiguity paralyses response and creates asymmetry: the aggressor acts with initiative; the target responds with debate.

Historical patterns reinforce this. The Quasi-War between the United States and France from 1798 to 1800 involved naval engagements, privateering, and tariff pressures without a formal declaration. President John Adams described the conflict as "half war, half negotiation", a candid acknowledgment of the shadow line mentality. The conflict's structure—deniable hostility combined with legal manoeuvring—anticipates many of the hybrid strategies visible today. The tools were different, but the incentives identical: assert national interest without risking escalation beyond control.

Hybrid conflict emerged because states recognised this truth early: power flourishes where ambiguity prevails. It is easier to deny involvement than to justify it. Easier to sow doubt than to rebut it. Easier to escalate by inches than to accept the burden of one decisive stride. The enduring motif across centuries is not technological sophistication but political psychology. Hybrid tactics endure because they grant the aggressor flexibility and the defender uncertainty.

The transition from overt to covert plays did not happen overnight. It evolved through small strategic experiments, from tribal militias used as buffers, to clandestine sabotage framed as accident, to political movements quietly funded from abroad. Every iteration demonstrated a version of the same insight: a deniable action creates room for manoeuvre. It allows a state to test boundaries, map reactions, and retreat without formal consequence. It encourages rivals to question their own intelligence assessments. It entrenches ambiguity as a strategic tool.

To grasp the origins of hybrid conflict is to see the structure beneath the shadows. Once states realised they could achieve influence without triggering full-scale retaliation, the sub-threshold battlefield became too valuable to abandon. The legacy of that discovery shapes the dilemmas of the present. The question that remains—unanswered and pressing—is whether the shadow line can hold when so many actors have learned to operate within it.

Defining Coercion Without War

At 04:46 on 12 May 2007, the Estonian government disconnected several of its online services after a wave of distributed denial-of-service attacks crippled banks, newspapers, and ministries across Tallinn. The outages lasted days. Data traffic spiked to over a thousand times the normal volume, overwhelming servers configured for routine administration rather than siege. When Estonia accused Russian-linked groups of orchestrating the assault in retaliation for relocating a Soviet-era monument, Moscow dismissed the claim. No soldiers crossed a border. No treaty was invoked. Yet the disruption forced Prime Minister Andrus Ansip to divert state resources, convene emergency committees, and confront the unnerving reality that his country had been strategically targeted by actors who refused to admit they had acted at all. Estonia had been pressured, but not in a way that traditional definitions could comfortably name. He watched systems stall.

Grey zone coercion occupies the shadow line between competition and combat. It is not peaceful by any meaningful measure, yet it is engineered to remain indistinguishable from routine friction, criminal activity, or misfortune. It unfolds in actions designed to impose measurable costs—economic delays, territorial nibbling, political destabilisation—while denying the political, legal, and moral vocabulary that would normally justify retaliation. A state seeks advantage but refuses to acknowledge the method. The paradox is that the behaviour resembles war in effect but mirrors peacetime in presentation.

Coercion without war becomes clearer when shown rather than theorised. In March 2010, South Korea's Cheonan corvette sank near Baengnyeong Island, killing forty-six sailors. The subsequent investigation, led by the Joint Civilian-Military Investigation Group, found fragments of a North Korean CHT-02D torpedo. Pyongyang rejected every assertion, calling the findings fabrication. The refusal to claim responsibility froze international deliberation. Should Seoul respond militarily to an attack the perpetrator insisted never occurred? That denial—performed repeatedly through state media—exemplified a strategy that measures success not only by inflicted damage but by the confusion it creates. The Cheonan case showed the mechanism: act, obscure, wait.

A counter-example illuminates the boundary. When Argentina seized the Falkland Islands in April 1982, its government embraced recognition of responsibility. The clarity allowed Britain to mobilise diplomatically and militarily. Deterrence functioned because the adversary did not attempt ambiguity. The conflict escalated along familiar lines because both parties accepted they were at war. This is what hybrid coercion avoids. Its practitioners reject clarity precisely to limit the defender's ability to calibrate a lawful, proportional reaction. The limitation of overt action is its transparency; the advantage of covert pressure is its doubt. This contrast reconciles the counter-example: hybrid tactics thrive when attribution is contested, flounder when actors concede authorship.

To define coercion without war is to pay attention to visible behaviours rather than stated intentions. A naval fleet increases its presence near disputed reefs. Patrol craft switch off Automatic Identification System transponders at coordinated intervals. Customs officers in a critical port begin "enhanced inspections" that delay specific categories of imports for eleven or twelve hours longer than the weekly average. A political party in a neighbouring state receives synchronised waves of anonymous donations routed through shell companies registered in Cork and Limassol. None of these acts individually breach international legal thresholds. Combined, they apply pressure as effectively as a conventional blockade or sanction but avoid the diplomatic backlash ordinarily triggered by such moves.

The blurred line between competition and combat becomes most vivid when examining decisions made within governments targeted by grey zone operations. Officials must decide whether to lodge formal protests, mobilise defensive units, or brief allies, yet each decision depends on a threshold the aggressor works hard to obscure. In February 2022, Lithuania recorded a surge of "instrumentalised migration" via its border with Belarus: groups flown from Baghdad and Istanbul, then encouraged to cross near Druskininkai. Minsk framed the flows as humanitarian. Vilnius classified them as coercion. The behaviour—the deliberate steering of vulnerable people into a geopolitical confrontation—demonstrated the elastic boundary between what is humanitarian and what is strategic. It exposed the way political theatre becomes a weapon when accountability is denied.

Legal frameworks struggle at this boundary. International humanitarian law presumes identifiable combatants, attributable acts, and a definable battlefield. Grey zone tactics upend these assumptions. When belligerents insist they are not belligerents, they exploit the requirement for high evidentiary thresholds before an action may be deemed unlawful. That insistence is a behaviour: public statements broadcast rapidly, diplomatic cables drafted with careful ambiguity, spokespeople reiterating the same line with choreographed discipline. The repetition casts doubt, and doubt delays action. The law's strength—its demand for clarity—becomes a vulnerability when an aggressor commits to opacity.

Moral challenges follow. If a state suffers a cyber breach that corrupts hospital appointment systems or contaminates water-treatment telemetry, lives are placed at risk, yet the absence of kinetic force allows the perpetrator to frame the incident as mere technical interference. Scholars such as Michael Schmitt have argued since 2017 that moral outrage often exceeds legal classification: if a hospital ward loses electricity because malware tripped a circuit, patients suffer regardless of whether the act meets the technical threshold of "attack". This reveals a tension at the heart of coercion without war. Harm is real. Intent is obscured. Responsibility floats in the fog.

Two examples clarify how the fog is thickened deliberately. During the 2014 occupation of Crimea, communications outages in Simferopol coincided with the seizure of government buildings by unmarked personnel. Vodafone Ukraine later acknowledged that fibre-optic cables had been cut. Russia denied involvement, attributing the blackout to "local activists". The visible behaviour—the synchronised disabling of communications—demonstrated coordination inconsistent with spontaneous crowds. In contrast, during the 2003 Northeast blackout in North America, cascading grid failures spread across eight U.S. states and Ontario. Investigators traced the cause to software errors and untrimmed vegetation. The event showed how easily a genuine accident can resemble sabotage. The reconciliation between example and counter-example lies in demonstrated intent. Hybrid coercion cultivates coincidence; genuine failure explains itself through engineering.

One motif threads through many of these cases: the *signal without signature*. A warning is delivered, but the sender remains obscured. States manipulate this tension because uncertainty forces victims to measure consequences rather than assign blame. A government asks: should we absorb the loss, escalate our rhetoric, or commit to defensive mobilisation? Choices must be made under informational pressure rather than strategic certainty. The aggressor's calculus relies on that discomfort.

A precise definition of coercion without war therefore rests on four observable characteristics. First, the action imposes a cost that is strategically meaningful. Second, the method is structured to remain below legal thresholds associated with armed conflict. Third, the perpetrator cultivates doubt to impede coherent response. Fourth, the cumulative effect of repeated actions shapes the adversary's decisions without resorting to force. To describe these characteristics is not to romanticise them. It is to articulate a pattern that recurs across domains: from naval harassment to cyber intrusion, from political interference to economic slowdown engineered through opaque regulation.

Moral challenges deepen further when considering civilian impact. When Russia conducted GPS jamming across northern Norway and Finland during NATO's Trident Juncture exercises in October 2018, the disruption affected commercial aircraft and regional search-and-rescue operations. Oslo protested. Moscow denied involvement. Pilots relied on alternative navigational systems. The episode illustrates how hybrid coercion often targets dual-use infrastructure—civilian systems with military relevance—to create pressure without open conflict. The moral dilemma is sharp: civilians experience the consequences while states debate whether a threshold has been crossed.

Grey zone coercion thrives because it exploits human and institutional caution. Decision-makers prefer certainty before they commit resources. Legislators prefer evidence before they authorise action. International organisations prefer unanimity before they condemn. A grey zone actor uses this preference as a strategic resource. Each delay gives the aggressor room to advance. One hour matters. Decisions drift.

Yet ambiguity is not an unlimited shield. The exposure of covert operations can reshape strategic calculations. When U.S. investigators traced the 2014 Sony Pictures hack to North Korea's Reconnaissance General Bureau, and President Barack Obama publicly attributed responsibility, Pyongyang's denial lost rhetorical force. The visibility of the act increased, and the domain shifted from covert coercion to overt diplomatic confrontation. Attribution punctures the shadow line. It transforms a hidden signal into an acknowledged act. That transformation can deter or escalate, depending on context.

Still, the core difficulty remains: how to classify behaviour that mimics war's effects while refusing its terms. The problem is not semantic. It is practical. If a state faces systematic pressure—harassment at sea, structural cyber disruption, orchestrated political interference—but cannot demonstrate intent beyond reasonable doubt, how should it respond? Mobilise fleets?

Issue indictments? Convene allies? These are costly decisions. They require clarity. Hybrid coercion operates in the gaps between costs and certainty.

The shadow line motif returns here. States step near it, test it, recoil from it, or advance past it before drifting back into ambiguity. The line moves because actors push it. The movement demands interpretation. And interpretation determines consequence.

The unresolved tension sits at the heart of strategic thought: when confronted with an adversary who insists *nothing is happening* even as pressure mounts, what threshold should govern a state's response?

Why Attribution Matters

Shortly after midnight on 23 December 2015, engineers at Ukraine's Prykarpattyaoblenergo power distribution centre in Ivano-Frankivsk watched their control screens twitch, freeze, and then execute commands they had not authorised. Circuit breakers opened one by one. Telephone lines flooded with calls as more than 200,000 residents lost electricity. When technicians attempted to override the sabotage manually, a second wave of intrusions disabled their remote terminals. Hours later, once systems were stabilised, investigators traced fragments of malware to infrastructure previously associated with the Sandworm group—a cluster of operators Western intelligence agencies linked to Russia's GRU. Moscow denied involvement. The forensic trail pointed in one direction; the political narrative pointed in another. The power was restored. The truth was not.

Attribution shaped every decision that followed. Kyiv convened emergency advisers yet hesitated to label the outage as an act of war without incontrovertible proof. Washington issued cautious statements, avoiding direct accusations. NATO limited its language, concerned that a premature declaration would expose gaps in alliance cohesion. The outage lasted a few hours. The uncertainty persisted for months. Five words mattered: *Who did this, and why?* Those questions lingered like smoke, obscuring the path to any coherent response.

The ambiguity seen in Ivano-Frankivsk illustrates a broader strategic pattern: hybrid coercion fractures the link between action and actor, turning the shadow line into both shield and weapon. When responsibility is obscured, states struggle to coordinate. They delay decisions, soften rhetoric, and recalibrate positions to avoid missteps. That delay is not accidental; it is cultivated. A grey zone actor sees value in the pause. Time buys advantage.

The most revealing examples come from cyber proxies—loosely affiliated groups that execute operations while maintaining plausible separation from states. In April 2012, a cluster identifying itself as the "Cutting Sword of Justice" launched destructive malware against Saudi Aramco, wiping data across 30,000 workstations. Within days, the group's online presence dissolved. Handles vanished. Servers were shut. Despite technical indicators linking the operation to Iranian-backed operators, Tehran dismissed the allegation as propaganda. The sequence demonstrated the elasticity of cyber proxies. They strike. They melt away. And by the time diplomats gather evidence, the trail has cooled. The visible behaviour—accounts disappearing, command-and-control servers blinking offline—creates a vacuum. That vacuum paralyses response.

Attribution matters because without it, deterrence falters. A state cannot calibrate proportionate measures if it cannot identify the perpetrator with confidence. Strategic analysts witnessed this difficulty in 2019 when Japan experienced a coordinated intrusion targeting Mitsubishi Electric. Forensic specialists identified malware variants long associated with China's Tick group, yet Tokyo opted for quiet diplomacy rather than public accusation. The absence of a definitive statement reflected a calculation: without certainty, escalation risked political embarrassment and economic repercussions. The ambiguity shaped behaviour. Silence became policy.

A counter-example clarifies the dynamic. When the United Kingdom publicly attributed the 2018 Salisbury nerve agent attack to Russia's GRU, naming officers Anatoliy Chepiga and Alexander Mishkin, the transparency unified allies. The Organisation for the Prohibition of Chemical Weapons corroborated key findings. Coordinated expulsions followed across twenty-nine capitals. Here, naming strengthened response. But the case also revealed a limitation: attribution can provoke retaliation. Russia denied responsibility and counter-expelled diplomats. Tensions rose. The public spotlight amplified the stakes. The motif returns: attribution illuminates, but illumination can burn.

Reconciling the counter-example requires recognising that attribution operates on two planes: forensic truth and political consequence. A state may possess strong technical evidence—matching malware signatures, correlating server behaviour, tracking encrypted keys—yet still weigh the diplomatic costs of revealing it. Attribution is therefore both an investigative act and a strategic choice. The decision to speak, or to stay silent, measures risk against necessity.

The difficulty intensifies when non-state actors mask state involvement. In January 2016, the group known as APT28 targeted the German Bundestag's network. Metadata routes pointed to infrastructure registered in Bulgaria but leased via intermediaries in Warsaw. The behaviour—logins during Moscow working hours, linguistic artefacts in Cyrillic—suggested state sponsorship. Yet Berlin withheld formal attribution until May 2020, when the Federal Public Prosecutor issued a warrant for GRU officer Dmitry Badin. The four-year delay showed the challenge: governments seek evidence that can survive public scrutiny and judicial standards, not merely intelligence assessments. Decisions require solidity.

The shadow line motif becomes visible again. Attribution drifts along that line, pulled by technical complexity and political timing. Each investigation asks the same question: *When does a hint become a fact?* Cyber proxies exploit the hesitation. They manipulate jurisdictional gaps—servers in Reykjavik, code compiled in Beijing, operators logged in through São Paulo VPNs. The difficulty is not simply tracing packets but interpreting a pattern designed to deceive.

This difficulty has implications far beyond the domain of cyber operations. At sea, unmarked vessels swarm contested reefs while coastguards nearby disclaim responsibility. In July 2016, Philippine patrols near Second Thomas Shoal recorded fishermen manoeuvring with military-style discipline, deploying powerful lights to disorient rival crews. Manila suspected coordination with the China Coast Guard but lacked definitive linkages to justify a formal protest under the UN Convention on the Law of the Sea. The visible behaviour created pressure; the deniability undermined collective response. Time passed. The reef's status changed by increments.

Naming and shaming can alter this trajectory. When governments attribute malicious activity publicly, they create a narrative fact that shapes markets, alliances, and political rhetoric. A credible statement commits the speaker. It invites allies to align or dissent. It pressures adversaries to respond. This is the power of visibility: it fixes what would otherwise float. Yet visibility also carries cost. A prematurely announced attribution risks error. Misattribution can undermine credibility for years. Scholars still cite the 2003 claim that Iraq possessed weapons of mass destruction—driven by flawed intelligence and political urgency—as a reminder of the dangers of overstatement. Even though that episode did not involve grey zone coercion, it demonstrates how public declarations can redefine strategic landscapes regardless of accuracy.

In hybrid conflict, misattribution can be even more destabilising. Suppose a coastal state blames a rival for disabling a radar system, only to later discover the fault stemmed from a contractor's overlooked firmware patch. The embarrassment erodes alliances. Markets react. Domestic critics gain ground. The state's future warnings carry less weight. Misstep once, and the shadow line thickens. The implication is stark: the urge to speak must contend with the obligation to be right.

Yet silence has costs too. When governments fail to name aggressors, proxies flourish. The 2015 hack of the U.S. Office of Personnel Management (OPM) compromised data on more than 21 million federal employees. For months, Washington refrained from attributing responsibility publicly, even as internal assessments pointed to China's Ministry of State Security. Only in 2018 did the Department of Justice indict two Chinese nationals. The delay reflected caution. It also revealed a consequence: strategic ambiguity expanded space for further intrusions. Each quiet month signalled that the risk of naming exceeded the benefit of clarity.

The dilemma is symmetrical. Naming may deter. Naming may escalate. Silence may preserve space for negotiation. Silence may invite further pressure. Attribution becomes a decision rather than a discovery. This decision is shaped by visible behaviours—troop movements, server activity spikes, regulatory timing—that must be interpreted within a contested narrative. It is rarely simple.

A recurring image captures this tension: the *finger pointing into fog*. States gesture toward a suspected actor, but the fog—technical, diplomatic, deliberate—limits visibility. The aggressor thrives within that fog. The defender gropes toward certainty. The question becomes: how much fog is tolerable before the defender's restraint becomes vulnerability?

The unresolved tension sits precisely there. When responsibility hides behind dissolving proxies and ambiguous signals, what standard should governments use to decide whether to call a shadow a shape, or a shape a threat?

Tech-Enabled Camouflage

At 07:13 on 14 February 2017, staff at Cloudflare's London office discovered that a stream of web requests had begun slipping through layers of their security filters with uncanny precision. The packets appeared normal. The timing was precise to the millisecond. Yet a deeper inspection revealed something unsettling: fragments of internal memory, including authentication tokens, were leaking into public traffic because a bug—later dubbed *Cloudbleed*—had been triggered by malformed HTML requests crafted with exacting detail. Within hours, researchers traced several of those malformed requests to servers registered under false identities in Kuala Lumpur and Bucharest. The operators vanished as soon as their activity became public. No state claimed involvement. No state denied it either. Instead, the exploit dissolved into the digital ether, reminding analysts that the modern battlespace favours those who can act decisively and disappear instantly.

That moment exposed a truth intelligence officers know too well: technology grants cover as effectively as terrain once did. Encryption shields intent. Offshore servers hide origin. Adaptive tools rewrite themselves mid-operation. Each capability deepens the fog, forcing investigators to measure shadows rather than illuminate shapes. The engineers fixed the bug. The actors behind it escaped scrutiny. Five facts survived.

Plausible denial becomes frictionless when digital infrastructure does the masking automatically. Show the behaviour: an operator launches a sequence of commands through a rented virtual private server in Reykjavik. Name the mechanism: end-to-end encryption. Explain the effect: the server sees packets, not purpose. Implication: any state, proxy, or individual can hide strategic intent behind a benign technical façade. Encryption was not created for conflict, yet conflict now depends on it. Intelligence units once compared handwriting or intercepted radio chatter; today they compare cryptographic hashes with no guarantee of meaning. The motif surfaces early here—the *mirror that reflects nothing.*

A second layer of camouflage emerges from offshore servers. In 2014, during the attacks on Sony Pictures Entertainment, investigators traced command-and-control infrastructure to leased systems in Singapore, Bolivia, and Cyprus. Each server was purchased with prepaid cards, routed through VPN chains, and hosted by companies that required little documentation. The behaviour—servers blinking online for minutes, then disappearing—gave investigators fragments, not patterns. When the United States attributed the attack to North Korea's Reconnaissance General Bureau, Pyongyang dismissed the claim, labelling the evidence fabrication. The servers themselves could not verify purpose. They could barely verify existence.

A counter-example demonstrates the limits. In March 2021, Microsoft disclosed that intrusions targeting its Exchange email servers were linked to a Chinese state-backed group known as Hafnium. Unlike more disciplined operators, Hafnium left logs and web shells in predictable locations, enabling rapid attribution once patches were distributed. The visible behaviour—repeated exploitation of the same vulnerability across thousands of domains—made the pattern easier to recognise. Yet this counter-example reinforces rather than negates the central claim: attribution succeeds only when an actor errs. The camouflage works until it fails. Once it fails, it forces actors to evolve. The reconciliation lies in the rhythm of adaptation: every exposure accelerates the sophistication of the next attempt.

Adaptive online tools compound the problem. Malware now rewrites its own signature every few seconds. Command sequences learn from defenders' patterns and adjust routes accordingly. In December 2020, investigators analysing the SolarWinds breach identified a backdoor—SUNBURST—that disguised itself within routine software updates. The behaviour was simple: mimic normal traffic. Name the tool: a supply chain Trojan inserted carefully months earlier. Explain the effect: defenders trusted the update because the vendor was legitimate. Implication: trust itself becomes a vulnerability. The *mirror that reflects nothing* returns, this time within legitimate code.

These mechanisms—encryption, offshore infrastructure, adaptive tools—grant hostile actors plausible denial not at the political level but at the technical one. Political denial becomes an afterthought. The real challenge arises long before states exchange accusations. Analysts must first determine whether an anomaly is malicious. If malicious, they must identify the operator. If they identify the operator, they must persuade policymakers that the identification is reliable. Each stage relies on sifting through digital noise crafted to mislead.

Intelligence agencies confront this noise with a mix of forensic patience and probabilistic judgement. They compare time zones of activity with known operator hours. They trace the lifespan of a domain—Was it registered minutes before use? Was it paid for using cryptocurrency familiar to specific groups? They examine metadata in compiled code, looking for linguistic artefacts. But these techniques are imperfect. An operator can schedule tasks to run when they sleep. They can outsource server registration. They can remove artefacts with a script. The smoke thickens.

Two examples illustrate the labour involved. During the 2018 VPNFilter investigation, the FBI found that routers infected by the malware called home to a server registered in Toronto but actually controlled from a hosting facility in the Netherlands. The behaviour—router LEDs blinking erratically—proved incidental. The crucial clue lay in a single hardcoded IP address. Naming the anomaly led investigators to a broader network associated with the group known as Sofacy. The implication was stark: one mistake becomes the thread that unravels a tapestry of obfuscation.

By contrast, intelligence analysts studying the 2017 NotPetya attack found themselves trapped in genuine ambiguity. The malware masqueraded as ransomware, yet its encryption routine was irreversible. The code included fragments linking it to previous operations attributed to Russian groups, but those fragments could be imitated. Even firms like Mandiant hesitated to declare attribution definitively until months had passed. Behaviour and signature pointed toward a likely actor, but the *mirror that reflects nothing* confused investigators long enough for the damage to cascade globally.

A recurring challenge arises from automation. Hostile actors deploy fleets of bots that scan thousands of addresses per hour, shifting identity with every connection. The behaviour—IP addresses flickering across regions—is mechanical. Naming the technique—fast flux hosting—captures the intent: overwhelm defenders with movement. The implication is profound. Analysts measure anomalies that last milliseconds. Their adversaries automate deception. The scale difference alters the nature of the hunt: humans pursue ghosts generated by machines that never sleep.

This technological camouflage affects state decisions directly. Policymakers rely on intelligence assessments that weigh evidence, identify probabilities, and present scenarios. But the absence of certainty produces hesitation. Should a government accuse another state when logs point through five jurisdictions? Should a foreign ministry issue a demarche when malware could originate from imitators? Decisions slow. Delays accumulate. The attacker benefits.

The difficulty is not confined to cyberspace. Encryption shields communication between maritime militias and command centres. Satellite links route through third-party relays. Identification systems are disabled or spoofed to imitate vessels from Panama or Belize. In June 2019, British surveillance aircraft patrolling the Strait of Hormuz recorded signals that seemed to originate from an Iranian patrol boat shadowing the tanker *Stena Impero*. Yet the vessel's AIS transponder broadcast coordinates more than twenty nautical miles away. The behaviour masked intent. The transponder misled sensors. Implication: even physical presence can be disguised digitally, turning the sea into yet another *mirror that reflects nothing.*

The camouflage is technological; the puzzle is human. Analysts sift through logs, compare build times, reconstruct server histories, and model communication graphs. They operate within constraints of uncertainty. Their task is to extract coherence from artefacts created to prevent coherence. When they succeed, attribution becomes possible. When they falter, the ambiguity shapes political space.

A credible counter-example reminds us that technology does not guarantee invisibility. In April 2022, the Conti ransomware group accidentally leaked its internal chat logs. The logs included operational details, payment records, and coded references to guidance from Russian officials. The visibility came not from failure of encryption but from human error: an insider leaked the material in response to the group's support for the invasion of Ukraine. Here, the *mirror that reflects nothing* cracked. The leak transformed speculation into evidence. It showed that sub-threshold operations remain vulnerable to old-fashioned betrayal.

Yet this counter-example reinforces a deeper truth. When attribution succeeds, it shocks because it is rare. The routine is ambiguity. Camouflage is the norm. Intelligence services operate within this norm, adjusting methods faster than doctrine. They deploy machine-learning models to cluster activity, but adversaries adapt by adding randomisation. They trace cryptocurrency flows using blockchain analytics, but actors shift to mixers or privacy coins. Every improvement triggers a countermeasure.

The unresolved tension at the heart of technological camouflage is simple to express and difficult to resolve: how do states commit to action when the evidence they see is routed through tools engineered to obscure causation?

Patterns Across History

On 7 July 1798, off the coast of Antigua, the U.S. frigate *Constellation* intercepted the French corvette *L'Insurgente*. The French captain, Michel-Pierre Barreaut, refused to yield, believing the Americans lacked authority to engage. No war had been declared between France and the United States. No formal hostilities existed on paper. Yet within minutes, broadsides tore through canvas and timber until *L'Insurgente* struck her colours. News of the clash reached President John Adams weeks later, forcing him to explain a paradox: the United States was fighting French vessels in the Caribbean while simultaneously negotiating with Paris. The "Quasi-War", as it later became known, existed in the liminal space between peace and formal conflict—a space where ambiguity did as much work as cannon fire. The guns spoke. The diplomats whispered.

The Quasi-War offers a sharp reminder that clandestine clashes have deep historical roots. Long before cyber intrusions or offshore servers, states recognised the value of operating below explicit thresholds. They probed, pressured, and provoked while denying intent. Show the pattern: unofficial blockades. Name the actors: early republics, emperors, mercantile empires. Explain the logic: minimise strategic risk while maximising influence. Implication: grey zone methods flourish whenever rulers fear that escalation may trigger consequences they cannot control.

Centuries earlier, the Venetian Republic engaged in a style of conflict that modern analysts would immediately recognise. In 1378, as tensions rose with Genoa, Venetian merchants financed and armed privateers operating out of Negroponte. These captains flew ambiguous flags, attacked Genoese convoys, and withdrew into friendly harbours long before formal declarations caught up with events. The behaviour was unmistakably strategic. Yet Venice insisted these were "entrepreneurs", not instruments of statecraft. The denial protected the republic from immediate retaliation while eroding Genoese confidence in Mediterranean routes. Venice gained months of manoeuvre. The pattern endured.

A similar rhythm shaped the Mughal–Maratha clashes of the late seventeenth century. The Maratha leader Sambhaji dispatched bands of light cavalry across Mughal lines around 1689, raiding supply depots near Burhanpur. Aurangzeb condemned the attacks as banditry. The Marathas countered that imperial officials failed to protect local populations. Both sides used ambiguity as leverage. Neither side wished to bear the political costs of committing fully to war. The raids continued. Negotiations drifted. The frontier became a theatre of competing narratives rather than set-piece battles. Again, the pattern endures: pressure without formal breach.

These examples show that clandestine conflict is not an aberration of the digital age. It is a recurring method shaped by structural incentives. States avoid open confrontation when they measure the risk of escalation as higher than the reward of clarity. They commit to deniable action because deniability itself provides manoeuvring space. In eighteenth-century Europe, privateers attacked merchantmen under letters of marque that blurred accountability. In nineteenth-century Central Asia, Russian and British agents disguised as pilgrims or scholars mapped territory, gathered intelligence, and stirred local loyalties. The Great Game's cartographers—such as Nikolai Przhevalsky and Thomas George Montgomerie—exploited plausible scholarly identities to penetrate regions where overt military presence would provoke crisis. Their journals hid strategic maps between ethnographic sketches. Their employers gained influence without firing a shot.

The counter-example that exposes the limits of clandestine manoeuvres is the Spanish–American War of 1898. There, ambiguity failed. When the USS *Maine* exploded in Havana harbour, U.S. officials framed the disaster as sabotage by Spain. Madrid denied responsibility and demanded arbitration. But neither side managed to keep the conflict within grey zone boundaries. Domestic pressure in Washington overwhelmed diplomatic caution. The conflict escalated rapidly into open war. This limitation matters: clandestine tactics depend on all parties accepting—or at least tolerating—ambiguity. When shock, outrage, or political incentives compel transparency, grey zone methods collapse into conventional confrontation.

Reconciling this counter-example reinforces the core principle: clandestine strategies thrive only when states believe they can control escalation. Where control is lost—through miscalculation, public fury, or technological accident—the grey zone narrows sharply. The lesson for history and for the present is the same: ambiguity is a strategic commodity, but a fragile one.

One motif threads through these episodes: the *hidden hand* that shapes outcomes while avoiding exposure. In medieval Japan, the Ashikaga shogunate relied on warrior-monks from Enryaku-ji to intimidate rivals without deploying official armies. Diplomatic exchanges described these monks as "autonomous actors", yet imperial court chronicles noted how conveniently their campaigns aligned with shogunal objectives. The tactic allowed Kyoto to influence regional disputes without breaching existing agreements. The behaviour remains visible even in contemporary statecraft: distance the principal, empower the proxy, deny the link.

By the twentieth century, the tools changed but the principles remained solid. During the 1956 Suez Crisis, British and French officials planned with Israel a sequence of moves designed to mimic independent Israeli action. Operation Kadesh began with Israeli advances into Sinai, prompting London and Paris to issue ultimatums and then intervene under the guise of restoring order. The choreography concealed coordinated intent. Here, the *hidden hand* widened into a full stage direction. The failure of the plan—due to U.S. opposition and rapid diplomatic exposure—illustrated how clandestine strategies can break when multiple actors misjudge political tolerance.

A second twentieth-century example, more successful, appeared during the Vietnam conflict. The Ho Chi Minh Trail ran through Laos and Cambodia, supplied by networks that Hanoi portrayed as popular support structures rather than logistical corridors. American reconnaissance pilots recorded truck convoys along Route 9 near Tchepone as early as 1961. Yet the North Vietnamese insisted these were local traders. The denial slowed international condemnation and allowed the trail to expand into a sophisticated supply chain. The behaviour—frequent movement at night, concealed depots, dispersed storage—revealed strategic clarity masked by rhetorical uncertainty. The trail endured because ambiguity served both sides: Hanoi gained operational depth; Washington avoided acknowledging that the war had effectively spilled into neutral states.

Across centuries, clandestine patterns reveal three consistent dynamics. First, states use intermediaries—privateers, militias, monks, traders—to create distance between intent and action. Second, they disguise operations within legitimate activity: commerce, pilgrimage, scholarship, or humanitarian movement. Third, they contest the narrative space vigorously. When Genoa accused Venice of supporting piracy, Venetian envoys flooded European courts with denials. When the United States accused France during the Quasi-War, Paris blamed rogue captains and shifted diplomatic posture. When modern states face allegations of cyber intrusion, they echo the same strategy: deny, delay, complicate.

The tools have changed. The principles have not. Wooden hulls have given way to leased servers. Secret orders have become encrypted channels. Pilgrims mapping mountain passes have been replaced by analysts scraping data from social platforms. Yet the *hidden hand* continues its subtle work, shaping decisions while avoiding the spotlight. Technology accelerates and expands what once required caravans or fleets. But the psychological calculus—apply pressure without triggering retaliation—remains identical.

The question that lingers, unresolved yet pressing, is whether today's actors still believe they can control the escalation their predecessors managed through narrative discipline and geographic distance. When the *hidden hand* moves at digital speed, what stops it from overreaching?

Chapter 2

Deniable Proxies in Operation

The convoy moved at dusk, its vehicles caked in the ochre dust of a frontier that officially belonged to no one. From a distance, the men appeared to be local fighters—ragged uniforms, mismatched rifles, the weary poise of those who live by improvisation. Yet the closer one looked, the more the details betrayed another story. Their radios were military-grade and recently imported. Their tactical formations reflected formal training. One of the rifles bore a serial number traced, months later, to a depot hundreds of miles across a national border. When journalists asked who these fighters were, their supposed commander replied with a shrug: "Volunteers." The sponsoring government, whose interests they advance so conveniently served, maintained the same line. It always does. Proxies thrive in the quiet space where truth bends.

A scene like this is hardly rare. The world's conflicts are crowded with actors who fight fiercely yet somehow avoid the burdens of official identity. Their flags are borrowed, their funding obscured, their loyalties understood only by those who trained and armed them. They are mercenaries who insist they are private contractors; rebels who insist they are patriots; militias who claim, with a straight face, that their sophisticated kit was purchased at the local market. They move through war zones as shadows with boots on. And at their back, in varying degrees of visibility, stands a sponsor state that claims innocence while steering events with a careful hand.

These deniable proxies form one of the defining features of the modern grey zone. They are as old as strategy itself yet newly potent in an age where governments seek influence without exposure, where conflict is easier to outsource than to justify, and where the line between combatant and civilian can be blurred with a press conference or an edited video. Their value is simple: they offer capability without accountability. A state can shape a conflict without owning it. It can escalate while feigning restraint. It can disavow, deflect, and deny even as the effects of its sponsorship become unmistakable. To study them is to enter the murky theatre of statecraft conducted by proxies, intermediaries, and masks.

The attraction for governments is both practical and political. Sensitive missions can be assigned to actors whose losses will not inflame public opinion at home, whose misdeeds can be dismissed as rogue excesses, and whose successes can be leveraged without bearing the diplomatic weight of authorship. When the Wagner Group appeared in eastern Ukraine in 2014—its fighters described as volunteers on "holiday"—the fiction served a purpose. It preserved the sponsor's plausible denial, confused international institutions, and bought time. That fiction hardened into a template replicated elsewhere: the use of disciplined yet disowned militias to contest territory, intimidate local leaders, and disrupt adversary plans.

Yet proxies are far more diverse than the caricature of masked gunmen implies. Some are mercenary outfits with formal corporate structures; others are ideological movements that align with a sponsor state's interests almost serendipitously. Some are militias embedded within diasporas; others are rebels whose grievances become strategically useful. Their categories shift, merge, and fracture, but their common trait endures: they are instruments of policy designed to keep the sponsor's fingerprints faint. Whether labelled "freedom fighters", "self-defence units", "anti-terror coalitions", or "local security committees", the variation in terminology only reinforces the underlying ambiguity. Language itself becomes a form of camouflage.

Behind the scenes, money moves with quieter purpose. Weapons are transferred through third countries. Training occurs in secluded camps or repurposed industrial sites. Shell companies fund logistics under the guise of construction, agriculture, or charitable outreach. Financial trails twist through jurisdictions with lax reporting requirements, leaving investigators with fragments instead of a map. The clandestine routes vary, but the logic is constant: complicate the forensic trail until certainty is impossible and accountability becomes negotiable. In conflict zones, crates arrive without markings; bank transfers bounce through four or five intermediaries; uniforms are deliberately mismatched to cultivate the illusion of local origin. War becomes an outsourced business with shifting ownership.

Yet every advantage carries a corresponding risk. A sponsor may believe it controls its proxies, only to discover that autonomy grows in the shadows. Proxies acquire their own interests—territorial ambitions, economic ventures, political influence—that may diverge sharply from the sponsor's script. A militia trained for "internal security" might intimidate civilians or execute reprisals that cross red lines the sponsor cannot publicly defend. The moral hazards multiply. A government may turn a blind eye to brutality because admitting involvement would be worse than denying agency. History is full of cases where a proxy's excesses forced sponsors into awkward denials, costly concessions, or spiralling escalation. Those who deploy shadows often find them difficult to gather again.

This is why investigators pay meticulous attention to the small, telling clues that reveal allegiance. A cluster of radios tuned to frequencies used by a neighbouring state's armed forces. Ammunition types inconsistent with local procurement. Medical supplies that match the packaging of foreign military stockpiles. Even speech patterns—slang, cadence, borrowed terminology—can betray a hidden lineage. Signals intelligence maps the chatter; financial forensics trace erratic flows of funds; field observers report inconsistencies that unravel official narratives. Attribution is painstaking, often incomplete, yet vital. For when the sponsor of a proxy is credibly exposed, the entire architecture of denial begins to crack.

If identification is the first step toward halting proxy conflict, ending it is far harder. Negotiators face a chessboard where pieces can refuse to move. Proxies may reject ceasefires that sponsors privately support. Regional actors may mediate to little effect because the real decision-makers sit far from the battlefield. International watchdogs struggle to enforce compliance when armed groups do not formally exist in legal terms. Off-ramps must be crafted with precision: incentives calibrated, guarantees verified, and face-saving mechanisms engineered for every party. In the grey zone, honour is as fragile as truth, and miscalculation can prolong violence by years.

The central irony is that while proxies allow states to avoid formal war, they often make exit more difficult. Once armed networks develop parallel economies and informal governance structures, they resist demobilisation. Once a state has denied sponsorship, it finds it awkward to negotiate directly. The contradictions accumulate. The conflict endures.

This chapter enters that terrain. It examines the identities and origins of proxies, the covert machinery that sustains them, the strategic calculus that makes them attractive, and the investigative craft required to pierce their disguises. It follows the tensions that define proxy warfare: control versus autonomy, influence versus deniability, short-term gain versus long-term instability. And it turns toward the difficult question that shadows the subject: how does one unwind a conflict built on actors who were never meant to stand in the light?

Proxies, after all, are more than tools. They are stories governments tell about themselves—stories of caution, restraint, plausible innocence. But every story breaks eventually. The reader now steps toward the battleground where author and instrument blur, where accountability flickers, and where the most consequential actions are carried out by those who claim to belong to no one.

Who Are the Deniable Proxies?

At dawn on 27 August 2014, Ukrainian soldiers manning a checkpoint near Novoazovsk spotted an armoured column advancing across flat steppe. The vehicles bore no national markings. The men wore mismatched fatigues stripped of insignia. Their speech—recorded later by journalists—carried the cadence of southern Russian military dialects, yet Moscow insisted they were "local volunteers" who had acquired their equipment through improvisation and luck. Within hours, the column had seized key intersections, opening a new front. Within days, the fighters had vanished back across a border others were forbidden to name. The field was silent. The fingerprints are absent. The effect is unmistakable.

Episodes like Novoazovsk reveal the essential puzzle of deniable proxies: armed actors who appear independent but move with the coordination and resourcing of a state. They sit in the grey zone between official force and plausible fiction. Their presence complicates diplomacy, distorts intelligence assessments, and reshapes conflicts without requiring governments to accept formal responsibility. To grasp their role, one must follow the *shadow line*—a recurring motif in proxy warfare—where actors exist, act, and inflict consequences while officially belonging to no one.

Deniable proxies come in several forms, though the boundaries between categories blur as frequently as they are policed. One form is the mercenary outfit—organisations that frame themselves as commercial security enterprises but operate in war zones with equipment and tactics far beyond private-sector norms. Executive Outcomes, deployed in Sierra Leone in 1995, demonstrated how a small, disciplined external force could stabilise a civil war more rapidly than international peacekeepers. Their behaviour—fast deployment, coordinated air-ground manoeuvres, strict operational secrecy—showed capabilities few corporations legitimately cultivate. States observed. They measured. And they learned that outsourced force could deliver results conventional diplomacy struggled to achieve.

Another form is the ideologically aligned militia: groups that emerge from local grievances but find themselves armed and advised by foreign states whose interests conveniently align. During the Lebanese Civil War in the 1980s, Iran cultivated Hezbollah not as a hired gun but as an ideological partner. Tehran provided training in the Bekaa Valley, funding routed through the Islamic Revolutionary Guard Corps, and doctrine that blended local resistance with regional strategy. The outcome was an organisation that claimed—and still claims—autonomous purpose while advancing the geopolitical aims of its sponsor. The proxy gained legitimacy at home. The sponsor gained reach abroad. Both denied dependency. Both benefited from the fiction.

A third category—more elusive—consists of "freedom fighters" whose narratives of liberation make scrutiny politically costly. In the 1980s, the United States channelled support to the Afghan Mujahideen through Pakistan's Inter-Services Intelligence Directorate. The arrangement allowed Washington plausible distance, Islamabad political leverage, and the Mujahideen matériel that far exceeded anything available on local markets. The training was systematic. The funding covert. The motivations complicated. When Stinger missiles downed Soviet aircraft over Khost in 1986, the evidence pointed toward a sponsor few would name openly. Here, the *shadow line* thickened, merging tactical collaboration with geopolitical secrecy.

Despite these categories, not all armed non-state groups qualify as proxies. Some militias remain genuinely autonomous, their funding local or criminal, their strategies improvisational. In parts of the Sahel, for example, community defence groups operate with little external support and often resist manipulation by state actors. Their autonomy matters: it reminds analysts that not every fighter with a foreign weapon is a proxy, and not every emergence of disciplined violence traces to a hidden sponsor. This counter-example tempers assumptions. It reinstates the need for evidence. And it reinforces that proxy status is not about composition alone but about direction, resourcing, and intent.

Yet even with this diversity, governments rely on proxies for consistent reasons. Some are strategic: a proxy offers deniability when a state measures the political cost of direct intervention as too high. Some are administrative: proxies can move faster than state institutions bound by oversight, procurement cycles, or legislative constraints. Some are domestic: casualties among proxies do not provoke the protests, budgetary debates, or scrutiny that state soldiers do. The decision to outsource violence is not driven by ideology; it is driven by feasibility.

Consider why states entrust sensitive missions to actors they pretend not to control. First, proxies create insulation. If a mission fails or draws condemnation, the blame can be redirected. When France supported Katangan secessionists in the Congo in the early 1960s, Paris denied involvement even as mercenaries under Jacques Schramme received French matériel. The denials allowed the government to reposition diplomatically when the crisis shifted. Second, proxies grant flexibility. They operate beyond the tempo of formal command structures, adapting to tactical openings without awaiting political approval. Third, proxies provide distance. A sponsor can commit influence, not flags; pressure, not declarations. The *shadow line* holds as long as the narrative remains plausible.

But proxies also carry risks, and those risks accumulate with time. Sponsors may lose control. A proxy may diverge from the script, pursuing local agendas that contradict the sponsor's objectives. The Pakistan-backed Afghan factions of the 1990s illustrate this vividly. After the Soviet withdrawal, Islamabad hoped to mould a post-war order favourable to its strategic depth doctrine. Yet its supported factions splintered repeatedly, leading to unpredictable violence and regional destabilisation. The sponsor's influence waned. Its investment became liability. The *shadow line* cut both ways.

The moral hazard is also substantial. When proxies commit atrocities—and many do—the sponsor must choose between acknowledging influence or denying involvement. In both cases, the sponsor's reputation suffers. During the Sri Lankan Civil War's final months in 2009, Tamil paramilitaries aligned with Colombo were accused of abductions and targeted killings. The government publicly distanced itself while continuing coordination behind the scenes. The contradiction proved unsustainable. International investigators documented patterns of cooperation, and the state faced prolonged diplomatic strain. Plausible denial eroded. Visibility replaced the shadow. The consequences were not easily reversed.

Still, the attraction persists because the machinery of proxy creation is well-practised and often concealed beneath layers of bureaucracy, private contracts, and informal networks. Weapons may arrive through third countries with falsified customs papers. Training camps may be hosted by "cultural associations" or "security consultancies" whose boards overlap strategically with intelligence veterans. Financial support may pass through charitable organisations registered in capitals where reporting thresholds are high and scrutiny episodic. These methods create the impression of distance. They shift the centre of gravity from overt sponsorship to carefully engineered ambiguity.

The quiet motif threading through all this is the *manufactured identity*: a fighter presented as a volunteer but trained by foreign instructors; a charity advertised as humanitarian but funded by a defence ministry; a movement that claims grassroots origins while using satellite phones distributed only through a neighbouring state's procurement channels. Each manufactured identity reinforces the proxy's usefulness. Each disguises the relationship long enough for the sponsor to deny it.

Yet even the most carefully disguised militia reveals itself in small slips. Uniforms that match no local supplier. Ammunition calibres not stocked in domestic arsenals. Mobile phone traffic that pings from foreign border towers moments before an attack. Investigators learn to measure these anomalies, compare them, commit them to pattern. Attribution becomes both art and evidence. And once a proxy's true allegiance is exposed, the strategic equation shifts. The fiction can no longer be sustained. The sponsor loses room for manoeuvre. The proxy loses its shield.

The open question, and one that defines the dilemmas of this chapter, is deceptively simple: How long can a state rely on proxies before the *shadow line* collapses, forcing it to choose between escalation and retreat?

Funding and Arming in Secret

On 4 May 1986, a chartered Boeing 707 touched down at Ilopango Air Base in El Salvador. The aircraft carried crates labelled as "agricultural equipment", yet the manifest omitted their true contents: rifles, night-vision devices, and medical supplies destined for Nicaraguan Contra fighters. The operation, run through a network overseen by retired U.S. Air Force officer Richard Secord, relied on covert financing and a web of shell entities including Lake Resources Inc., registered in Switzerland. When the aircraft was later shot down and its sole surviving crewman captured, the CIA denied involvement. Washington insisted the supply chain was private. The plane smouldered. The lie held. The logic behind it endures.

This scene sets the rhythm for one of the grey zone's most defining practices: the covert supply of weapons, training, and money to actors a state claims not to command. It is a rhythm built on indirection—crates mislabelled, contracts signed in far-off capitals, payments bouncing through banks that specialise in discretion. To follow these routes is to trace the *ghost lines* of statecraft, the quiet but deliberate channels through which governments outsource conflict while distancing themselves from its consequences.

States arm proxies for reasons that, when stripped of rhetoric, are bluntly practical. Open involvement in a conflict invites risk: diplomatic backlash, sanctions, escalation, and domestic scrutiny. Covert involvement, by contrast, offers strategic influence without the same visibility. Show the behaviour: a government supplies anti-tank weapons to a militia across its border. Name the structure: a logistics chain disguised as humanitarian aid. Explain the effect: influence without ownership. Implication: the state gains leverage while preserving a veneer of innocence.

This pattern appears in many theatres. During the Soviet–Afghan War, the United States funnelled weapons to the Mujahideen through Pakistan's Inter-Services Intelligence Directorate. The route relied on Pakistani depots, Gulf donors, and CIA funding approved in tranches that left minimal paper trail. The performance of neutrality mattered. Washington avoided direct fingerprints, Islamabad gained leverage over Afghan factions, and the fighters acquired matériel far beyond local supply. It was a system calibrated to protect the sponsor's distance while amplifying its power. The *ghost lines* ran through Karachi warehouses and into the Hindu Kush.

A second clear example surfaced when Iran equipped Hezbollah after 1982. Israeli intelligence intercepted convoys of Fateh and Fajr rockets moving through the Bekaa Valley, yet Tehran framed its support as "advisory" and routed funds through charitable foundations such as the Imam Khomeini Relief Committee. The behaviour—consistent shipment schedules, training rotations, and encrypted communications supplied by IRGC officers—revealed an institutional relationship. The narrative insisted otherwise. The gap between narrative and reality is where deniability breeds.

Not every case fits neatly. A counter-example lies in the British arming of Kurdish Peshmerga forces during the fight against the Islamic State in 2014. London publicly acknowledged the transfer of machine guns and ammunition, even inviting journalists to view the crates at Erbil airport. The clarity here challenges the assumption that all proxy arming is hidden. But reconciliation is simple: deniability is a tool, not a requirement. When a state measures reputational gain higher than secrecy, it arms openly. When it measures political cost higher than transparency, it arms covertly.

The method shifts with incentives; the *ghost lines* appear or disappear accordingly.

To supply weapons secretly, states rely on multi-layered logistical routes. One starts with training: discreet camps run by intelligence agencies or private contractors. In Angola in the 1970s, apartheid South Africa trained UNITA rebels at remote bases near Rundu, flying them in at night to minimise detection. The training included small-unit tactics, communications discipline, and mine warfare—skills that mirrored the South African Defence Force's own doctrine. The behaviour was meticulous. The intent unmistakable. Official acknowledgment absent.

Another begins with procurement. States purchase weapons through intermediaries—exporters in Eastern Europe, surplus dealers in the Balkans, or sanctioned manufacturers willing to operate through cutouts. In Yemen, some Houthi units were found using rifles marked as Bulgarian production, delivered via shipments nominally destined for the UAE. The routed path—Sofia to Dubai to the Red Sea—camouflaged the original relationship. When confronted, each intermediary offered a variation of the same answer: paperwork irregularity, routing confusion, or rogue brokers. The *ghost lines* thickened through bureaucratic fog.

Money, however, is the lifeblood of these operations. And money moves more quietly than weapons. States use shell companies registered in permissive jurisdictions—Belize, the Seychelles, the British Virgin Islands—to shift funds into conflict zones without triggering compliance alerts. During the Balkan conflicts of the 1990s, arms brokers such as Viktor Bout moved millions through companies like Trans Aviation Network Group, exploiting gaps in regulatory oversight across the UAE and South Africa. Each transfer masked intent. Each invoice disguised origin. The financial behaviour created distance that policymakers later exploited: "We do not control every company incorporated by our citizens."

Charitable fronts further obscure the trail. Organisations purporting to provide humanitarian relief have channelled funds, uniforms, vehicles, and communications gear to proxies. In Syria, several charities registered in Istanbul between 2012 and 2014 were later found by Turkish investigators to have diverted donations toward equipment purchases for armed factions along the border. Delivery manifests listed blankets and medical kits. Border inspections recovered ammunition and encrypted radios. Donors spoke of aid. Fighters spoke of supply. The tension between declared purpose and material reality was stark, but the fiction protected the sponsor from direct blame.

Despite the sophistication of these routes, the operations leave traces. Intelligence agencies use forensic techniques to follow money through correspondent banks—examining payment timings, currency conversions, and unusual routing decisions. Signals intelligence captures chatter from training camps or encrypted command channels. On-ground observers note uniform patterns, weapon serial groupings, and convoy movement rhythms. Each clue is small. Together, they expose the *ghost lines* that sponsors hope remain invisible.

Yet the secrecy comes with risks that states underestimate at their peril. First is blowback: weapons supplied covertly often circulate beyond the proxy's intended use. The U.S. Stinger missiles provided to Afghan fighters in the 1980s resurfaced decades later in black markets, prompting expensive buyback operations. Second is moral hazard: proxies perceive support as permission. In 2018, UN investigators documented abuses by South Sudanese militias backed covertly by regional actors, including forced recruitment and targeted killings. The sponsors denied knowledge. Victims dismissed the denial as insult. The *ghost lines* became moral fault lines.

Third is diminished control. Proxy groups develop internal economies—taxation networks, smuggling routes, patronage structures—that make them resistant to external pressure. The Liberation Tigers of Tamil Eelam financed their insurgency partly through diaspora contributions routed via front organisations in Canada and Switzerland. Even when sponsors attempted to alter the group's trajectory, they found limited leverage. Proxies grow opaque. Sponsors lose grip.

Yet the appeal remains powerful because covert arming allows states to calibrate involvement finely. They can increase or decrease support by adjusting delivery schedules, training deployments, or cash transfers. They can test an adversary's tolerance by arming lightly or altering the tempo of supply. They can reverse course quickly if caught. The flexibility is seductive. The accountability is thin.

One more strand complicates the picture: digital finance. Cryptocurrencies, particularly privacy-focused coins, have entered the toolkit of some proxy networks. In 2020, U.S. Treasury investigators traced fundraising for Hamas's military wing through Bitcoin wallets that used mixing services to obscure origin. The sums were modest—measured in tens of thousands, not millions—but the pattern was important. It showed that *ghost lines* can now run through decentralised systems that resist conventional scrutiny. States observe this evolution. Some will adapt it. Others already have.

A counter-example reminds us that opacity is not absolute. In 2017, after the Rohingya crisis escalated in Myanmar, several Southeast Asian charities were accused of funnelling support to Arakan Rohingya Salvation Army fighters. The Malaysian government launched public investigations, froze accounts, and released findings that contradicted the charities' claims of innocence. The exposure mattered: it demonstrated that vigilant oversight can pierce the veil. But such clarity is rare. And it arrives late.

Throughout these cases, the motif persists: the *ghost lines* that allow states to act without appearing to act. Lines that stretch across jurisdictions, financial systems, and diplomatic narratives. Lines that are often faint but consequential.

The unresolved question is this: if covert supply chains continue to evolve faster than oversight mechanisms, how long can states rely on *ghost lines* before they must confront the instability they themselves have fed?

Advantages and Risks for Sponsors

At 16:40 on 9 January 2018, a convoy of armoured pickups rolled into the outskirts of Deir ez-Zor. They flew no national flags. Their insignia had been stripped. Their fighters—many of whom spoke Russian—wore a mix of civilian and military kit. Satellite images reviewed later by the United Nations showed that the vehicles had crossed from al-Tabiya oilfield, an area overseen by Syrian government forces. Yet Moscow insisted that the men belonged to a private military company, Wagner, and not to the Russian state. When, a month later, scores of these fighters were killed during a clash with U.S. forces at Khasham, the Kremlin offered condolences while denying responsibility. The ambiguity held because the design demanded it. Moscow gained influence in Syria without the domestic fallout that body bags from an official deployment might have triggered. The dead were shadows. The sponsor remained untouched.

This incident captures the paradox at the heart of proxy sponsorship: by acting through intermediaries, states extract strategic gains while distancing themselves from the consequences. The *double mask*—a motif threaded through the proxy relationship—allows governments to speak the language of restraint while prosecuting interests with considerable force. Yet behind the mask lies a ledger of risks: actors who drift out of control, reputational damage when brutality is exposed, and blowback that reshapes security landscapes for years.

States employ proxies because the payoff can be immediate and substantial. Show the behaviour: a sponsor deploys fighters to seize resource-rich territory without crossing a formal border. Name the logic: reduced accountability. Explain the effect: strategic influence without legislative approval or diplomatic penalties. Implication: the proxy becomes a flexible extension of state policy, manoeuvring where official troops cannot. The Wagner presence in Libya after 2019 illustrates this dynamic. Fighters supported Khalifa Haftar's advance on Tripoli, installing air defences and operating artillery systems previously linked to Russian hands. Moscow maintained the fiction of distance, insisting these were "private contractors". The result was predictable. Russia gained a foothold. Libya absorbed the cost.

Another advantage lies in adaptability. Proxies move with a tempo state militaries struggle to match. They bypass procurement cycles, operate beyond bureaucratic oversight, and improvise tactics without the political risk of admitting failure. Iran's support for Shi'a militias in Iraq after 2003 demonstrates this flexibility. Tehran provided advisers from the Quds Force, smuggled weapons through Khuzestan, and funded operations targeting coalition forces. When a militia overreached or fractured, Iran adjusted support accordingly—strengthening some factions, sidelining others. The sponsor shaped the battlefield without declaring war. The *double mask* held fast.

Yet the power of proxies rests not only in what they allow but in what they obscure. A state can feign innocence when a proxy carries out a controversial mission. It can deny involvement in sabotage, covert assassinations, or territorial encroachment. The sponsor can step forward or backward depending on international reaction. This malleability is useful. It is also dangerous.

The risks begin with loss of control. A proxy armed for strategic leverage may pursue its own agenda. Pakistan's sponsorship of various Afghan factions in the 1990s offers a clear example. Islamabad hoped to create a stable, pliable government in Kabul that would provide strategic depth against India. Instead, factions splintered. In 1994, Mullah Omar's Taliban emerged, initially with Pakistani support, but soon evolved into an uncontrollable force whose decisions repeatedly clashed with Pakistan's interests. The behaviour—independent governance, severe social policies, refusal to align with Islamabad's diplomatic cues—revealed a shift from instrument to autonomous actor. The *double mask* slipped, exposing the sponsor to geopolitical consequences it could neither steer nor undo.

A second risk is blowback: the unintended arrival of consequences in the sponsor's own territory. The United States learned this after the Soviet–Afghan War. Weapons funnelled to the Mujahideen, particularly Stinger missiles supplied after 1986, circulated in black markets long after the conflict ended. By 2003, intelligence reports indicated that some missiles had migrated into networks hostile to U.S. interests, prompting costly retrieval operations. The metric—millions spent on buybacks—revealed the long shadow of what had once seemed a low-cost, high-gain strategy. The sponsor lost control of matériel. The consequences returned home.

The most corrosive risk is moral hazard. When states deny responsibility for their proxies, those proxies may interpret the distance as licence. Violence escalates. Restraint evaporates. In 2005, during operations in Sudan's Darfur region, the Janjaweed militias supported by Khartoum engaged in scorched-earth campaigns against villages thought to harbour rebels. Human Rights Watch documented patterns of coordinated attacks supported by aerial strikes from Sudanese aircraft. Khartoum denied direction, claiming that tribal conflicts had spun beyond the state's reach. Yet photographs of uniforms, satellite analyses of air–ground synchronisation, and eyewitness testimony told a different story. The sponsor turned a blind eye to brutality because acknowledging it would collapse the architecture of plausible denial. The villages burned. The *double mask* concealed political intent while revealing moral retreat.

A counter-example helps refine the argument. Not all sponsorship descends into chaos. The United States' support for Kurdish Peshmerga forces fighting the Islamic State from 2014 to 2017—implemented through openly acknowledged training programmes and conditional funding—maintained clearer lines of accountability. Washington monitored operational decisions, restricted the use of supplied weapons, and maintained formal communication channels. The result was a proxy relationship with fewer deviations and less moral hazard. Yet this case is the exception. It demonstrates that when a sponsor accepts responsibility, the *double mask* loosens; the proxy operates in an environment of oversight rather than ambiguity. It shows that the very measures designed to reduce risk require relinquishing some deniability. The reconciliation is simple: states can have flexibility or control, but rarely both.

Still, sponsors continue to choose ambiguity because it offers one more advantage: deniable escalation. A state facing diplomatic constraints can use proxies to test boundaries. It can commit operations that, if challenged, it claims to have neither ordered nor sanctioned. Turkey's support for Syrian rebel factions around Afrin in early 2018 illustrated this. While Ankara deployed its own forces openly, it also facilitated the movement of allied militias whose conduct diverged widely across fronts. When reports emerged of looting and detainee abuse, Turkish officials distanced themselves, framing the militias as autonomous local actors. Yet their coordination with Turkish units suggested otherwise. The *double mask* provided room for manoeuvre, but not immunity from reputational cost.

Attribution, once credible, transforms risks into liabilities. A sponsor exposed through weapons tracing, leaked communications, or captured fighters faces diplomatic fallout and potential sanctions. The behaviour of international bodies shifts. Allies apply pressure. Adversaries seek leverage. In 2020, after Russia's Wagner Group fighters were captured in Libya and their passports circulated publicly, Moscow faced heightened scrutiny at the United Nations Security Council. Even silence carries weight. The exposure narrowed Russia's diplomatic options in the conflict and altered negotiations with other regional actors. The *double mask* protected Moscow until it didn't.

But even with these risks, proxies persist because they allow states to calibrate involvement with remarkable precision. A government can increase pressure by adding advisers. It can signal retreat by slowing ammunition deliveries. It can reposition without announcing a shift. The efficiency—measured in political cost saved per intervention achieved—is considerable. Yet each calibration nudges the proxy's sense of autonomy, creating feedback loops that sponsors struggle to anticipate.

The thread binding all these cases is the fragile architecture of denial: the *double mask* that lets a state wield force while shrinking responsibility. It is a structure that can enable strategy but also incubate long-term instability. It offers influence at a discount but often charges interest later.

The unresolved question, the one every sponsor must face eventually, is stark: how long can a state tolerate a proxy's behaviour before the *double mask* becomes a trap—forcing a reckoning between claiming the proxy and condemning it?

Detecting Hidden Affiliations

At 02:17 on 25 June 2018, a patrol from the United Nations Panel of Experts on South Sudan entered the outskirts of Mayom. The village had suffered an attack two days earlier. The assailants claimed to be a spontaneous local militia protesting taxation. Yet on the ground, investigators recovered rifle casings stamped with factory codes used by Sudan's Military Industry Corporation and fragments of radio equipment linked to the National Intelligence and Security Service in Khartoum. The militia vanished into the bush. The sponsors denied involvement. But the matériel remained, and *the imprint of origin*—a motif that threads through every clandestine conflict—whispered a truth the denials could not erase.

This moment illustrates the central tension of proxy warfare: violence carried out by actors who insist they act alone, and sponsors who insist they have no hand in events. The work of investigators begins in that tension. They examine fragments—frequencies, payment chains, serial numbers, convoy timings—and stitch them into patterns that reveal hidden affiliations. The patterns are rarely perfect, often incomplete, but they matter. They break the spell of plausible denial that sustains proxy operations. They turn shadows into evidence.

Signals intelligence is often the first crack in the façade. Show the behaviour: a militia communicates on encrypted radios during an operation. Name the method: spectrum analysis that captures bursts of traffic at specific frequencies. Explain the significance: those frequencies align with a neighbouring state's procurement catalogue. Implication: coordination suggests sponsorship. This dynamic played out in eastern Ukraine in 2015, when NATO analysts intercepted command instructions to separatist fighters using encryption modules previously documented in Russian military exercises near Rostov-on-Don. The packets were short, disciplined, and timed with movements on the ground The intercepts, released publicly months later, didn't prove control beyond doubt, but they undermined claims of spontaneous insurgency. The *imprint of origin* surfaced through radio waves.

Financial forensics provide another route. Money leaves trails even when routed through labyrinthine structures designed for concealment. Investigators track transfers through correspondent banks, analysing timing anomalies and transaction clusters. During the Balkan wars of the 1990s, the UN's Sanctions Assistance Missions uncovered payment routes linking Serbian paramilitaries to offshore companies registered in Cyprus and the Isle of Man. The behaviour—regular disbursements in matching increments—revealed a payroll disguised as commercial activity. Naming these entities exposed a network that Serbian officials had denied for years. The implication was far-reaching: once financing became visible, pressure on the sponsor intensified, and the paramilitaries' ability to operate with impunity eroded.

A second example lies in Syria after 2012. Turkish investigators traced funds from a charity registered in Gaziantep to purchases of communications gear for armed groups near Aleppo. The charity claimed humanitarian purpose. Bank ledgers suggested something different. The behaviour—payments issued hours before large-scale offensives—offered a rhythm too precise to be incidental. Naming the pattern created diplomatic friction, but it also disrupted the flow of matériel. This is the quiet power of financial forensics: it turns anonymous transfers into political liabilities.

Yet there are limits. Not all financial flows reveal their origins. Cryptocurrency fundraising for militant groups, such as Hamas's al-Qassam Brigades identified by the U.S. Treasury in August 2020, demonstrates how anonymity frustrates tracing efforts. Wallet addresses mutate. Mixing services erase trails. The technology obscures the *imprint of origin* more effectively than offshore accounts once did. Reconciling this counter-example clarifies the challenge: forensic methods improve, but evasion evolves. No single technique is decisive. Convergence matters.

Beyond signals and finance, investigators rely on painstaking field observation. Behaviour on the ground—uniform stitching, weapon handling, formation discipline—betrays training lineages. In Mali in 2021, analysts from MINUSMA observed militia units employing fire-and-manoeuvre tactics identical to those used by Wagner personnel in CAR the previous year. The cadence of movement, the spacing of fighters, the choice of ambush sites—all aligned with Russian doctrine rather than local patterns. Show the detail: boot prints that matched foreign-made soles unavailable in Malian markets. Name the implication: external training. Explain the consequence: the militia's façade of autonomy weakened. Implication: revelations shifted diplomatic conversation, prompting ECOWAS to recalibrate negotiations with Bamako.

Weapons analysis remains one of the most reliable anchors. Serial numbers, metallurgy, and component design provide unique signatures. Conflict Armament Research (CAR), a field-based investigative organisation, documented Iranian-manufactured Qiam missile components used by Houthi forces in Yemen in 2017. The parts contained fusing mechanisms identical to those recovered from Iranian military tests. Tehran denied involvement. The material evidence told another story. This is the strength of tracing: anonymity falters when physical artefacts speak plainly. The *imprint of origin* becomes tangible.

But attribution is not merely technical; it is interpretive. Analysts compare behaviour across theatres, measure timing, and assess plausibility. If a militia gains access to advanced weapons beyond the reach of local markets, if its strategic choices align with a neighbour's geopolitical aims, if its communications spike during diplomatic crises, a pattern emerges. The pattern is the argument. In Colombia in the early 2000s, forensic evidence linking right-wing paramilitaries to elements within the Colombian military—shared ammunition stockpiles, overlapping checkpoints, synchronised patrols—forced Bogotá to confront internal complicity. The state's response, shaped by exposure, led to demobilisation agreements and a partial dismantling of paramilitary networks. Here, attribution did not simply diagnose the conflict; it reshaped it.

Investigators must also contend with deception. Sponsor states increasingly imitate the signatures of rivals to deflect scrutiny. Malware coded in Cyrillic can be seeded by actors in Tehran. Ammunition with Balkan markings can be shipped through third countries to mimic criminal networks. The risk is misattribution. A credible counter-example demonstrates this danger: in 2014, early reports incorrectly linked weapons captured from ISIS fighters near Mosul to Syrian military stockpiles. Later analysis by CAR revealed many had been seized from Iraqi depots during the group's rapid advance. Incorrect attribution risked inflaming regional tensions. Reconciliation lies in humility: evidence must surpass inference. Precision matters.

Despite these challenges, exposing hidden affiliations remains indispensable. When a sponsor is credibly identified, the strategic terrain shifts. Diplomatic pressure increases. Sanctions gain traction. Proxy forces lose the narrative protection that shields recruitment and fundraising. The disruption is often subtle: weapons arrive late, salaries shrink, morale dips. In Nigeria, after the Financial Action Task Force highlighted links between regional donors and Boko Haram in 2013, banks tightened oversight, and several fundraising channels collapsed. The effect, measured in reduced cross-border cash transfers, demonstrated how attribution constrains covert networks.

Signals intelligence, financial forensics, and field investigations are not separate streams but converging currents. Their interplay forms a composite picture. A radio intercept aligns with a timing anomaly in a payment chain.

A payment chain aligns with a shipment of weapons. A shipment aligns with a militia's sudden improvement in tactical sophistication. Each detail reinforces another. The *imprint of origin* emerges not from a single clue but from accumulation.

And yet a deeper question lingers beneath the craft: once investigators expose a sponsor's identity, what then? States must decide whether to confront, deter, negotiate, or retaliate. Exposure destabilises the equilibrium of deniability. It forces sponsors into a narrower set of choices. It pulls shadows toward the light.

The unresolved tension sits precisely here: if attribution disrupts covert activity but risks escalation, how far should states commit to revealing the *imprint of origin* when the truth itself may narrow the path to restraint?

Ending Proxy Wars

On 12 October 2016, in the humid air of Luanda, negotiators from the International Conference on the Great Lakes Region met to address a conflict that officially did not exist. The Democratic Republic of the Congo insisted that rebel groups crossing its eastern frontier were backed by neighbouring states. Rwanda denied everything. Uganda denied everything. Yet the militias continued to move, fight, and fragment, their supply chains hinting at patrons who would not enter the room. The diplomats drafted communiqués, scheduled verification missions, and proposed troop disengagement lines. The militias ignored them. By the evening, one Angolan official, stepping out for air, murmured the refrain that haunts every mediation of indirect conflict: "How do you negotiate with actors who won't admit they're there?" His question lingers still.

Proxy wars confound the very logic of peacemaking because they operate beneath the surface on which diplomacy usually stands. When sponsors disown their proxies, negotiations fracture into layers: the visible dispute between states, the hidden dispute between patrons, and the lived conflict between armed groups on the ground. The *broken silhouette*—a motif that captures the mismatch between what actors claim to be and what they are—follows every attempt to construct a settlement. Mediators must stabilise shadows as well as armies.

Ending such conflicts begins with the uncomfortable recognition that proxy wars are rarely terminated by battlefield exhaustion alone. They end when incentives change. Show the behaviour: a sponsor reduces weapons shipments and restricts training access. Name the mechanism: conditional de-escalation. Explain the effect: the proxy's operational tempo falters. Implication: negotiations become viable precisely because the sponsor adjusts, not because the proxy relents. This dynamic shaped the 1988 Geneva Accords, which ended the Soviet–Afghan War. The accords nominally concerned Kabul and Islamabad, yet the critical movement came when Moscow signalled—through phased troop withdrawals and limited funding reductions—that its willingness to sustain the conflict was ebbing. Public statements shifted. Logistics shrank. The *broken silhouette* grew sharper: the states spoke in diplomatic terms, but the real pivot occurred backstage.

Regional agreements serve as another channel. In West Africa, ECOWAS interventions during the Mano River conflicts (1990–2003) demonstrated that neighbouring states can impose collective discipline on sponsors. Liberia's use of proxies in Sierra Leone, and Sierra Leone's reciprocal backing of Liberian factions, created circular violence that mediation alone could not stop. ECOWAS deployed ECOMOG, established monitoring blocs, and pressured Charles Taylor through sanctions and travel bans. The behaviour changed: financial flows slowed, cross-border movement shrank, and proxy commanders lost access to supply corridors. The implication was decisive: once sponsors felt the cost of continuation rise, political settlement followed. Here, the *broken silhouette* narrowed until sponsorship could no longer be denied.

International watchdogs play a quieter but often decisive role. Panels of Experts, arms-monitoring missions, and investigative bodies compile evidence that exposes covert ties. Their reports do more than name violations; they shift bargaining power. When the UN Panel of Experts on Libya released documentation in 2020 linking foreign contractors to violations of the arms embargo, those findings influenced negotiations within the Berlin Process. States adjusted positions subtly, retreating from expansive claims and adopting more cautious language. Behaviour changed because visibility changed.

Yet watchdogs face sharp limitations. They can document patterns, but they cannot compel compliance. A credible counter-example illustrates this: in 2013, the UN Group of Experts on the DRC produced detailed evidence that M23 rebels received backing from Rwandan officials. Kigali refused the findings, dismissed the documentation as selective, and raised procedural objections. For months, the reports generated diplomatic heat but little movement. Reconciliation lies in the recognition that transparency is not enforcement. Documentation weakens deniability, but it does not dissolve ambition. The *broken silhouette* remained fragmented until military pressure mounted and Rwanda recalculated its interests.

On-ground observations remain essential because proxy groups, unlike states, fragment in unpredictable ways. Mediators must measure cohesion: are commanders obeying orders? Are factions splintering? Are supply lines still intact? In 2007, during the Juba peace talks between the Ugandan government and the Lord's Resistance Army, regional monitors reported inconsistencies in LRA participation. Some units attended discussions; others raided villages along the Congolese border. Their behaviour revealed internal fractures. The implication was immediate: agreements signed in Juba would bind only slices of the organisation. Mediators adjusted expectations. Off-ramps had to be tailored, not general.

Off-ramps themselves are fragile constructions. They require sponsors to step forward without admitting what they previously denied. They require proxies to commit to deals they did not publicly negotiate. They require regional actors to guarantee processes whose legitimacy may be contested. To build an off-ramp is to persuade actors operating in the grey to make commitments in the light.

One technique is compartmentalised negotiation. During the Dayton Accords in 1995, U.S. envoys dealt separately with Slobodan Milošević, Franjo Tuđman, and Alija Izetbegović while addressing the role of Bosnian Serb forces indirectly. Serbia denied command over the Army of Republika Srpska, yet Milošević agreed to terms that directly constrained its operations. The *broken silhouette* became a tool: mediators used the ambiguity to secure concessions from the sponsor without forcing explicit admissions that could collapse the talks.

Another method is phased demobilisation tied to verifiable benchmarks. During the 2005 Comprehensive Peace Agreement in Sudan, the disarmament of southern militias occurred in stages, monitored by regional observers from IGAD. The behaviour—progress measured in cantonment numbers and weapons recovered—provided a metric for trust. The implication was structural: when sponsors saw their commitments reciprocated, they relaxed. When proxies saw progress acknowledged, they complied. Yet even here, the shadow lingered; some armed groups retained hidden stockpiles, anticipating future reversals. In proxy environments, demobilisation is never perfectly linear.

Counter-examples, however, reveal the structural fragility of such arrangements. The collapse of Yemen's 2018 Stockholm Agreement demonstrated how insufficient leverage over proxies stalls peace. The agreement mandated redeployment from Hodeidah and joint monitoring mechanisms. But the Houthi movement, with support networks that extended beyond the formal negotiation framework, resisted compliance. Their behaviour—partial withdrawals, delayed access for monitors, selective cooperation—showed that without strong pressure on sponsors, agreements remain aspirational. The implication is uncomfortable: peace processes involving proxies require more than goodwill. They require sustained constraint on the unseen actors who feed the war.

This is why disrupting sponsor support becomes central to ending proxy conflicts. When fuel for war shrinks—whether weapons, salaries, training, or sanctuary—proxies lose operational stamina. In 2016, after Nigeria, Niger and Chad tightened border controls and financial oversight, Boko Haram factions splintered. Movement became costly. Funding inconsistent. Violence dipped temporarily. The lesson is empirical: pressure on sponsors recalibrates the battlefield more than pressure on proxies alone.

Yet the difficulty of ending proxy wars lies precisely in the incentives that create them. Sponsoring states rarely admit involvement because admission carries diplomatic cost. Proxies rarely accept limits because their legitimacy depends on resistance. Mediators rarely possess enough leverage to push both sides simultaneously. The *broken silhouette* endures: actors visible enough to influence events, invisible enough to evade obligations.

Negotiation frameworks must therefore work within ambiguity rather than presume its absence. They must craft agreements that allow sponsors to save face, provide proxies with credible guarantees, and offer regional actors roles that align with—rather than contradict—their security interests. This often means allowing language that papers over contradictions, sequencing commitments to avoid public humiliation, and relying on quiet diplomacy rather than dramatic accords.

Yet even the best frameworks cannot resolve the core dilemma: off-ramps demand ownership from actors who have spent years operating without it. The question, sharpened by every failed truce and partial redeployment, remains unresolved: can a conflict built in shadows be dismantled in daylight, or must endings be negotiated in the same half-light that sustained the war?

Chapter 3

Cyber Ops and Ransom Attacks

Just after midnight on 27 June 2017, employees at the Danish shipping giant Maersk opened their laptops to find a stark red screen. Files were locked. Systems frozen. Within hours, terminals from Rotterdam to Mumbai stalled, ships idled offshore, and logistics chains—normally coordinated to the hour—buckled. The malware responsible, later dubbed NotPetya, masqueraded as ransomware but carried the destructive signature of something more strategic. No demands were issued that could plausibly be fulfilled. No decryptor existed. For Maersk, the world's largest container carrier, the attack erased weeks of operational capacity in a single morning. The company's engineers eventually rebuilt its entire network from a lone surviving domain controller in Ghana, flown overnight on a USB drive. The episode revealed a truth governments and corporations had been slow to accept: the battlefield of the twenty-first century is increasingly silent, borderless, and instantaneous, and the opponents that shape it may never announce themselves.

Cyber operations sit at this intersection of invisibility and consequence. Their power lies in the ability to slip through systems unnoticed—an accountant's laptop, a misconfigured server, an outdated printer driver—and escalate from nuisance to sabotage without crossing any physical frontier. Zero-day vulnerabilities, unknown even to their creators, are bought, sold, and stockpiled like rare munitions. Advanced persistent threats embed themselves deep within networks, moving laterally with patience that human adversaries rarely muster. The digital intruder waits. Watches. Listens. The motif that recurs across this terrain is the *quiet breach*: a presence that becomes dangerous long before it becomes visible.

Yet the economics of this battlefield are no longer the exclusive domain of states. Ransomware has democratised disruption. A small criminal group can inflict the damage of a mid-sized military unit with little more than off-the-shelf encryption tools, leaked intelligence manuals, and the nerve to deploy them. The Colonial Pipeline attack in May 2021—executed by actors linked, loosely and deniably, to the DarkSide ransomware syndicate—halted fuel transport across the eastern United States and forced the company to pay a multimillion-dollar ransom. The incident exposed how quickly localised extortion could cascade into national concern. It also illustrated how state-linked hackers piggyback on criminal methods, hiding sophisticated espionage behind the chaotic opportunism of ransomware crews. When attribution becomes crowded, truths blur. Responsibility dilutes.

This chapter examines that dilution. For even when digital fingerprints exist—IP traces, malware families, compiler time stamps—the link between hacker and sponsor remains negotiable. Cyber forensics resemble a puzzle with pieces deliberately obscured: spoofed servers, compromised routers, code written to imitate another actor's signature. In 2016, during investigations into the breach of the Democratic National Committee, competing intelligence assessments struggled to untangle multiple layers of obfuscation, each designed to confound. Analysts traced patterns across regions, time zones, and behavioural profiles, yet the process took months. The delay mattered. Ambiguity became a political instrument.

Defence, meanwhile, has entered an arms race of architectures and discipline. Network segmentation reduces blast radius. Encryption protects data even when attackers breach the perimeter. Threat intelligence teams harvest signals from the darker edges of the internet, comparing chatter, correlating anomalies, and sharing indicators of compromise across sectors. The most successful defences resemble coordinated ensembles rather than fortified walls. One of the more instructive examples came from a coalition of European energy firms in late 2020, which repelled a state-linked intrusion attempt by rapidly exchanging telemetry, isolating infected nodes, and deploying patches within hours. Victory was measured not in heroics but in preparation—the disciplined routines that turn crisis from catastrophe into inconvenience.

And yet the more societies rely on digital infrastructure, the more cyber conflict strains our legal and ethical frameworks. Policymakers wrestle with questions inherited from kinetic war but transformed by the nature of code. What constitutes an armed attack when no blood is drawn but hospitals shut down? Can a state retaliate when attribution remains probabilistic rather than absolute? Does sovereignty extend to servers hosted abroad but owned by domestic firms? Jurisdictions collide. Laws lag. Calls for "cyber norms" echo in diplomatic halls, yet enforcement remains aspirational. Proposals for ceasefires in cyberspace—temporary retreats to allow patching or humanitarian access—sound sensible but rest on trust that is rarely present and verification that is rarely possible.

The deeper tension lies in how cyber operations fuse the criminal, the political, and the strategic into a single continuum. A teenage coder in Minsk may use ransomware for profit; a state intelligence unit may exploit the resulting chaos to mask its own intrusion; a multinational corporation may pay a ransom, inadvertently funding future attacks. Each actor occupies a different moral and legal space, yet their actions converge on the same infrastructure. The *quiet breach* recurs here too: a faint disturbance that grows in significance as layers of intent accumulate.

This chapter follows these layers—silent infiltration, opportunistic extortion, contested attribution, defensive ingenuity, and legal ambiguity—not as isolated topics but as interlocking facets of a domain where every decision carries strategic weight. Cyberspace erases the conventional distances that once protected states from one another. It collapses escalation ladders. It empowers actors previously too small to matter and gives large actors plausible masks behind which they operate with impunity.

What follows is an exploration of both the threat and the opportunity: the threat posed by a domain where malicious action can be global and instantaneous, and the opportunity to craft resilience in ways that blend technology, governance, and strategic restraint. The reader stands at the threshold of a battlefield where the frontline may be a workstation, a cloud server, or a supply-chain partner several countries away. The next pages trace how these assaults unfold and what they reveal about the shifting architecture of power. The deeper question—how societies can protect themselves without surrendering openness—remains unresolved. The direction, however, is clear: the invisible battlefield is no longer distant. It has already arrived.

The Invisible Battlefield

At 08:07 on 12 May 2017, radiologists at the National Health Service Trust in Lancashire stared at screens that flickered, froze, and then displayed a single, crude message: their files had been encrypted, and a Bitcoin payment was demanded for their release. The malware—later identified as WannaCry—raced through networks that morning, crippling more than 80 NHS Trusts across England. Ambulances diverted. Operations postponed. The cost, compiled by the Department of Health (2018), ran into tens of millions of pounds. Most striking was the method: the attackers never stepped inside a hospital, never crossed a perimeter fence, never issued a threat in their own voices. They slipped into Britain's health infrastructure through a vulnerability in outdated Windows systems, exploiting a tool first developed by the U.S. National Security Agency and leaked online two months earlier. Hospitals stopped. Life slowed. The adversary remained unseen.

Cyberspace rewards this invisibility. It is a theatre where intruders penetrate without noise, map vulnerabilities without detection, and sabotage at a distance. The intrusion rarely begins with grand gestures. It may start with one spear-phishing email, one misconfigured port, one unpatched printer left exposed on a Friday evening. The breach is quiet. The breach grows. The breach becomes intent. That slow, deliberate drift—the *footfall no one hears*—is the motif that defines this domain. It appears first as inconvenience; it can end as paralysis.

Zero-day exploits sit at the heart of this dynamic. They represent flaws unknown to the software creator, traded on markets as discreetly as smuggled antiques. When Stuxnet struck Iran's Natanz enrichment facility in 2010, it relied on multiple such vulnerabilities, slipping into the system via compromised USB drives before sabotaging centrifuge speeds. Its creators, never officially acknowledged, used the element of surprise as both shield and sword. Show the behaviour: code designed to mimic legitimate instructions. Name the mechanism: a zero-day exploit chain. Explain the effect: physical infrastructure responds to a ghost within the machine. The implication is simple yet profound: cyber weapons operate before defenders even know the battlefield exists.

Advanced persistent threats (APTs) embody this patience. Groups such as APT29, linked to Russia's Foreign Intelligence Service, have infiltrated Western networks for years, often with the subtlety of legal auditors rather than saboteurs. During the SolarWinds breach discovered in December 2020, APT29 embedded malicious code into software updates distributed globally. The method was elegant in its subtlety. Thousands of firms and government departments installed the compromised update themselves, trusting a product they believed safe. The behaviour showed no haste. The adversaries measured timelines, picked targets, and navigated with care. They lingered for months. They took what they needed. The implication: on the invisible battlefield, intrusion is not an event but a residency.

The risks transcend intelligence gathering. In March 2021, the Irish Health Service Executive fell victim to the Conti ransomware group. Files locked.

Networks corrupted. Staff forced to revert to pen-and-paper records. The attackers demanded payment, and while the Irish government refused on principle, the disruption persisted for weeks. This episode exposed the paradox of ransomware: groups with limited resources can cripple systems vital to millions, yet their motivations—financial, opportunistic, apolitical—are often exploited by states seeking to mask their own campaigns. When state-linked actors piggyback on criminal infrastructure, attribution blurs. The *footfall no one hears* echoes through multiple corridors at once.

Yet for every high-profile incursion, there are quieter operations that reveal the limits of invisibility. Consider the 2014 breach of Sony Pictures Entertainment. The attackers, later attributed by U.S. authorities to the Lazarus Group linked to North Korea, left behind a trail of operational mistakes—hard-coded IP addresses, reused encryption keys—that investigators pieced together over time. Here, a credible counter-example emerges: the façade of invisibility cracked. But reconciliation is straightforward: mistakes by criminals do not imply weakness among state-backed APTs. The implication is that invisibility is not absolute; it is probabilistic. Some actors trip. The most disciplined do not.

Cyber operations shift the balance of risk. For the intruder, costs remain minimal: a few servers, a skilled team, a willingness to experiment. For the defender, costs accumulate through constant vigilance—patch cycles, training schedules, audits, simulations, segmented architectures. Decisions become behavioural metrics: how many hours before a breach is detected? How many endpoints isolated before lateral movement spreads? How quickly do teams deploy updates? Each number marks a posture on the invisible battlefield.

The complexities multiply when intrusion becomes sabotage. In 2015, Ukraine's power grid fell to a coordinated cyberattack attributed to Sandworm, a Russian military intelligence unit. Operators watched as their mouse cursors moved independently on-screen, shutting down substations. This was not simple theft of data; it was an adversary demonstrating physical impact through digital means. The *footfall no one hears* became thunderous. Yet even here, a second layer defines the conflict: the attackers withdrew before causing lasting structural damage. The implication: cyber operations frequently serve strategic messaging as much as destruction.

The question of counter-examples resurfaces when states misjudge the power of code. In 2012, Saudi Aramco suffered the Shamoon attack, which wiped data on 30,000 computers. The incident showed that even a blunt digital tool can induce chaos. But it also showed a limitation: although devastating to office systems, the malware did not touch industrial infrastructure. The sponsor—suspected by U.S. intelligence to be linked to Iran—achieved spectacle rather than sustained disruption. Reconciliation lies in recognising that cyber operations are shaped by both ambition and constraint. Precision grows, but not uniformly.

In this space, the distinction between peace and conflict dissolves. Cyber intrusions occur daily, hourly, continuously. They do not adhere to declarations, treaties, or ceasefires. An APT may enter a system during diplomatic talks without violating any formal rule. A ransomware group may hit a hospital during a humanitarian crisis without crossing a recognised red line. Behaviour becomes the defining metric: what systems are targeted, what data is exfiltrated, what disruptions tolerated. The implication is stark: cyberspace produces a continuum of contestation with no natural boundary.

For defenders, the challenge is as psychological as technical. They must detect anomalies that scarcely ripple the surface: a file transfer a few kilobytes too large; login activity in an unexpected time zone; a subtle shift in registry values. They hunt for that faint *footfall no one hears*—the motif that binds this domain. Detection demands curiosity as much as code.

But defenders also confront choices with strategic consequences. When a multinational firm such as CNA Financial paid a ransom of approximately $40 million in March 2021, it did so to restore operations quickly. The decision addressed an immediate crisis but fuelled a long-term one, signalling to other groups that profitable targets remained willing to comply. Trade-offs harden. The battlefield grows.

The technical sophistication of the attackers, meanwhile, continues to evolve. Machine learning models assist intrusion detection, but adversaries use similar tools to automate reconnaissance. Encryption protects data, yet attackers increasingly rely on double-extortion tactics: stealing files first, then encrypting networks, threatening exposure if ransom is refused. Defensive architectures mature. Offensive creativity keeps pace.

As we navigate this terrain, the unresolved question becomes sharper: how do societies function in a space where conflict is constant, adversaries are faceless, and escalation may originate from a keyboard rather than a command centre? The next sections examine that question in depth, but the contours are already visible. Silence can be strategic. Presence can be concealed. And the first sign of an attack may be the moment everything stops.

Ransom Tactics and Escalation

At 05:54 on 7 May 2021, Colonial Pipeline's control-room screens froze. Operators in Alpharetta, Georgia, watched status panels blink and vanish as the DarkSide ransomware group seized the firm's billing network and threatened to encrypt operational systems next. Within hours, the company halted pipeline flow along the eastern seaboard of the United States, disrupting fuel distribution across multiple states. The attackers demanded a payment in Bitcoin; Colonial Pipeline paid roughly $4.4 million shortly after the intrusion. The ransom bought a decryption tool so slow and unreliable that engineers rebuilt systems manually instead. The trade was stark: millions paid for a key that barely worked, and millions more spent recovering afterwards. The attackers, meanwhile, retreated behind their screens. They left few traces. They acted with the composure of a group that understood how much leverage silence affords.

Ransomware works because it twists a universal vulnerability—dependence on data—into a vector for coercion. The criminal logic is simple: encrypt, threaten, wait. It is the digital equivalent of seizing the only copy of an archive and charging for its return. Yet ransomware also thrives because the attack posture is fluid. Some groups strike opportunistically; they search the internet for exposed remote desktop ports, outdated VPN appliances, or misconfigured cloud buckets. They do not stalk particular victims. They scan, find, and strike. Their behaviour is measured in hours: entry at dawn, encryption by noon, negotiation by evening.

Others operate with slower purpose. They lurk, map networks, exfiltrate sensitive files, and execute what specialists now call *double extortion*: encrypting systems while simultaneously threatening to publish stolen data. In 2020, the REvil group deployed this tactic against Travelex in London. Systems collapsed. Branches closed. Data leaked. The firm entered administration months later. The attack demonstrated how hostage-taking of data now extends far beyond operational paralysis; it includes reputational blackmail and legal exposure. The motif that threads through these cases—the *sealed door*—captures the moment a victim realises that access to its own information has been locked from the inside.

State-linked hackers exploit this ecosystem. They mimic it. They hide within it. The Lazarus Group, tied to North Korea, used ransomware variants like WannaCry in May 2017 not primarily for extortion—its payment infrastructure was haphazard—but as a distraction and a revenue experiment. By adopting the grammar of criminal activity, the group obscured the strategic intent behind the attack. Show the behaviour: code signed with amateurish ransom notes. Name the actor: a unit linked to a state intelligence bureau. Explain the advantage: plausible deniability amid global confusion. The implication is unsettling: by piggybacking on criminal methods, state actors can test cyber weapons or retaliatory strategies without immediate attribution. They disappear into the noise.

The HydraLocker campaign, active across parts of Eastern Europe in 2016, demonstrated a different pattern. Investigators traced the malware to a small criminal crew in Kyiv, whose tools were later found embedded—modestly modified—in a breach targeting a Baltic government ministry. Analysts saw overlapping infrastructure: shared command-and-control servers, similar obfuscation routines, identical encryption libraries. The fingerprints suggested a state actor had borrowed the criminals' scaffolding to mask its operations. Yet attribution remained uncertain because the scaffolding itself was widely circulated on underground forums. Limitation becomes lesson: the ubiquity of ransomware tools creates camouflage even for sophisticated sponsors.

Victims face excruciating decisions. Some firms refuse to pay as a matter of principle. The Irish Health Service Executive in May 2021 rejected the Conti group's demand, choosing disruption over capitulation. Staff worked with paper charts. Clinics postponed appointments. Engineers rebuilt systems line by line. The cost was high, but the message—visible behaviour in the face of coercion—sent a signal: the state would not reward criminal extortion. Yet several months later, smaller Irish service providers were hit by copycat attacks, illustrating a counter-example: refusal does not guarantee deterrence. Criminal groups measure opportunity, not honour.

But paying carries its own risks. When CNA Financial in Chicago transferred roughly $40 million to ransomware affiliates in March 2021, it unwittingly demonstrated to others that high-value payouts were achievable. Analysts from multiple cybersecurity firms observed a surge in big-game hunting shortly afterwards; attackers shifted focus towards insurance, healthcare, and supply-chain firms with deep pockets and low tolerance for downtime. The implication is blunt: ransom payments reshape the market. Every transaction signals profitability. Every profitable attack encourages more attackers.

Governments grapple with this tension. Regulators in the United States warned in late 2020 that companies paying ransoms to sanctioned entities could violate federal law. The behaviour here—hesitant payments, delayed negotiations—introduced new frictions into the ransomware economy. But the limitation is clear: sanctions complicate decisions without dismantling the incentive structure that fuels the attacks. Criminals adapt; they insert intermediaries; they relocate wallets; they launder through mixers. The *sealed door* appears again, this time representing the opacity of financial flows as much as encrypted data.

State-linked piggybacking introduces yet another escalation. When Russia's Sandworm unit deployed NotPetya in June 2017, it disguised a destructive worm as ransomware. Victims saw ransom notes; they searched for decryption keys; they attempted negotiations. But there was no path to recovery. The malware overwrote master boot records irreversibly. Companies like Maersk suffered global outages costing hundreds of millions of pounds. Show the behaviour: pseudo-ransomware disguised as criminal activity. Name the strategy: sabotage under the mask of extortion. Explain the effect: confusion, delay, and misattribution. The implication: ransomware techniques have become a language states can imitate to deliver strategic blows while maintaining deniability.

Even when attribution eventually succeeds, it arrives too late to alter the immediate costs. Forensic investigations take time—weeks for malware analysis, months for tracing crypto transfers, years for establishing patterns across intrusions. In the meantime, firms negotiate, pay, restore, and review procedures. Every hour lost deepens the attacker's advantage. The asymmetry is structural: defenders must maintain constant vigilance; attackers need only one opening.

Victims respond with varied behaviours that shape the broader ecosystem. Some negotiate aggressively, reducing ransom demands to a fraction of initial claims. Others involve insurers, transforming the process into a cost-benefit calculation. Still others opt for silence, paying discreetly to avoid reputational fallout. But each behaviour alters the attackers' expectations. Criminal groups track public reports. They measure payout frequency. They compare negotiation patterns. They refine their targets accordingly. Ransomware, at scale, becomes a market with feedback loops.

A credible counter-example tempers this determinism. In 2022, the Costa Rican government refused to pay Conti during a large-scale attack on multiple ministries. Instead, it declared a national emergency, hardened networks, and worked with international partners to rebuild. The attackers published data, issued taunts, and eventually dissolved into successor groups. Reconciliation emerges: while refusal does not eliminate risk, co-ordinated national resilience reduces the appeal of targeting a state incapable of being coerced financially. The *sealed door* opened—but on the government's terms, not the attackers'.

Ransomware escalation follows predictable yet adaptive patterns. Criminals innovate to overcome defensive measures; states mimic criminal techniques to disguise geopolitical manoeuvres; firms react under pressure, sometimes inadvertently funding future attacks. The cycle accelerates when payments flow readily and slows when attackers face friction—technical, legal, reputational.

Yet across these variations, one unresolved question lingers: when the next ransom demand appears on a screen, encrypted files locked behind a threat written in imperfect English, what calculation should guide the response? Every choice carries consequences. Every payment echoes outward. And the attackers, waiting in silence, need only watch how the door is opened.

Attribution vs. Plausible Deniability

At 02:13 on 20 December 2015, engineers in Ukraine's Prykarpattyaoblenergo control room watched their cursors move without being touched. One by one, substations disconnected. Phone lines jammed. A blackout spread across Ivano-Frankivsk, leaving more than 200,000 residents without power. The attackers vanished as swiftly as they appeared. Initial forensics pointed tentatively towards the BlackEnergy malware family. Later analysis by the Slovak firm ESET identified links to the group now known as Sandworm. But the crucial question—who authorised the attack—remained unresolved for months. Russia denied involvement. Ukraine insisted otherwise. Western agencies debated quietly. The breach became a symbol of a deeper problem: in cyberspace, even when you know *what* happened, proving *who* stands behind it is an altogether different challenge.

Attribution is the art of naming the unseen. It is a process that blends technical forensics, behavioural profiling, geopolitical context, and educated inference. Yet even this combination often yields only probability, not certainty. States exploit this ambiguity deliberately. They outsource attacks to proxy groups, route traffic through compromised infrastructure, imitate the code signatures of rivals, and stage operations at hours that mimic foreign time zones. These behaviours are not by-products of secrecy; they are strategic tools designed to complicate the very act of confirmation.

The motif running through such cases—the *vanishing hand*—captures how sponsors intervene decisively, then withdraw into a mist of digital misdirection.

The complexity becomes clearest when examining how cybersecurity forensics function in practice. Analysts begin with indicators of compromise: malicious files, IP logs, registry edits, command-and-control communication trails. They measure patterns. They compare samples. They correlate anomalies with known threat actors. Yet the evidentiary chain is fragile. When APT10 targeted managed service providers across Europe and the United States between 2016 and 2018, investigators eventually tied the campaign to China's Ministry of State Security. The behaviour matched prior incidents: familiar dropper tools, reuse of certain encryption routines, operational hours consistent with GMT+8. But the attribution required months of cross-referencing between government agencies and private firms such as PwC and BAE Systems. It was not one smoking gun; it was a mosaic assembled painstakingly from fragments.

The implication is profound: attribution in cyberspace relies less on definitive proof than on converging likelihoods. That leaves room for dispute, denial, and diplomatic performance.

One case illustrates this with stark clarity. The 2014 Sony Pictures breach began with crude threats and destructive malware. Early indicators pointed to North Korea: Korean-language artefacts, code similarities to prior Lazarus campaigns, and IP addresses occasionally linked to the region. But these clues could have been planted. Analysts from several private firms noted inconsistencies. Why leave Korean strings visible? Why rely on infrastructure traceable to Pyongyang when stealthier options existed? For weeks, the *vanishing hand* frustrated investigators. Only after the FBI combined technical indicators with classified intelligence—including human reporting—did the U.S. government publicly attribute the attack to North Korea on 19 December 2014. Even then, scepticism persisted within parts of the cybersecurity community. The limitation was clear: open-source forensics alone rarely produces certainty.

Reconciliation lies in recognising that attribution occupies a spectrum. At one end sits definitive confirmation, typically possible only when intelligence agencies possess privileged visibility—SIGINT, HUMINT, or insider leaks. At the other end lies ambiguous inference, where circumstantial evidence is strong but not conclusive. Most cases fall in the grey between.

Consider the NotPetya incident of June 2017. The malware appeared to be ransomware, but its pseudo-ransom mechanism lacked functional design. Forensic analysis showed near-identical code segments to tools previously used by Sandworm. Ukrainian targets dominated the early wave of infections. Traffic logs suggested preparatory reconnaissance months earlier. Western governments eventually attributed the attack to Russia's military intelligence service, the GRU. Yet the attribution took time, in part because NotPetya rapidly leapt beyond Ukraine into global supply chains—Maersk, Merck, and FedEx, among others. The sheer breadth of victims diluted the clarity of initial assessment. The *vanishing hand* exploited this confusion: a global catastrophe masked an operation born of a specific geopolitical rivalry.

A credible counter-example complicates this narrative. The 2018 Marriott breach exposed data from approximately 500 million guests. U.S. agencies later linked the intrusion to China's Ministry of State Security, citing shared infrastructure with prior MSS campaigns. Yet the operation's target profile—global travellers across sectors—suggested an intelligence motive rather than sabotage. Some analysts questioned whether criminal actors might have sold or shared parts of the toolkit. Here, attribution remained contested because the behavioural signals overlapped between espionage and opportunistic crime. The reconciliation is pragmatic: cyber signatures are often recycled, traded, or reverse-engineered, making it dangerous to treat code similarity as proof of sponsorship.

This interpretive fog grants states a powerful strategic asset. Plausible deniability allows them to operate beneath thresholds of open conflict. Sponsorship becomes a rumour rather than a declaration. Deterrence weakens. Response options shrink. When the United Kingdom publicly attributed the 2020 SolarWinds campaign to Russia's SVR, the statement arrived long after the intrusion had achieved its objectives. It served diplomatic signalling rather than operational defence. The *vanishing hand* had done its work.

Cybersecurity forensics wrestle constantly with shadows. Analysts trace malware families—Turla, APT28, APT34—not because names provide certainty, but because categorisation brings order to a domain built on deception. They match timestamps: an intrusion that consistently operates between 9 a.m. and 6 p.m. Beijing time suggests, though does not confirm, a Chinese-language actor. They examine compilation metadata: a file compiled on a Russian-language machine may indicate origin, unless the adversary manipulated these values intentionally. They follow money trails through cryptocurrency mixers, sometimes identifying wallets tied to sanctioned entities. Each behaviour measured offers a clue. Each clue interpreted introduces risk.

The implication is that attribution is never merely technical. It is geopolitical theatre. States weigh the decision to accuse another government against potential retaliation or diplomatic fallout. They sometimes hold back information to avoid exposing intelligence sources. They sometimes delay statements to coordinate allies or reinforce international norms. In 2018, the Netherlands publicly named GRU officers caught attempting to hack the Organisation for the Prohibition of Chemical Weapons in The Hague. Dutch authorities displayed taxi receipts, Wi-Fi logs, and confiscated equipment. The evidence was unusually detailed—a rare moment when the *vanishing hand* became visible not through code but through human clumsiness. Yet such clarity is exceptional.

The question of plausible deniability deepens when states exploit criminal ecosystems. Groups such as Evil Corp, based in Russia, operate with relative impunity. Their leaders, like Maksim Yakubets indicted by the U.S. Department of Justice in December 2019, allegedly collaborated with domestic intelligence in exchange for protection. Here, behaviour shows partnership; naming confirms state–criminal entanglement; explanation reveals a hybrid model; implication suggests that dismantling criminal networks may also require confronting state sponsors—an escalation few governments are willing to risk.

Attribution's difficulty generates a policy dilemma. If states cannot reliably confirm responsibility, how do they calibrate responses? Too firm a stance risks punishing the wrong adversary. Too soft a stance invites further attack. The threshold for retaliation shifts. Norms erode. Deterrence becomes performative rather than preventive.

This dilemma sharpened after the 2021 Microsoft Exchange Server compromise, attributed to the Chinese group Hafnium. The attack combined espionage with indiscriminate exploitation, leaving thousands of systems worldwide vulnerable. Yet the United States and its allies waited months before issuing coordinated attribution. The delay reflected internal debates: How strong was the evidence? How would Beijing respond? What signal would joint attribution send? The *vanishing hand* shaped statecraft not through action but through uncertainty.

For investigators, the enduring challenge lies in distinguishing camouflage from genuine signature. Malware authors increasingly plant false flags—

fragments of foreign-language code, deliberate use of rival actors' tools, mimicked operational tempos. One forensic team at Kaspersky Lab noted in 2019 that an intrusion in East Asia used Russian-language artefacts but matched none of the behavioural profiles associated with Russian APTs. False flags do not simply mislead; they corrode confidence in the very frameworks analysts rely on.

The unresolved question emerges from this haze: if attribution remains probabilistic, how should states respond when the next intrusion hits critical infrastructure? Should they rely on cumulative intelligence? Should they announce with measured caution? Or should they accept a world where some acts of aggression may never be traced to an identifiable sponsor at all? The *vanishing hand* persists, shaping the battlefield not through visibility, but through doubt.

Technology Defences That Help

At 06:42 on 16 December 2020, engineers at FireEye's headquarters in Milpitas, California, noticed an anomaly: a two-kilobyte jump in outbound traffic from a workstation that had no reason to communicate externally. The packet was encrypted, the destination obscure, the timing precise. Minutes later, a second deviation appeared—again small, again faint. Those fragments were the first visible signs of the SolarWinds intrusions, later traced to a supply-chain compromise affecting thousands of organisations. Yet FireEye did not fall victim in the way so many others did. Its security controls—segmented networks, behavioural analytics, disciplined logging—caught what most missed. The subsequent investigation helped unravel one of the decade's most sophisticated espionage campaigns. It was a rare moment when a defender, not the attacker, dictated the pace of escalation.

That success story matters because technical defences often appear futile against determined intruders. Zero-days bypass patches. Social engineering defeats even diligent staff. Persistence outmatches vigilance. But FireEye's experience shows something else: resilience begins not with perfect detection, but with architectures that contain damage when detection inevitably fails. The quiet motif that threads through such cases—the *spare key*—captures the idea of layered safeguards designed to recover control even when the front door has been quietly forced.

Encryption sits at the centre of this philosophy. Properly implemented, it protects data even when attackers breach the network. When the UK's National Cyber Security Centre reviewed the 2018 compromise of

Heathrow Airport's USB data leak, investigators noted that encrypted files recovered from the device remained useless to journalists who obtained them. The behaviour—strong encryption at rest—converted a potentially damaging incident into an inconvenience. Naming the principle—cryptographic isolation—reveals its power: defenders assume breach but prevent exploitation. The implication is straightforward: confidentiality becomes resilient rather than conditional.

Yet encryption is only as strong as its discipline. The 2019 breach of Capital One, executed by a former Amazon Web Services employee in Seattle, exploited misconfigured access permissions that granted visibility into encrypted customer data. Encryption existed, but the keys and privileges were managed poorly. This credible counter-example tempers the celebration of cryptographic solutions. Reconciliation lies in understanding that encryption must be paired with secure key management, least-privilege access, and continuous audits. Without these behaviours, encryption becomes a locked safe with the combination taped to the front.

Network segmentation represents another form of the *spare key*. Instead of assuming that a perimeter firewall can hold indefinitely, segmentation divides infrastructure into compartments. When attackers penetrate one section, they cannot simply walk into others. During the 2017 NotPetya outbreak, several European banks experienced intrusions, yet avoided catastrophic damage because their transactional systems remained isolated from administrative networks. Show the behaviour: lateral movement blocked by firewall zones. Name the technique: micro-segmentation. Explain the effect: malware contained before reaching high-value assets. The implication: defenders limit strategic fallout by narrowing the battlefield.

Segmentation also exposes attackers who expect frictionless access. In 2020, the Norwegian parliament (Stortinget) disclosed a breach linked to APT28. Logs revealed that the attackers attempted to pivot across isolated domains, encountering repeated permission failures. Those stumbles generated alerts. The segmentation acted not only as a shield but also as a sensor, identifying intrusion through frustration rather than explicit signature. Failing quietly, attackers reveal intent.

Threat intelligence completes this triad of defences. Rather than waiting for unusual alerts, defenders cultivate external awareness—collecting indicators from global partners, sharing telemetry, and studying adversary behaviour. The European Energy Information Sharing and Analysis

Centre (EE-ISAC), established to support grid operators, demonstrated the value of this approach in February 2020 when it coordinated alerts about a phishing campaign targeting SCADA administrators. Operators in Belgium, Spain, and Denmark compared suspicious emails within hours. The behaviour—rapid cross-border intelligence exchange—allowed firms to block domains before payloads executed. Naming the mechanism—shared situational awareness—clarifies its advantage: defences grow stronger through collective knowledge. The implication: the *spare key* is not held by one entity alone but by a network of partners acting in concert.

A successful coordinated defence stands out as a rare but illuminating example. In late 2020, a consortium of European telecom operators detected scanning activity against exposed 5G core components. Rather than respond in isolation, they pooled logs into a central analysis hub, identified patterns suggesting reconnaissance by a group later associated with APT41, and implemented joint mitigations across networks. The attackers, expecting fragmented responses, instead encountered harmonised resistance: patched endpoints, blocked IP ranges, and deceptive honeypots. Their campaign dissipated without achieving operational foothold. This episode demonstrated something often overlooked: attackers measure ease. When defenders commit to collective action, the cost of intrusion rises sharply.

A counter-example reveals the fragility of such coordination. During the WannaCry outbreak in May 2017, the NHS struggled not because defences were absent, but because key systems lacked timely patching and segmentation. Some hospitals had modern controls; others relied on outdated Windows XP machines integrated into essential equipment. The inconsistency created pathways for rapid lateral spread. Reconciliation emerges when understanding that resilience is not additive; it is contingent on weakest links. Technology defences succeed only when uniformly adopted and rigorously maintained.

Detection, though vital, cannot shoulder the full burden. Behavioural monitoring catches anomalies, yet attackers increasingly mimic legitimate workflows. Machine learning models detect statistical deviations, yet adversaries tune their operations to stay within expected ranges. Intrusion detection systems flag suspicious signatures, yet ransomware groups constantly rotate payloads. This dynamic pushes defenders toward resilience rather than reliance on alarms. It shifts the question from "How do we stop every breach?" to "How do we ensure breaches do not cripple us?"

This shift manifests in concrete decisions: the frequency of backups, the distance between production and recovery systems, the testing of failover procedures, the number of minutes required to isolate a compromised node, the scale of redundancy built into critical services. Each behaviour becomes a measure of preparedness, not perfection. The *spare key* returns: resilience is the pre-arranged ability to reopen doors attackers believe they have sealed.

Legal and regulatory structures increasingly support this orientation. The EU's NIS2 Directive requires essential service providers to adopt risk-based security controls, conduct regular assessments, and report incidents within strict deadlines. These obligations translate abstract risk into tangible routines: documented patch cycles, auditable access controls, encrypted communication channels. Yet regulation cannot anticipate every threat. The limitation, again, is uneven implementation: mature organisations embrace resilience; resource-constrained ones struggle to meet minimum baselines.

The unresolved tension lies here: defences grow stronger through collaboration, yet attackers adapt by probing the seams between institutions, sectors, and states. If coordination falters, even briefly, the advantage shifts. Thus the forward question becomes unavoidable: when the next intrusion attempts to slip quietly into a network—small traffic spikes, obscure destinations, faint anomalies—will the *spare key* be ready, or will defenders discover too late that the door was never secured at all?

Legal and Ethical Dilemmas

At 14:23 on 15 February 2021, lawyers inside the Dutch Ministry of Foreign Affairs received a detailed briefing from investigators who had spent weeks tracing an intrusion into the internal systems of the Hague-based Organisation for the Prohibition of Chemical Weapons. The breach, attributed publicly in 2018 to officers of Russia's GRU, had raised a question that no courtroom could yet answer: was this espionage, sabotage, or an attempted act of war? The evidence—Wi-Fi logs, cloned MAC addresses, forged diplomatic plates on the attackers' rental car—painted a clear picture of intent. But the legal framework lagged behind. There was no treaty defining what constituted a hostile cyber act; no tribunal equipped to weigh digital footprints as evidence; no global standard for proportional response. The gap between harm and law, visible in that quiet meeting room, remains the central dilemma of cyber conflict.

That gap is not accidental. Cyberspace evolved faster than the norms meant to govern it. The laws of armed conflict, framed originally in The Hague Conventions of 1899 and 1907 and refined after 1945, presuppose physical damage—territorial incursions, kinetic attacks, or casualties. Yet modern intrusions rarely fit these criteria. They corrupt data, not buildings; they interrupt services, not borders. Policymakers must therefore decide whether doctrines built for artillery and airstrikes can meaningfully apply to attacks executed through code. The motif that binds these dilemmas—the *unfinished rulebook*—captures the tension between action and interpretation, between what states *do* and what the law can meaningfully *name*. It surfaces repeatedly, because every cyber dispute touches something the rulebook never anticipated.

The Tallinn Manual, first published by NATO's Cooperative Cyber Defence Centre of Excellence in 2013 and updated in 2017, offers one attempt to bridge the gap. It provides scholarly interpretations of how existing international law might extend into cyberspace. Show the behaviour: experts debate whether a power outage triggered by malware qualifies as an "armed attack" under Article 51 of the UN Charter. Name the product: the Tallinn Manual 2.0. Explain the effect: guidance without enforcement. The implication is structural—states may cite its principles when convenient but ignore them when inconvenient. Without binding status, the manual embodies the *unfinished rulebook*: ambitious in scope, limited in force.

Jurisdiction deepens the problem. Cyber operations rarely originate and land within the same legal domain. When North Korea's Lazarus Group breached Bangladesh Bank in February 2016, routing fraudulent SWIFT transfers through accounts in Manila, the investigators stretched across three jurisdictions within days: Bangladesh, the Philippines, and the United States. Each state held different legal standards, cooperation thresholds, and evidentiary requirements. Even the definition of "cybercrime" varied. Behaviour collided with borders. Naming the difficulty—jurisdictional fragmentation—reveals the scale. The implication is stark: countermeasures must navigate a legal maze before they can even begin.

The paradox becomes sharper when states consider retaliation. The UN Charter permits self-defence only against an "armed attack". But can the sabotage of a hospital network qualify? What about a ransomware strike that paralyses a fuel pipeline? In May 2021, when the Colonial Pipeline hack halted petrol supplies across parts of the United States, policymakers debated whether the intrusion constituted a national security incident or an elaborate extortion. The FBI urged caution; the White House considered defensive cyber options; legal advisers warned against escalating without definitive attribution. The *unfinished rulebook* again limited action: without categorical language, decision-makers risk miscalibrating responses.

Two contrasting examples illuminate this inconsistency. In 2015, the U.S. government indicted five officers of China's PLA Unit 61398 for cyber espionage against American companies. The move treated cyber intrusions as criminal acts, prosecutable in domestic courts even when suspects remained beyond reach. Show the behaviour: indicting foreign officers by name. Name the logic: law-enforcement framing. Explain the effect: political signalling rather than direct punishment. The implication: legal tools become rhetorical tools when enforcement is impossible.

Contrast this with the 2020 EU Cyber Sanctions regime, under which the European Council imposed asset freezes and travel bans on individuals linked to major cyberattacks like WannaCry, NotPetya, and Cloud Hopper. This approach treated cyber operations as violations of international norms rather than crimes. Here, states embraced a diplomatic framework, not a judicial one. Both strategies—criminalisation and sanctioning—attempted to fill gaps left by the *unfinished rulebook*. Neither fully resolved them.

A credible counter-example demonstrates the limits of legal measures. In 2012, Saudi Aramco suffered the Shamoon attack, which erased data on more than 30,000 machines. The malware displayed a burning American flag on infected systems—an unmistakable act of political messaging. Yet no state offered a formal legal pathway to prosecution. Saudi Arabia blamed Iran; Tehran dismissed the accusation. With no established tribunal for cyber sabotage, the dispute stalled. The reconciliation emerges when we recognise that cyber law lacks not only rules but also institutions. Without a venue to litigate allegations, norms remain aspirations.

These dilemmas extend into ethics. Scholars increasingly argue that cyber operations blur the threshold between espionage—historically tolerated—and warfare—legally constrained. What is the moral weight of an intrusion that disables a hospital's radiology equipment? What is the ethical status of a worm that spreads globally, harming neutral states unintentionally? The 2017 NotPetya attack, attributed to Russia's GRU, caused an estimated $10 billion in global losses (White House estimates, 2018). Maersk, Merck, TNT Express, and hundreds of smaller firms suffered collateral damage. Behaviour: destructive code built to punish Ukraine. Name the ethical breach: indiscriminate spillover violating proportionality principles.

Explain the implications: cyber operations struggle to remain contained; their ethics collide with their physics.

Such spillover also challenges sovereignty. If a worm deployed by one state damages infrastructure in another without intent, has the second state been attacked? Or merely inconvenienced? Traditional legal doctrines do not distinguish between intentional and unintentional harm when foreign forces cross borders. Yet cyber tools travel in ways no tank or aircraft can. The *unfinished rulebook* strains again.

All of this raises the question of whether states could ever enforce "retire-from-cyberspace" rules—treaties that prohibit offensive cyber operations or mandate digital ceasefires. In 2015, the U.S. and China reached a bilateral commitment to refrain from cyber-enabled theft of intellectual property for commercial advantage. For several months, analysts observed a drop in Chinese intrusion activity targeting U.S. firms. But by 2017, activity resumed, albeit with different operational tactics. The agreement reshaped behaviour but did not stop operations. It offered discipline without permanence.

A more ambitious attempt emerged at the UN Group of Governmental Experts (UN GGE), which debated global norms for cyber behaviour from 2010 to 2021. Agreements encouraged restraint against critical infrastructure, cooperation on incident response, and adherence to international law. Yet these norms lacked inspection regimes or penalties. When Russia launched cyberattacks against Ukrainian banks and ministries in February 2022, hours before the wider invasion, no enforcement mechanism existed to penalise the breach of established norms. The limitation here is fundamental: norms rely on voluntary compliance from actors who benefit most from their violation.

A counter-example softens the pessimism. In 2020, after a series of ransomware attacks against hospitals during the COVID-19 pandemic, several major cybercriminal groups publicly pledged to avoid targeting healthcare. While some violated their own declarations, others adhered. Behaviour showed partial restraint. Naming the phenomenon—self-imposed ethical boundaries—suggests that norms can emerge informally even among adversaries. Yet the reconciliation is sober: voluntary boundaries are brittle when profitability and geopolitics provide incentives to overstep them.

As jurisdictions multiply, the enforcement challenge intensifies. The Budapest Convention on Cybercrime, signed in 2001, provides a framework for extradition and cooperation, but major powers such as Russia, China, and India have refused to ratify it. Without shared standards, mutual assistance stalls. Investigators pursuing a ransomware gang in St Petersburg may find themselves blocked by sovereignty arguments. States invoke jurisdictional shields to prevent external scrutiny. The *unfinished rulebook* stretches again, unable to compel cooperation where strategic interests diverge.

For policymakers, the dilemmas converge into a single question: how do you legislate for a battlefield that is everywhere and nowhere? They measure thresholds—how many systems must fail before defensive force becomes justified? They compare risks—retaliation might expose classified capabilities or escalate conflict. They commit to frameworks—sanctions regimes, diplomatic advisories, joint statements—but each framework reflects compromise rather than clarity.

The unresolved tension is whether meaningful restraint is even feasible in a domain built on anonymity, deniability, and speed. If states cannot reliably attribute an attack, how can they punish it? If they cannot punish it, how can they deter it? And if they cannot deter it, what mechanism remains to prevent escalation? The *unfinished rulebook* lies open. The next intrusion may write its own rule before policymakers can draft theirs.

Chapter 4

Lawfare and Treaty Manipulations

The hearings at the Permanent Court of Arbitration in The Hague in July 2016 offered an image that has lingered in diplomatic memory: legal teams hunched over thousands of pages of maritime charts, affidavits, and expert testimony, attempting to redraw the meaning of a treaty signed decades earlier. The Philippines had brought its case against China under the UN Convention on the Law of the Sea, asking arbitrators to decide whether expansive maritime claims could be justified by historical narrative rather than legal entitlement. The tribunal's findings unsettled more than the two parties involved. They revealed how law itself had become a battleground, with states employing litigation not as a final resort but as an instrument of strategy—one in which persuasion, interpretation, and procedural endurance mattered as much as facts. The courtroom looked calm. The stakes were anything but.

Lawfare begins in moments like these: where power adopts legal form, and where legal form disguises power. It is not simply the use of law to settle disputes; it is the reshaping of law to produce strategic advantage. A government may abide by the letter of a treaty while eroding its spirit. Another may invoke norms it has no intention of following, solely to constrain a rival. The move is deceptively elegant. No soldier crosses a border. No warship fires a shot. Yet the balance of influence shifts as surely as it would in any conventional campaign. Legal arguments become artillery. Tribunal schedules become tactical timelines. Even filing fees can carry the weight of coercion.

This chapter enters that terrain—the quiet theatre in which states press their interests through courts, councils, clauses, and committees—while insisting they are merely upholding international order. It is a theatre where ambiguity is a resource, precedent a weapon, and delay a form of pressure. It is also a theatre where outcomes often hinge on who has the stamina to remain inside the process the longest. Legal scholars sometimes speak of "normative power," but in its more strategic form it resembles something different: a kind of institutional judo, the leveraging of procedures designed for fairness to produce advantage through friction.

One sees this most starkly in boundary disputes. Treaties drafted in haste or hope leave behind seams, and seams invite manoeuvre. A clause written to ensure flexibility becomes a gap large enough for expansive claims. A term meant to encourage cooperation becomes a shield behind which a state can move incrementally, knowing that each small step is easier to tolerate than to contest. Legal bodies, bound to deliberate carefully, cannot match the speed of geopolitical ambition. That mismatch creates a grey zone in which subtle violations accumulate until they acquire the appearance of normality. The longer a breach remains unchallenged, the more it looks like practice—and the harder it becomes to overturn.

Yet lawfare does not stop at borders. It extends into the chambers of international courts, where litigation can serve as a slow-acting constraint. Some governments initiate suits not to win, but to exhaust. A case filed before the International Court of Justice or an investment arbitration panel can freeze a rival's assets, cast reputational shadows, or deter investors simply by existing. The process itself becomes the punishment. In certain cases, corporations have even deployed this logic against states, using investor–state dispute mechanisms to challenge environmental regulations or infrastructure decisions. The suits may fail on the merits, but success lies elsewhere: in signalling cost, in buying time, in forcing a recalibration of policy. The courtroom becomes a lever, not a venue for closure.

Treaties, too, invite tactical manipulation. Vague provisions tempt states to stretch their meaning, claiming compliance while edging into violation. When bodies like the UN Security Council or regional organisations respond slowly—as they often must, due to diplomatic sensitivities—those stretches can accumulate into de facto rights. A state that repeatedly conducts patrols in contested waters, or establishes facts on the ground while claiming they are temporary, knows that the burden of proof falls on the accuser. Without immediate evidence, protest becomes performance rather than remedy. The ambiguity is deliberate. Power grows in the space between what is forbidden and what can be proven.

International forums add yet another layer to this strategic ecosystem. Committees, rapporteurs, and voting blocs can be marshalled to shape global narratives. Governments form alliances not only for shared interests but for procedural leverage: the ability to set agendas, determine the order of debate, or draft resolutions that frame events to their advantage. When a state lobbies successfully for a condemnation of a rival—sometimes over an incident still under investigation—it shifts diplomatic gravity without deploying a single asset. Reputation becomes terrain. Public statements become sanctions in softer form. The chamber's acoustics amplify power without exposing its sources.

Viewed together, these dynamics raise a difficult question: how does the international system preserve legitimacy when law itself becomes a strategic asset? Treaty designers must decide whether to tighten clauses, risking rigidity, or preserve ambiguity, risking exploitation. Legal resilience demands adaptability—mechanisms to update agreements quickly, procedures to sanction subtle violations, dispute-resolution bodies capable of rapid, credible action. Yet every improvement encounters resistance. States guard their sovereignty fiercely. They demand rules for others and flexibility for themselves. The guardianship of order becomes entangled with the pursuit of advantage.

Still, the search for resilience cannot be abandoned. Without credible treaties, the temptation to manipulate grey areas grows stronger. Without agile dispute mechanisms, stalling becomes a competitive strategy. Without shared norms, forums turn into battlegrounds rather than meeting places. The challenge—felt in The Hague, in New York, in countless regional councils—is how to design frameworks that accommodate geopolitical reality without surrendering to it entirely. That is the tension running through this chapter: the recognition that law can be both shield and sword, constraint and conduit, ideal and instrument.

What follows explores that tension in depth. It traces how states weaponise clauses, courts, and committees; how ambiguity becomes a currency; how legal structures built to stabilise the world can be bent into tools of pressure. It also considers what resilience might realistically look like, and why the future of global order may depend not on eliminating lawfare—an impossible task—but on managing it with clarity and resolve. The question is not whether states will continue to fight in courtrooms and council chambers. They already do. The question is what rules, if any, will shape that fight.

Legal Instruments as Weapons

The hearing room at the Permanent Court of Arbitration in The Hague on 12 July 2016 felt strangely subdued for a moment that would recalibrate regional power. Lawyers for the Philippines laid out maritime charts showing reefs and shoals in the South China Sea, while China—having declined to participate—remained an absent presence looming over every exhibit. When the tribunal ruled that China's "historic rights" claim had no legal basis, it handed Manila a sweeping victory. Yet the outcome revealed something larger still: law itself had become a battlefield. States could now project influence through case law as effectively as through patrol boats. The maps on the tribunal's screens marked more than disputed waters; they mapped the emergence of lawfare as a strategic craft.

The term "lawfare" gained currency in the early 2000s, but the practice has deep roots. It describes the deliberate use, manipulation, or selective enforcement of legal instruments to secure geopolitical advantage. Its potency lies in paradox: it converts legal restraint into strategic opportunity. A state may argue that its actions are compelled by treaty obligations even as it interprets those obligations to suit its aims. Another may weaponise international law not to settle disputes but to impose costs, delay rivals, or create a veneer of legitimacy. Law becomes a shield and a blade at once.

The appeal of this approach is obvious. Litigation costs less than mobilisation. A cleverly constructed legal argument can shift diplomatic equilibrium without triggering armed retaliation. The performance of compliance offers protection: a state that claims merely to follow the rules gains moral cover even as it stretches them. The motif running through these manoeuvres is the quiet movement through grey zones—spaces where law is not violated outright but contorted just enough to change its meaning. These grey zones recur throughout the modern system; they are its seams, and seams invite pressure.

Consider how treaties lend themselves to such manipulation. Many were drafted in periods of relative optimism, when negotiators assumed that clarity could be inferred from spirit rather than spelled out in text. Yet ambiguity is not an oversight; it is often a diplomatic necessity. Vagueness allows competing signatories to claim victory at home. But in practice, it provides ample room for redefinition. A clause requiring "due regard" for another state's interests becomes a licence to obstruct. An article obliging "peaceful intentions" turns into a shield for coercive patrols presented as routine. What begins as interpretation becomes slow, cumulative revision.

The 2016 South China Sea arbitration illustrates this dynamic. Under the UN Convention on the Law of the Sea (UNCLOS), states are guaranteed certain maritime entitlements. But the Convention left unresolved the relationship between historical claims and legal zones, assuming courts would handle such ambiguities case by case. China interpreted this grey space expansively, insisting that past usage amounted to sweeping jurisdiction, while the Philippines argued that historical narrative must yield to legal delineation. The tribunal agreed with Manila. Yet the case also showed the limits of lawfare's clarity: Beijing rejected the ruling outright, proving that even decisive judgments can become symbolic victories rather than practical constraints. The risk of lawfare is that when law becomes visibly instrumentalised, its authority weakens.

A second pattern emerges around selective enforcement. States frequently uphold treaties when enforcement serves their interests and downplay them when it does not. This is not hypocrisy so much as the structural design of international law, which lacks a central enforcer. Powerful states can comply à la carte, turning norms into strategic resources. When the United States refused to recognise the International Criminal Court's jurisdiction over its personnel in Rome Statute cases, it was practising a form of defensive lawfare—securing treaty exemptions to shield itself from legal vulnerability. When Russia cited the 1999 Kosovo intervention to justify its recognition of Abkhazia and South Ossetia in 2008, it engaged in imitative lawfare—appropriating Western legal rhetoric to justify its own geopolitical aims. These examples show how law can be invoked to widen policy options rather than narrow them.

The flip side is enforcement through excess. A state may press legal claims aggressively, not to win but to complicate. Filing a boundary case before the International Court of Justice can impose diplomatic and economic burdens on the target. Even if the claimant anticipates defeat, the process itself constrains a rival's actions. During the 1979 maritime delimitation dispute between Libya and Malta, Tripoli filed suit partly to assert symbolic authority over contested waters in the central Mediterranean. Although Malta eventually prevailed in 1985, Libya leveraged the years-long uncertainty to bolster its bargaining position in regional negotiations. The litigation acted as strategic fog—a delay mechanism that bought time for manoeuvre.

Yet lawfare does not always succeed. A counter-example lies in the 2002 Eritrea–Yemen arbitration over the Hanish Islands. Both states sought to frame historical presence and maritime rights in expansive terms, deploying seasoned legal teams and substantial archival evidence. The arbitral decision, however, was decisive, carefully balanced, and accepted by both sides. Instead of prolonging dispute, the legal process closed it. The limitation here is instructive: lawfare can be blunted when tribunals act swiftly, wield clear legal standards, and benefit from political willingness to abide by outcomes. The implication is that lawfare thrives where ambiguity meets reluctance; it falters where clarity meets commitment.

Still, even clear rulings can be strategically manipulated after the fact. Governments may comply selectively, implementing only the least costly obligations while ignoring the rest. Such behaviour reveals a darker truth: treaty compliance is often a political calculation, not a legal obligation. It is measured by visible decisions—coastguard deployments, resource licences withheld or granted, construction paused or accelerated. When compliance becomes conditional, rival states adjust their expectations accordingly, preparing for contests that unfold not on the battlefield but in the conference room and legal brief.

This brings us back to the quiet motif underlying lawfare: the courtroom becomes a proxy for the battlefield. Arguments replace artillery, but the objectives remain strikingly similar—gain ground, constrain rivals, defend positions, shape narratives. The tools differ; the logic does not. In legal settings, states measure credibility through evidence submitted, experts retained, and procedural tactics deployed. A government that refuses to appear before a tribunal may signal disdain, or strength, or a desire to deny the court legitimacy. The absence itself becomes strategy.

Complexity intensifies when multinational treaties intersect with regional ambition. The European Union, for instance, regularly invokes legal instruments to challenge member state deviations on rule-of-law issues. Critics claim this is political interference; defenders insist it is institutional preservation. Meanwhile, in Africa, overlapping treaty systems—the African Union, subregional communities, bilateral agreements—create a mosaic of norms that can be interpreted in multiple ways. A state seeking strategic advantage can select whichever legal instrument most favours its claim and frame compliance accordingly. Lawfare flourishes in such plural systems because fragmentation breeds opportunity.

The challenge for policymakers is acute: how to strengthen treaties without turning them into rigid traps; how to encourage compliance without enabling exploitation; how to maintain legitimacy when legal frameworks become tools of strategy. Attempts to revise treaties often meet resistance from states wary of limiting their future manoeuvrability. Efforts to clarify definitions may unsettle compromises painstakingly built over years. The pursuit of resilience encounters political geometry—angles, not straight lines.

A deeper dilemma shadows the entire system. If law becomes an openly strategic weapon, will states still trust it to provide stability? Trust is not rhetorical here; it manifests in behaviour: accepting judgments, refraining from opportunistic reinterpretation, submitting to monitoring. When that trust erodes, incentives shift towards unilateralism. Power fills the vacuum. Yet abandoning lawfare is impossible. States will always exploit the legal environment because it offers unique advantages: low cost, low visibility, high legitimacy. The task is not to eliminate lawfare but to manage its consequences, to create structures where legal contestation strengthens rather than corrodes the international order.

The unanswered question—one that frames the future of global governance—is whether the international community can design institutions nimble enough to respond to strategic legal manoeuvres without descending into procedural trench warfare. If law can be weaponised, can it also be armoured? Or will states continue to treat treaties as malleable documents, bending them until the line between compliance and coercion becomes indistinguishable?

Suing Rivals into Submission

On 16 January 2013, the International Centre for Settlement of Investment Disputes in Washington, D.C., registered *Yukos Universal Ltd. v. The Russian Federation*, a case that would sprawl across nearly a decade and consume thousands of pages of filings. What began as a claim by former shareholders seeking compensation for the dismantling of the Yukos oil conglomerate soon hardened into one of the largest arbitral awards ever issued—US$50 billion in July 2014. Yet the real consequence lay not in the number but in the process. For Russia, the arbitration became a diplomatic irritant, a reputational hazard, and a strategic distraction. For the claimants, it was a drawn-out campaign designed as much to tie up Moscow's legal bandwidth as to secure compensation. The case drifted through appeals, counter-appeals, and enforcement battles in Amsterdam, The Hague, and multiple national courts. Years passed. The judgment rose, fell, then rose again. The law, in this instance, outlasted the politics.

Strategic litigation has long served as a weapon of states seeking to complicate an adversary's agenda without resorting to force. The logic is deceptively simple: file a claim that cannot be ignored, then let procedure—slow, meticulous, and resource-intensive—do the work. The battlefield shifts to hearing rooms, legal teams, and interim measures. The quiet motif throughout is delay. Delay drains budgets. Delay constrains diplomatic choices. Delay generates uncertainty. A state tied up in legal disputes finds its attention divided, its officials distracted, and its reputation questioned before allies and investors. Litigation becomes an attritional campaign executed in plain sight.

International courts and tribunals inadvertently assist in this process. Their procedural architecture is designed for fairness, not speed. Each motion requires a response. Each evidentiary dispute invites expert analysis. Each interlocutory decision becomes a foothold for appeal. A claimant intent on stalling can multiply filings; a respondent determined to resist can do the same. The judiciary, bound by rules of due process, cannot simply dismiss these manoeuvres as vexatious. Time becomes a commodity, and the party best able to manipulate it gains advantage.

A second example illustrates the tactic from another angle. In 2004, Nicaragua filed suit against Colombia at the International Court of Justice over maritime boundaries in the Caribbean Sea. The process stretched across multiple phases, culminating in a 2012 judgment that redrew the maritime map, granting Managua significant waters but leaving sovereignty over islands with Bogotá. The verdict spawned a series of follow-on applications, counter-claims, and jurisdictional disputes that continued well into the following decade. Throughout, Colombia maintained naval patrols and asserted that the Court lacked authority to alter its constitutional geography. The litigation became a diplomatic choke-point: talks froze, investments stalled, and both governments devoted political capital to explaining an evolving case to domestic audiences. Victory mattered less than narrative control, and narrative control depended on exploiting the procedures of the Court itself.

Such strategies reveal how lawsuits can be deployed not to win but to burden. A legal claim forces an adversary to assemble teams, hire counsel, collect evidence, and recalibrate diplomatic messaging. These behaviours have measurable costs: billable hours, diverted staff, postponed initiatives. Even when a state is confident of eventual victory, the journey itself can strain institutional capacity. The implication is stark: a lawsuit becomes a theatre of operations where the goal is not adjudication but exhaustion.

Corporations, too, find themselves entangled in these contests, sometimes as pawns, sometimes as proxies. The case of Chevron's prolonged dispute with Ecuador is instructive. What began as litigation over environmental damage in Lago Agrio escalated into a labyrinth of international claims, counter-claims, and enforcement bids spanning courts in Quito, New York,

The Hague, and Toronto. By 2018, arbitral tribunals had ruled in Chevron's favour, citing procedural irregularities and alleged misconduct in the Ecuadorian judgment. Yet Ecuador's government endured reputational blows, activist campaigns, and diplomatic friction throughout the process. The corporation, though legally vindicated, had spent years—and vast financial resources—waging a legal war of attrition. The limitation here is clear: lawfare through litigation carries risks for all parties, for the very reach of international jurisdiction means reputational fallout spreads quickly and unpredictably. Still, the dynamic reinforces the core point: strategic lawsuits have become instruments for shaping political and economic terrain.

States deploy these actions with a degree of plausible deniability. They may argue that domestic law obliges them to defend their interests in court, or that they are merely upholding treaty rights. Yet when litigation becomes serial, targeted, and timed to strategic moments, intent becomes visible. One need only observe the filing patterns: cases launched on the eve of negotiations, motions submitted during periods of diplomatic pressure, appeals lodged when enforcement approaches. These behaviours reveal a strategic choreography. Litigation is not reactive but deliberate.

A counter-example underscores that this tactic is not infallible. In the 2015 Mauritius v. United Kingdom arbitration concerning the Chagos Archipelago, London faced claims that its creation of a Marine Protected Area violated the rights of displaced Chagossians. The tribunal ruled partly in Mauritius's favour in 2015, and a related 2019 advisory opinion by the International Court of Justice further undermined the UK's position. Rather than buying time, the British legal strategy backfired, galvanising international support for Mauritius and creating long-term diplomatic costs. Here, the attempt to delay produced acceleration: scrutiny increased, and political space for manoeuvre shrank. This example shows how poorly calibrated lawfare can invert its purpose. Still, even in misfire, the process consumed years—time that could be used to adjust policies, negotiate terms, or manage reputational fallout.

The corporate-versus-state dimension extends the reach of this strategy. Consider the 2016 ICSID award in *Rockhopper Exploration plc v. Italy*, in which the British oil company claimed losses after Italy banned offshore drilling near its coast. Italy found itself litigating across multiple forums while managing domestic environmental politics and EU regulatory obligations. For Rockhopper, the case became both a legal remedy and a pressure mechanism, signalling to other governments the financial consequences of abrupt regulatory change. The lesson was unmistakable: litigation can serve as a warning as much as a remedy, shaping behaviour beyond the immediate dispute.

The common thread across these cases is that legal confrontation creates a form of reputational gravity. Once a state is drawn into prolonged litigation, the narrative becomes sticky. Investors monitor filings. Allies ask pointed questions. Civil society mobilises. The matter gains momentum independent of the original grievance. The courtroom becomes a stage in which credibility is measured through visible decisions: disclosure levels, cooperation with tribunals, consistency of argument. Even silence becomes meaningful, as when a state refuses to attend proceedings, signalling both disdain and possible vulnerability.

This brings us back to the quiet motif that runs through strategic litigation: the slow tightening of time. Unlike kinetic conflict, where escalation is rapid and destructive, lawfare through lawsuits advances by accretion. Each brief adds weight. Each hearing adds delay. The target may not feel crisis, but it feels drag—a steady pull on capacity and attention. For policymakers, the dilemma is whether to fight on procedural terrain or seek negotiated exits. Settlement brings speed but concedes narrative. Litigation preserves principle but surrenders time.

The unresolved question, and one that frames the remainder of this chapter, is simple but consequential: when does legal defence become strategic entanglement, and how does a state decide whether to escalate, settle, or step back from a confrontation that may last longer than the dispute that triggered it?

Subtle Treaty Violations

At dawn on 24 May 1997, Indonesian and Malaysian patrol boats edged uneasily around the waters off Sipadan and Ligitan, two small islands in the Celebes Sea whose ownership had become a matter of finely drawn treaty interpretation. Neither side fired a shot. Neither crossed a visible boundary. Yet both quietly adjusted the facts on the ground. Malaysia erected small structures—lighthouses and shelters—arguing they constituted lawful administration under ambiguous colonial-era agreements. Indonesia protested but hesitated to escalate, aware that the treaties guiding the dispute, including the 1891 Convention between Britain and the Netherlands, were studiously vague about sovereignty over minor features. It took until December 2002 for the International Court of Justice to award the islands to Malaysia. By then, Malaysia's incremental steps had created a record of "effective control" that proved decisive. A subtle violation, or a subtle fulfilment, depending on perspective. What mattered was not the scale of the actions but the silence that met them.

Such manoeuvres speak to a broader truth: treaties often contain language designed to appease negotiators rather than constrain behaviour. Clauses refer to *reasonable measures*, *due regard*, or *appropriate steps*—phrases capacious enough to accommodate contradictory interpretations. States exploit these openings with a delicate choreography. They commit acts small enough to avoid outrage but significant enough to shift precedent. The quiet motif here is erosion: a slow wearing away of norms through repetition rather than rupture. Each step is modest; the cumulative impact is transformative.

The attraction of subtle violations lies partly in plausible deniability. When a state positions survey vessels just outside a neighbour's territorial sea, or conducts "routine inspections" of ships in areas governed by overlapping claims, it can insist it operates within treaty bounds. Ambiguous text supports flexible explanations. Enforcement bodies such as the UN or regional organisations must tread cautiously, for accusing a state of violating treaties requires compelling evidence—evidence that is often fleeting, contested, or deliberately obscured. Minor infractions rarely meet the threshold for sanctions or formal censure. The risk of false accusation looms large, encouraging restraint even when infractions are obvious to those closest to them.

Consider China's incremental expansion in the Spratly Islands throughout the 1990s and early 2000s. Beijing maintained that its activities—building small shelters, deploying fishing fleets under state direction—were lawful under its interpretation of historic rights and UNCLOS provisions. Rival claimants disagreed, yet global responses remained muted. The acts were too dispersed, too marginal, and too clouded by legal complexity to galvanise collective action. By the time larger structures appeared in the mid-2010s, the pattern had been normalised. What once seemed aggressive now appeared familiar. The implication is stark: slow reactions do not simply fail to deter subtle violations—they entrench them.

A second example illustrates this drift from ambiguity to precedent. In 2010, Ethiopia began constructing the Grand Ethiopian Renaissance Dam on the Blue Nile. Egypt, citing colonial-era treaties from 1929 and 1959, argued that Ethiopia required its consent. Ethiopia countered that those treaties excluded it and that modern principles of equitable utilisation applied. For years, negotiations proceeded in fits and starts. Meanwhile, construction continued. Each additional turbine, each milestone reached, shifted leverage. No tribunal moved swiftly enough to clarify rights before the facts changed. The limitation here is instructive: even when law is clear, institutions often act too slowly to shape events. The dam became a symbol of how strategic patience can trump formal rules.

The challenge of proving subtle violations compounds this inertia. Treaty breaches often manifest through behaviours rather than declarations. Extra customs checks at a border crossing, selective enforcement of fishing quotas, the quiet deployment of unmarked security personnel—these acts generate patterns, not incidents. Intelligence agencies may detect anomalies, but evidentiary standards for international condemnation require verifiable attribution. A vessel's transponder goes dark. A document is leaked without metadata. A patrol's nationality remains technically "unconfirmed". Immediate proof dissolves, replaced by inference.

States exploit these evidentiary gaps with calculated precision. When Russia deployed "little green men" in Crimea in February 2014—armed personnel without insignia—Moscow initially denied involvement, claiming they were local defence groups. The statement was implausible, yet difficult to debunk instantly. International organisations called for investigation. Investigation required time. Time allowed structure: referendums organised, administration absorbed, narratives fixed. The subsequent admission of involvement did not alter the strategic outcome. The cost of acting early had seemed higher than the cost of acting late; this imbalance is lawfare's most enduring advantage.

Yet subtle violations can falter when transparency overrides ambiguity. A counter-example emerges from the 2005–2006 border dispute between Cameroon and Nigeria following the ICJ's ruling on the Bakassi Peninsula. Despite years of grey-zone manoeuvring by both sides, the presence of UN observers and sustained diplomatic engagement limited opportunities for minor infractions to accumulate meaningfully. Where monitoring is visible, and reporting rapid, the calculus shifts. Violations become harder to normalise. Still, the exception underlines the rule: only with sustained oversight do treaties regain weight.

The consequences of unchecked subtle violations ripple far beyond the immediate dispute. Norms weaken as they adapt to repeated bending. Allies begin to reassess the reliability of legal commitments. Smaller states, observing inconsistent enforcement, adjust by hedging—seeking new patrons, diversifying partnerships, or building capacities once guaranteed under treaty protection. Such shifts reveal the behavioural metric of eroding trust: states start to measure obligations against the probability of betrayal rather than the promise of law.

The phenomenon also exposes the structural tension within international governance. Treaties require flexibility to accommodate changing realities, yet flexibility invites exploitation. Enforcement bodies require consensus to act, yet consensus is often impossible when major powers benefit from ambiguity. Attempts to tighten wording may provoke walkouts; attempts to strengthen monitoring may be framed as threats to sovereignty. The architecture of global governance rests uneasily on these contradictions.

The unresolved question, the one that threads through every example, is precise and unsettling: at what point do subtle violations cease to be exceptions and become the baseline upon which future conduct is measured?

Weaponising International Forums

On 23 March 2021, the Human Rights Council chamber in Geneva filled with a familiar choreography: delegates adjusting earpieces, interpreters steadying their microphones, aides sliding final notes across polished desks. Minutes later, the United States tabled a resolution condemning China's actions in Xinjiang with EU support. What followed was not a legal debate but a diplomatic battlefield. China's delegation moved quickly, lobbying member states from Africa, the Middle East, and Southeast Asia. Within hours, a counter-statement—framed as a defence of sovereignty—gathered more signatures than the original motion. No treaty was rewritten. No sanctions were imposed. Yet the reputational balance shifted. Beijing avoided formal censure not by military projection but by mobilising voting blocs, shaping perceptions, and signalling the high cost of alignment with its critics. The outcome was as strategic as any naval deployment.

This episode captures how international forums, ostensibly designed for deliberation, can be repurposed as competitive theatres. Resolutions become tools of pressure. Committee appointments morph into contests of influence. Voting patterns reveal loyalties that states prefer to mask elsewhere. The quiet motif running through these manoeuvres is visibility: the moment a vote is cast, a state's alignments surface, and those alignments carry consequences. A rival may find itself isolated not through force but through arithmetic.

The shape of this practice is consistent across institutions. States cultivate networks long before any vote. They commit to development projects, forgive debts, coordinate trade deals, or offer favourable visa regimes. In return, they expect diplomatic support—sometimes explicit, often implied. These behaviours form a ledger of informal obligations. When crisis looms, that ledger is called in. The implication is unavoidable: influence in international forums is accumulated incrementally, then deployed decisively.

Consider how the Organisation of American States (OAS) became a battleground in 2017 over Venezuela's political direction. The United States and several Latin American states sought a resolution condemning Caracas for democratic backsliding. Venezuela, backed by Bolivia and Nicaragua, campaigned to block the motion. Both sides lobbied aggressively, courting smaller Caribbean nations whose votes could swing the outcome. Offers of energy assistance, development aid, and future trade arrangements circulated discreetly. In the end, the resolution fell short of the supermajority required. The limitation here is instructive: even when a clear majority supports action, procedural thresholds can shelter a state from censure. Yet the political impact endured. The voting record exposed regional fractures and signalled the shifting weight of influence across the hemisphere.

A parallel example emerged at UNESCO in 2016, when Israel and the United States objected to a resolution regarding cultural heritage sites in Jerusalem. Israel argued the resolution minimised Jewish historical links to the Temple Mount. Diplomatic efforts intensified immediately. Tel Aviv appealed to African and Asian states, emphasising shared concerns over politicised heritage claims, while Arab states rallied support by framing the issue as a protection of cultural rights. The vote passed, but only narrowly. The episode demonstrated that cultural institutions—often perceived as neutral—can become instruments of geopolitical narrative-setting. Each paragraph of the adopted text carried symbolic weight; each member's vote revealed strategic calculations extending far beyond archaeology.

Such cases show how states manipulate agendas even before motions arrive on the floor. Committees decide which issues receive airtime, which are quietly deferred, and which become multiyear projects. A well-placed ally in a procedural subcommittee can ensure an item appears late in the session when attendance wanes or push it onto a crowded agenda where it is overshadowed. These behaviours are visible in meeting minutes: sudden schedule rearrangements, unusual requests for additional consultations, or repeated calls for "technical clarifications". Each procedural decision may appear bureaucratic but often masks deliberate strategy.

At times, manipulation moves from agenda-setting to punishment. When Turkey criticised Saudi Arabia's handling of the Jamal Khashoggi murder in late 2018, Riyadh responded not through diplomatic rupture but through coordinated voting and lobbying at the Organisation of Islamic Cooperation (OIC). Proposals favourable to Turkish positions stalled; discussions Turkey hoped to elevate were downgraded to working groups. The measures were subtle but cumulative. Ankara found its traditional influence diluted across committees where Saudi alliances held sway. Punishment took the form of procedural invisibility.

A counter-example, however, offers a reminder that weaponisation is not always successful. In 2020, China sought to prevent a World Health Organization vote that would allow Taiwan to attend the World Health Assembly as an observer. Despite significant lobbying, including appeals to African and Pacific states, several countries publicly resisted. They argued that Taiwan's pandemic response offered valuable expertise during a global crisis. The motion did not pass, but China's campaign created unexpected backlash. Some states began calling for reforms to observer criteria, while others signalled unease with perceived overreach. The limitation is evident: when lobbying becomes too forceful or too transparent, it can trigger resistance that undermines its purpose.

Beneath these strategic battles lies a structural vulnerability in global governance. International forums rely on procedural neutrality, yet neutrality depends on member states restraining their competitive instincts. When committees become arenas for strategic alignment, norms weaken. States begin to measure institutions not by their principles but by their utility. This shift manifests through visible behaviours: shrinking participation in debates, rising abstentions, and growing reliance on informal caucuses instead of formal negotiation. Once process becomes politicised, substance follows.

The corporate versus state dimension occasionally surfaces here too. Multinational firms, especially in extractive industries, often petition UN bodies or regional organisations to influence regulatory debates. States may use these corporate interventions tactically—inviting statements that support national positions or delegitimising rivals' arguments through sponsored research. These tactics reveal how influence radiates beyond formal diplomatic channels. The quiet motif of visibility returns: even non-state actors become instruments in shaping global perception.

Monitoring these manoeuvres requires forensic attention to detail. Analysts track changes in voting blocs, tally abstentions, measure shifts in language across successive resolutions, and compare sponsorship patterns. A single state moving from "abstain" to "oppose" can signal new alignments. A coalition dissolving across votes suggests negotiations elsewhere have faltered. This form of diplomatic measurement reflects a deeper truth: influence is observable in patterns long before it is declared.

The unresolved question shadows every forum: when does strategic engagement become manipulation, and when does manipulation erode the very legitimacy that states rely upon to condemn their rivals?

Building Legal Resilience

The Permanent Court of Arbitration in The Hague faced an unusual procedural hurdle on 12 July 2016. As the tribunal prepared to deliver its ruling in *Philippines v. China*, the judges were acutely aware that their award—rejecting China's extensive South China Sea claims—would have no binding enforcement arm. The Philippines gained a decisive legal victory. China refused to recognise the judgment. Yet the ruling reshaped diplomatic behaviour across Southeast Asia, influencing defence partnerships, investment patterns, and maritime practices. The tribunal exposed a structural tension: international law can deliver clarity, but not always compliance. That gap between principle and power remains the central problem of legal resilience.

This scene signals a deeper question. Treaties rely on wording that aspires to universality, yet states interpret text through the prism of sovereignty. A phrase like "due regard" or "reasonable measures" can swing billions of dollars in resource rights, but its meaning depends on context, politics, and precedent. When global bodies hesitate to react, ambiguity hardens into custom. The sea becomes a ledger of competing narratives rather than settled rules. *Rules drift.* That motif recurs throughout the story of treaty fragility.

Strengthening treaties begins with acknowledging how they fail. When states exploit vaguely drafted clauses, they usually point to textual fidelity. The behaviour appears as formal compliance—states issue lengthy memoranda, submit counter-maps, cite previous resolutions—while simultaneously altering reality on the ground. Naming this pattern matters. For example, after the 1994 Energy Charter Treaty came into force, several European states used its investor-protection provisions to challenge regulatory changes they argued were discriminatory. The resulting arbitration surge by the early 2010s revealed how clauses drafted with post-Cold War optimism proved ill-suited for complex environmental transitions. The implication is stark: vague or overly flexible treaty language invites reinterpretation that undermines collective goals.

Closing such wording gaps requires deliberate craftsmanship. Analysts study how specific verbs—"shall", "should", "endeavour to"—anchor obligations with varying degrees of precision. Negotiators measure the impact of each choice by modelling compliance scenarios. A clause that mandates emissions monitoring every quarter is stronger than one requiring "periodic review". The metric is behavioural: how often must a state report, and what happens when it does not? The Oslo Convention on Cluster Munitions (2008) offers an instructive example. By imposing clear national reporting requirements and a fixed timeline for stockpile destruction, it constrained the wiggle room states might have sought. Critics highlight its limitations—several major powers refused to join—but among signatories, clarity strengthened follow-through.

The challenge intensifies when enforcement mechanisms lag behind violations. The European Court of Human Rights (ECHR) illustrates both promise and constraint. In cases such as *Ilgar Mammadov v. Azerbaijan* (2014), the Court ordered the release of a political prisoner, yet compliance took years and required sustained pressure from the Council of Europe. The counter-example is compelling: even strong institutions falter when political incentives overshadow legal obligations. And yet, the Court's continuing scrutiny showed why resilience depends not on instantaneous power but on sustained visibility. Each delayed response generated reports, plenary debates, and diplomatic costs. The motif of rules drift becomes rules resisted.

Financial measures can tighten enforcement. Sanctions regimes linked to treaty violations—such as the UN's Article 41 mechanisms—work best when automated triggers are built into agreements. If a state misses a deadline for chemical weapons disclosure, for instance, monitoring bodies can escalate the matter without requiring new consensus. Behaviour then becomes measurable: missing reports, restricted site access, contradictory declarations. Yet this system has a limitation. Powerful states can obstruct consensus or cast doubt on findings, as seen in Security Council disputes over Syrian chemical weapons investigations from 2017 onward.

Reconciling this limitation leads to a critical insight: enforcement must diversify. Regional bodies, independent labs, and cross-institutional panels can corroborate evidence when global unanimity collapses.

Legal resilience also depends on flexible dispute-resolution mechanisms. Traditional tribunals move slowly; cases can stretch a decade. During that time, the strategic environment shifts, evidence degrades, and fait accompli behaviours become entrenched. More agile pathways exist. The 1982 UN Convention on the Law of the Sea offered optional "special chambers" for faster maritime boundary rulings. Similarly, the East African Court of Justice, despite limited jurisdiction, pioneered faster interim orders to prevent irreversible harm while cases proceed. These innovations reveal a broader implication: speed is not a luxury in geopolitics; it is a safeguard. A tribunal that delivers a ruling too late risks irrelevance.

Still, speed cannot erase the tension between sovereignty and collective rules. Many states fear that tightening treaty language or accelerating enforcement will erode their autonomy. This fear shows through specific behaviours: reservations attached at ratification, interpretive declarations filed with depositaries, late submission of annual reports. These acts are signals of caution. They reflect political realities rather than malice. Sympathising with this complexity is essential. International law must not prescribe uniformity where none exists; it must instead construct pathways through which diverse states can commit without feeling cornered.

Confidence-building can help. The Chemical Weapons Convention (1997) introduced structured "clarification requests" that allow states to raise concerns without launching immediate formal disputes. This mechanism lowers the diplomatic temperature and offers political cover for compliance. Information-sharing, technical exchanges, and verification training deepen institutional memory. The behaviour to watch here is participation: when states send capable delegations, share national data, and host inspections, treaty resilience grows. When they send minimal teams or delay responses, drift reappears.

A more durable reform may lie in hybrid oversight. Independent scientific bodies, civil-society monitors, and regional organisations can complement treaty institutions by providing parallel evidence streams. The International Commission on Missing Persons (ICMP), originally formed in 1996 for the Balkans, expanded its mandate as states recognised the value of impartial forensic capabilities. Its documented DNA identifications—over 22,000 by 2020—created a trusted factual layer that courts, families, and governments could rely on. Though not a treaty body, its method offers a blueprint. Evidence gathered by multiple actors reduces the scope for manipulation and accelerates accountability.

Yet even the most refined legal architecture confronts a final dilemma: treaties operate in a competitive world. States exploit ambiguity because ambiguity offers advantages. They delay compliance because delay grants leverage. They reject rulings because obedience would cost them territory, prestige, or resources. The task of building legal resilience, therefore, is not to pretend that law can transcend power but to ensure that law shapes power's trajectory. The question, then, lingers: can future treaties be drafted with enough precision, backed by enough agility, and supported by enough political will to prevent the next quiet slide from rules to drift—and can they do so before the drift becomes entrenched?

Chapter 5

Maritime Militia Tactics

At dawn on 9 March 2014, officers aboard the Philippine Coast Guard cutter *Maragatan* watched a slow-moving fishing trawler drift across the mouth of Second Thomas Shoal. The vessel's deck was cluttered with nets, faded buoys, and stacks of plastic pails—props of a normal working boat. Yet its manoeuvres were anything but routine. It shadowed the cutter's path, altered speed in perfect sync, and maintained a deliberate distance of sixty metres, just beyond the threshold that might compel a formal boarding. No flag. No call-sign. No acknowledgement. The officers logged the encounter, aware that this modest hull—more workhorse than warship—was acting with a discipline learned elsewhere. A civilian silhouette carried the intent of a state.

This quiet theatre of pressure has become a defining feature of maritime contestation. Fishing fleets double as paramilitary vanguards. Cargo vessels run patterns that look more like reconnaissance than commerce. Offshore, the line separating ordinary livelihoods from covert power projection grows faint enough to dissolve. It is a contradiction that unsettles seasoned naval commanders: how do you respond to aggression that hides behind an innocent profile? The world's oceans hold this riddle in plain sight.

Maritime militias thrive in ambiguity. Their power rests not in armour or firepower but in the protective shell of normality. Commercial paint schemes and mended nets form a kind of camouflage that no conventional naval vessel can reliably interpret at first glance. This presents a strategic problem with profound consequences. If a state can mobilise an informal flotilla to advance territorial claims while denying any official connection, it gains a pressure tool that is both flexible and deniable. The sea becomes a grey zone—an operating space shaped less by formal fleets than by legions of plausible civilians.

The rise of these militias embodies a broader shift in how states test boundaries. Coercion no longer needs a destroyer or a frigate; it can move through hulls that would not look out of place in a postcard of coastal life. A fishing captain who receives quiet instructions via a provincial liaison office, a merchant vessel that adjusts AIS signals for a "maintenance failure", a cluster of trawlers forming a barrier in disputed waters—all these create strategic faits accomplis without the spectacle of gunfire. The stakes are high. A state that appears absent can steer events from the shadows. A rival that seeks to resist must do so without escalating into open conflict. The motifs of disguise and pressure recur.

These tactics frustrate conventional maritime doctrine because they manipulate the rituals of normality. A naval officer expects to interpret codes, radar signatures, call-signs, and hull numbers—not smoke from a galley stove or the shape of a net stack. Yet these are now meaningful indicators. A tanker that drifts erratically near a contested reef can be conducting pattern surveillance. A pair of trawlers lingering on a shipping lane may be probing response times rather than chasing fish. The difference between routine and strategic intent hinges on behaviours too mundane for formal rules of engagement to address swiftly.

A pattern emerges across theatres. In 2019, unmarked vessels clustered near Scarborough Shoal in a manner that resembled a blockade but lacked the explicit qualities of one. In the East China Sea, Japanese patrol boats observed similar formations: civilian fishing boats manoeuvring with military precision, retreating the moment a coastguard cutter approached. Such cases highlight a core problem. International maritime law presumes good faith conduct by non-military vessels. When a fishing fleet behaves like a disciplined auxiliary force, that presumption collapses, yet the legal tools to address the breach remain blunt.

False flags heighten the confusion. A militia boat may fly a national ensign one hour, a provincial flag the next, and no flag at all when shadowing a rival's coastguard. This shifting identity disrupts attribution. States deny responsibility, attributing actions to private operators or rogue captains. These claims, while disingenuous, resonate because the vessels look civilian. In contested waters, identity becomes a weapon. The absence of a flag is not an oversight; it is a tactic that forces opponents to hesitate.

Deception extends beyond appearance. Electronic warfare plays an increasingly central role. Spoofed AIS transponders create phantom fleets miles away from their true position. Radio silence disables the usual cues used to assess intent. Dual-use cargo—spare engines, fuel drums, construction materials—can service both fishing operations and rapid island fortification. Maritime domain awareness, once a matter of tracking predictable military assets, now must map a seascape of unpredictable hybrid actors.

The significance of these developments reaches far beyond the world's flashpoints. If civilian fleets become instruments of statecraft, the moral architecture of maritime law strains under the weight of conflicting interpretations. Freedom of navigation, once secured by clear distinctions between military and civilian traffic, becomes vulnerable to manipulation. Even peaceful maritime regions feel the ripple effects. Nations invest in new sensors, algorithmic anomaly detection, and joint patrols, aware that subtle provocations could unfold anywhere.

Yet countermeasures exist. Some states strengthen coastal radar networks to detect unusual patterns of movement—clusters of boats appearing at odd hours, vessels maintaining suspiciously tight formations. Others pursue multinational exercises designed to practise responses to hybrid maritime threats. The logic is clear: no single navy or coastguard can manage a problem built on ambiguity. Coordination must replace unilateralism. Historical precedents, from anti-piracy coalitions in the Gulf of Aden to combined fisheries patrols in the North Atlantic, show that agile partnerships can constrain elusive actors. The lesson is not that militias can be eliminated, but that their room for manoeuvre can be narrowed.

What makes maritime militias formidable is their alignment with the rhythms of the sea. Oceans have always been spaces where authority thins and improvisation thrives. When states weaponise routine behaviour, the surface calm becomes an illusion. The chapter ahead explores how covert fleets expand strategic options while burdening global maritime governance with puzzles it was never designed to solve. The question that follows is both practical and philosophical: how do we safeguard open waters when the vessels that challenge order look indistinguishable from the ones that sustain it?

Covert Naval Power

In April 2019, officers aboard the Vietnamese Fisheries Surveillance vessel *Kiem Ngu 214* watched a peculiar convoy slip across Vanguard Bank. The lead ship resembled a working trawler—rust along the bow, a lattice of nets drying in the sun—yet it moved with a discipline more akin to a naval auxiliary. Two similar hulls trailed behind it in a loose echelon, each adjusting course the moment the lead altered speed. None displayed a national ensign. None broadcast an Automatic Identification System

(AIS) signal. When *Kiem Ngu 214* altered its bearing, the convoy matched it, closing the gap to a controlled forty metres before peeling away in a manoeuvre that looked rehearsed. The encounter ended without incident, but it left a distinct imprint on the officers: these were not fishermen improvising on the waves. Someone had choreographed this.

Such fleets are built on contradiction. They look harmless but behave like instruments of policy. Civilian exteriors mask strategic agendas. The effect is potent because it exploits the visual grammar of normality at sea. Ordinary fishing boats travel in groups, sometimes with erratic patterns. Small cargo vessels linger near reefs while awaiting transhipment. These facts give wide cover for states seeking to project influence without triggering formal military responses. The sea is expansive, the traffic informal; ambiguity is easy to cultivate. States measure the advantages and commit to the masquerade.

The term *maritime militia* captures a layered phenomenon. It refers to civilians—or civilians in appearance—mobilised to advance state interests while maintaining a façade of independence. This may involve state-issued stipends, navigation training, or covert communications links disguised within ordinary equipment. When deployed in contested waters, such vessels gather intelligence, trail foreign coastguard ships, shield state construction efforts, or form blockades that, while not declared as such, carry all the functional properties of one. The motif of disguise recurs: hulls clad in chipped paint, crews in rubber boots, vessels that lack the steel and radar signatures of warships yet display uncommon coordination.

One clear example illustrates both the method and its impact. In 2012, during the height of the Scarborough Shoal standoff, Philippine authorities confronted a cluster of ostensibly civilian vessels that prevented them from arresting poachers. At first, the boats appeared to be ordinary fishing craft. But their behaviour—tight formations, disciplined withdrawal, and synchronised movements—aligned more closely with naval training. Scholars such as Andrew S. Erickson (US Naval War College, 2013) later documented the extensive role of what he termed the "People's Armed Forces Maritime Militia". The point was not the vessels' capabilities; it was their identity. They occupied legal grey zones that complicated Manila's response. A coastguard cutter cannot simply ram or arrest a civilian boat without taking on heavy political and legal risk.

The principle is straightforward: plausible civilians constrain professional militaries. A destroyer's rules of engagement rely on clear indicators of threat—flags, armaments, patterns of approach. These militias omit all three. They use behaviour rather than hardware to shape the encounter. If a fishing boat shadows a naval vessel at thirty metres, is it gathering intelligence or merely inexperienced? If it drifts across a contested shoal, is it trespassing deliberately or avoiding rough water? States exploit such ambiguities because every hesitation they induce extends their strategic manoeuvring room.

Two further cases underscore the pattern. In the East China Sea in 2016, the Japan Coast Guard reported that more than 300 Chinese fishing vessels had entered waters around the Senkaku/Diaoyu Islands. Many lacked AIS signals, a violation that ordinarily implies negligence or malfunction. Yet the vessels manoeuvred with surprising coherence, responding swiftly to Japanese patrols. Tokyo could not treat them as naval combatants; that would invite escalation. Nor could it ignore them; their presence reinforced competing claims. The ambiguity was the point.

A second case—less widely reported but equally telling—occurred off Natuna in 2020. Indonesia deployed its navy after a flotilla of foreign trawlers operated deeply inside its exclusive economic zone. Video footage later revealed that the flotilla's lead vessels received guidance from a distant ship consistent with a command-and-control platform. The fishermen did not hide; they invoked their right to work. The sponsoring state denied involvement. But the choreography was too precise to fit any spontaneous enterprise. The sea yielded a pattern of intent without a legally admissible author.

The appeal for states is obvious. Maritime militias offer influence without the liabilities of open force. A government can deny involvement, delaying diplomatic fallout while continuing to shape events on the water. If confronted, it points to private economic actors, domestic licensing disputes, or navigational errors. Meanwhile, the militia accomplishes its task: marking presence, deterring rivals, escorting survey ships, or asserting control over sensitive areas. Because the vessels appear civilian, rivals must treat them with care. Any misstep risks being framed as aggression against innocent mariners.

The danger, of course, is slippage. Not all fleets are equally disciplined. In 2017, Vietnamese fishermen near the Paracels clashed with a group of foreign vessels that allegedly sought to ram them. Hanoi avoided formal protest, likely wary of escalation, but the incident revealed a critical limitation in militia strategy. Civilians—even trained auxiliaries—do not always respond predictably under pressure. A misjudged manoeuvre can escalate a standoff or damage the sponsor's diplomatic posture. States weigh these risks but often judge the strategic benefits to outweigh the occasional embarrassment.

Yet the underlying logic remains resilient because it transforms the maritime environment itself. Instead of a stage for conventional naval encounters, the sea becomes a theatre of micro-interactions where intent must be deduced from patterns rather than armaments. A fishing boat blocking a channel at dusk may be performing a dual function—gathering catch while also positioning itself as a physical barrier to foreign patrols. A cargo vessel drifting near disputed reefs may be conducting hydrographic mapping under the guise of mechanical delay. Each behaviour sows hesitation, which in turn erodes the clarity that naval doctrine depends upon.

This ambiguity strains legal norms. The United Nations Convention on the Law of the Sea (UNCLOS) assigns rights and responsibilities based on vessel category: warship, government non-commercial vessel, or private craft. Maritime militias intentionally blur these distinctions. A state can insist that a boat remains legally a private vessel even as it executes tasks associated with state authority. The mismatch between conduct and classification renders enforcement difficult. A coastguard ship may suspect a militia role but cannot act on suspicion alone. The sponsor relies on this friction.

Critics sometimes argue that not every cluster of fishing boats deserves geopolitical interpretation. Storms, depleted fish stocks, and shifting currents can concentrate vessels in unexpected places. Equipment failures can disable AIS transmissions. These facts serve as a counterweight to claims of omnipresent state direction. And they matter: if analysts interpret every irregularity as strategy, they fall into the trap of over-attribution. To reconcile this tension, investigators examine behavioural consistencies. Ordinary fishermen scatter when approached by large patrol vessels; militias close in. Commercial vessels rarely maintain tight formation across extended distances; militias do. The veil is thin but discernible.

One motif helps anchor understanding: the silhouette. A silhouette at sea tells only part of a story. It reveals the hull shape and approximate size but says nothing about intent. States that deploy maritime militias weaponise this gap between appearance and purpose. The silhouette becomes both shield and signal—shielding the sponsor from accountability while signalling presence to rivals. The motif repeats across theatres, a reminder that coercion need not look like coercion to function.

Countermeasures are evolving, though they lag behind the ingenuity of covert fleets. Some states integrate satellite imagery with machine-learning tools to map anomalous movements. Others coordinate patrols with allies to reduce blind spots. Yet even the best sensors struggle to decode intent. Radar can plot a course; it cannot read instructions whispered during a port visit. The challenge is structural: the sea offers room to manoeuvre and room to hide.

As maritime militias continue to operate, states face a persistent dilemma. Respond too softly, and the pattern spreads. Respond too firmly, and an incident involving "civilians" can spiral into diplomatic crisis. The question for policymakers and naval commanders alike remains unresolved: how does one challenge covert power when it refuses to appear as power at all?

Hiding Behind Everyday Activities

At first glance, the satellite images from 21 March 2021 looked unremarkable: a scatter of small, white flecks moored in loose rows at Whitsun Reef, part of the Spratly archipelago in the South China Sea. Analysts in Manila and Washington zoomed in, expecting to see weather fronts or data artefacts. Instead, they counted hulls—dozens at a time—clustered tightly inside the atoll. Official statements later described them as fishing boats sheltering from rough seas. Yet the weather was calm. The vessels did not deploy nets. For days, then weeks, they remained stationary, lights burning through the night. No flag markings were clearly visible in many of the photographs. Ordinary boats. Extraordinary behaviour. The paradox was obvious to anyone who studied the patterns: an activity that looked routine was producing a very deliberate map.

This kind of scene has become a template. Fishing, shipping, coastal transport—each offers a plausible script that states can adopt to advance strategic aims without the visual cues of traditional power projection. The sea is full of noisy, everyday movement. Barges shuttle ore. Tankers wait for berths. Trawlers zigzag across rich grounds. Within that churn, it is remarkably easy to hide intent. A boat that drifts across a disputed reef can claim to be seeking shelter. A cargo vessel that slows near contested waters can cite engine trouble. A flotilla of trawlers idling in a tight cluster can insist on "normal operations". The motif that threads through such episodes is the *mask of routine*: activity that looks unremarkable but quietly redraws the balance of control.

Routine fishing has long intersected with geopolitics. Coastal communities depend on stocks that rarely respect legal boundaries; for centuries, boats have strayed across invisible lines in search of better catch. What is new is how governments now harness those routines. In some states, fishing captains receive subsidies to operate in contested zones, fuel vouchers that make long-range trips economically viable, and quiet assurances that coastguard support will be nearby if trouble arises. The visible behaviour—nets in the water, lanterns at night—appears unchanged. The hidden layer—reporting requirements, pre-arranged rendezvous points, radio codes—transforms an economic activity into a strategic presence.

Whitsun Reef illustrated this shift starkly. Philippine military patrols reported that the moored vessels maintained regular spacing, had unusually bright deck lighting at night, and showed no signs of fishing gear in active use. This did not prove state direction beyond doubt. But it strongly suggested a different mission: to establish a quasi-permanent cluster of "civilian" hulls inside a disputed feature, thus normalising a presence that would be politically riskier if asserted by grey-painted warships. The *mask of routine* did two things simultaneously. It made any robust response look disproportionate—who wants footage of coastguard ships harassing "fishermen"?—and it created facts on the water that could later be framed as evidence of longstanding use.

Cargo traffic offers similar cover. A bulk carrier can alter course by a few degrees and suddenly transit through waters another state considers sensitive. A tanker can slow just outside an exclusive economic zone and hover there for hours, "awaiting instructions". Container ships can use port calls in disputed regions as opportunities to gather signals intelligence or test radar coverage. None of this, taken alone, proves malign intent. Ships divert for weather, mechanical checks, or scheduling delays. But when such diversions repeatedly trace the same contested shoals or straits, they form their own cartography—a paperless chart of what a state considers negotiable.

One example, noted quietly by maritime analysts, involved a pattern of small oil tankers pausing near the Paracel Islands while ostensibly en route between Chinese and Southeast Asian ports. Their declared reasons—congestion, minor repairs—varied, but their positions coincided with survey lines previously used by government research vessels. Here, the normal rhythm of trade became a tool of familiarisation. Officers aboard these tankers observed local traffic, tested communication channels, and, by their very presence, underscored a claim to unconstrained passage in waters others regarded as disputed. The ships did not need to act aggressively. They just had to be there often enough that their presence ceased to attract attention.

Territorial marking at sea depends heavily on repetition. On land, a fence or a road can signal control. At sea, there is no equivalent of razor wire. Instead, control is demonstrated through patterns of presence: who fishes where, whose boats anchor where, which coastguard responds first when a distress call is made. Routine activities write these patterns over time. A cluster of foreign trawlers that returns season after season to the same reef turns a contested zone into something closer to a working ground. If the coastal state objects, it is portrayed as obstructing livelihoods. If it tolerates the incursions, those incursions gradually acquire the patina of normality. The *mask of routine* becomes a slow-moving instrument of annexation.

This creates dilemmas for states whose vessels encounter unmarked or ambiguously marked ships in disputed waters. A coastguard commander spotting a line of unflagged trawlers has limited choices. Boardings and seizures risk confrontation and international criticism. Warnings over radio go unanswered. Shadowing the vessels consumes fuel and time, stretching limited patrol assets. Ignoring them cedes psychological ground. Every option carries cost. Traditional naval doctrine offers little comfort. Rules of engagement are geared toward clearly identified threats, not silent boats hauling nets—or claiming to.

A short example from the Senkaku/Diaoyu area illustrates the bind. Japanese coastguard crews have repeatedly reported encounters with clusters of Chinese fishing vessels, some flying flags only intermittently, some not at all, operating just inside or at the edge of Japan's claimed territorial waters. These vessels perform recognisable tasks—setting lines, hauling catch—but also execute manoeuvres that look suspiciously like drills: coordinated turns, bracketed approaches toward Japanese patrols, deliberate "near misses" that test response thresholds. To treat them as ordinary fishermen would be naïve. To treat them as hostile combatants would be inflammatory. Stuck between those poles, Japan resorts to verbal warnings, photographs, and diplomatic protests. The unmarked hulls return the following season.

Of course, not every suspicious pattern is proof of state orchestration. Storms can push fleets off course. Overfishing can drive desperate crews into forbidden areas. Smugglers exploit maritime law for entirely private gain. A credible counter-example helps keep analysis honest. In 2015, a cluster of Vietnamese fishing boats appeared off the coast of Malaysia, prompting speculation about coordinated incursions. Subsequent investigation revealed a more prosaic cause: a middleman had misrepresented stock conditions and fuel subsidies, luring crews far from their usual grounds. The episode did not involve state sponsorship, but it did leave Malaysian authorities wary. The reconciliation lies in methodology: patterns must be assessed cumulatively, not assumed from single incidents. The *mask of routine* can hide both strategy and accident.

Still, the strategic use of everyday activity remains hard to ignore. Resource seizure under cover of fishing is perhaps the most obvious example. Trawlers can vacuum high-value stocks from contested waters, undermining the economic base of coastal communities that rely on them. Clam diggers and sand dredgers can strip reefs and shoals, damaging ecosystems while providing materials for island-building projects. All of this can be framed as labour, not coercion. Arrests become politically charged. Images of handcuffed fishermen play poorly on evening news broadcasts.

Territorial marking goes beyond presence. Floating markers—buoys, improvised beacons, even anchored rafts—appear in disputed zones, ostensibly to aid navigation. In practice, they function as quiet claims. Remove them, and the sponsoring state protests interference with safety. Leave them, and charts slowly accommodate their existence. Even radio chatter has a marking function: when patrol vessels from one state consistently answer mayday calls within a contested area, mariners begin to treat that state as the de facto authority there. Over time, habit hardens into expectation.

All of this confounds the usual toolkit of maritime law. The United Nations Convention on the Law of the Sea assumes categories—warship, government vessel, merchant ship, fishing boat—that map clearly onto roles. When those roles are blurred, enforcement agencies lose their bearings. A frigate cannot inspect every small craft it encounters. A coastguard service cannot chase every lightly laden cargo ship that veers slightly off standard lanes. The gap between what is technically possible and what is operationally sustainable widens. States exploiting everyday activity understand this arithmetic. They push just hard enough to stretch patrol capacities, never hard enough to provoke a military response they do not want.

The motif of the *mask of routine* returns most starkly in the question of intent. Intent is inferred from behaviour—distance kept from patrol vessels, compliance with radio instructions, patterns of seasonal return.

Yet these indicators are inherently ambiguous. A captain who kills his AIS transponder might be evading sanctions, avoiding pirates, or following instructions from a maritime militia coordinator. A freighter that slows abruptly could be calibrating sensors, waiting for port clearance, or loitering to observe a foreign exercise. The same outward act can carry different purposes. For analysts and commanders, this is the heart of the problem.

As maritime militias and opportunistic fleets become more sophisticated, coastal states are experimenting with new ways to read and challenge the mask. Some deploy drones to photograph decks up close, looking for signs of unusual equipment. Others work with commercial satellite firms to track loitering behaviour across months, not days. A few have begun to publish detailed reports on incursions, hoping that international exposure will deter the most blatant abuses. Yet each of these responses carries costs—financial, diplomatic, and operational. Making routine suspicious can sour relations with legitimate fishermen and traders, whose livelihoods are already precarious.

The unresolved tension hangs over every patrol report from disputed waters: when a radar screen fills with small, slow-moving returns, which blip is merely a boat seeking a better catch, and which is a piece in a larger territorial play? And if the only way to know is to treat all of them as potential instruments of strategy, how long before the sea's everyday commerce becomes collateral in a contest it never chose to enter?

False Flags and Denial

When the Philippine Coast Guard intercepted a cluster of vessels near Sabina Shoal in May 2023, officers expected the predictable choreography of contested waters: shouted warnings, slow withdrawals, perhaps a close pass for intimidation. Instead, they found boats with their flags lowered, names freshly painted over, and Automatic Identification System (AIS) transponders running irregularly or not at all. The moment the patrol attempted to document the encounter, several vessels raised flags that did not match earlier sightings. Others maintained silence and drifted away, as though indifferent to the unfolding standoff. The scene captured the essential puzzle of grey-zone maritime tactics: ships present and active, but identities unstable, affiliations concealed, intent masked by studied ambiguity. Five words, noted in one patrol log, captured the frustration: *We cannot confirm anything today.*

Flag manipulation is as old as maritime conflict. In 1588, English privateers shifted ensigns to confuse Spanish galleons off the Channel Islands, exploiting the few seconds of hesitation a mismatched flag could induce. The contemporary variant is more calibrated. Vessels linked informally to state-run maritime militias raise flags selectively, switch to registries in states with minimal oversight, or sail with no visible markings at all. A flag, in theory, confers nationality and legal accountability. Remove it, and a boat becomes a ghost—still physical, still consequential, but harder to trace within the legal frameworks that underpin maritime order. The motif that threads through these behaviours is the *vanishing signature*: the deliberate effort to erase the clues that tie visible conduct to political command.

One reason flag manipulation endures is its plausible deniability. When a flagged vessel behaves provocatively—shadowing a research ship, obstructing an oil exploration survey, or cutting across a patrol boat's bow—a sponsoring state can claim that it is a private actor pursuing its own agenda. The denial is often delivered through careful phrasing. No direct link is acknowledged; no responsibility accepted. Instead, statements refer to "civilian fishing communities", "commercial organisations operating independently", or "mariners exercising traditional rights". Each phrase nudges the encounter back into the civilian sphere, away from the charged world of state-directed operations. *We do not control them*, officials remark. Whether the claim is true matters less than its capacity to slow diplomatic escalation.

A well-documented pattern emerged in 2019 around the Natuna Islands, when Indonesian authorities repeatedly confronted Chinese fishing vessels accompanied by coastguard cutters. Several of the fishing boats flew Chinese flags at the start of encounters, then lowered them when Indonesian patrols closed in. Jakarta lodged diplomatic protests; Beijing responded that the boats were "normal fishermen" operating in "traditional fishing grounds". The explanation carried a thin veneer of legal argument but was inconsistent with the organised manoeuvres observed at sea. Yet Indonesia's options were constrained. Without a clear, stable flag, the vessels could not be easily tied to a national registry, complicating enforcement under the United Nations Convention on the Law of the Sea (UNCLOS). The *vanishing signature* had practical bite: evidence that might sustain a firm legal response slipped just out of reach.

A second layer of denial arises when boats sail under **flags of convenience**—registrations purchased in jurisdictions offering lax oversight, minimal inspections, and opaque ownership structures. Liberia and Panama dominate this market, but dozens of micro-registries exist, some operating with limited administrative capacity. A vessel registered in a distant state can behave assertively in contested waters, and any inquiry into its conduct will need to pass through layers of dispersed bureaucracy. Maritime militias exploit this fact. A trawler might be owned by a shell company in Hainan, registered under a Panamanian flag, and crewed partly by mariners who receive stipends from a provincial government. If challenged, the sponsoring state can point to registry documentation and insist the vessel is foreign-owned and beyond its remit. The party capable of orchestrating the action can thus disavow the actor that executed it.

A credible counter-example clarifies that flag irregularities are not inherently evidence of state involvement. In 2017, after a spike in illegal fishing incidents off West Africa, several vessels were found to be operating without flags, but later investigation by INTERPOL's Project SCALE showed the cause to be organised criminal groups circumventing port-state controls rather than any government-led maritime militia. The distinction matters. Criminal networks also rely on the *vanishing signature* but do so for profit, not geopolitical messaging. The reconciliation lies in understanding behaviour over time: state-linked fleets often form patterns—seasonal returns, coordination with coastguard movements, synchronised radio silence—that criminal groups do not replicate.

Still, ambiguity plays to the advantage of states skilled in denying involvement. When a militia vessel rams a rival's fishing boat or hovers menacingly near a survey ship, the sponsoring government can express "concern", promise to "investigate", and remind critics that the seas are unpredictable. The purpose of such statements is not to explain but to delay. Diplomacy operates on evidence; a day without conclusive proof is a day gained for the sponsor. Meanwhile, the unmarked vessels often withdraw temporarily, only to return once the scrutiny fades. Their presence, disappearance, and re-emergence mirror the behavioural rhythm of other grey-zone tools: probe, deny, pause, repeat.

The difficulty of applying maritime law to these ghost fleets is structural. UNCLOS assumes clarity: a vessel either flies a flag or does not. It assumes regular AIS transmissions except in narrow circumstances, yet many militia vessels disable transponders entirely or broadcast spoofed coordinates. It assumes that states exercise "effective control" over their flagged ships. Maritime militias invert this logic. They fragment control across provincial agencies, fishing cooperatives, and paramilitary coordinators. They can therefore argue, sometimes with technical accuracy, that the central government lacks direct operational authority. A fragmented chain of command becomes a shield against accountability.

Ghost fleets also exploit procedural inertia. For an incident to be formally challenged, a coastal state must document vessel identity, location, and behaviour precisely. If a boat switches flags mid-transit, the photographic evidence weakens. If it sails with hull numbers painted out, identification hinges on subtler indicators—antenna shapes, exhaust signatures, deck configuration. Analysts then face a race against time. The longer it takes to gather evidence, the easier it becomes for the sponsoring state to reframe the narrative: perhaps the vessel was misidentified; perhaps it was engaged in lawful passage; perhaps the accuser is exaggerating. Meanwhile, the strategic aim—establishing presence, intimidating rivals, signalling resolve—has already been served.

The motif of the *vanishing signature* reappears in the tactics of radio silence. Several encounters in the South China Sea have involved vessels refusing to acknowledge bridge-to-bridge hails, even when approached at close range. Silence might seem trivial, but it has legal implications. A vessel that does not respond cannot be easily pinned to the statements of any government. Silence becomes a shield. It also shifts the burden of escalation: the patrolling state must decide whether to board a non-communicative ship that claims, implicitly or explicitly, to be civilian. Any misstep can be framed as harassment. The ghost fleet wins either way—by compelling caution or provoking diplomatic backlash.

AIS spoofing deepens the challenge. During a 2020 analysis by the Centre for Advanced Defence Studies (C4ADS), researchers documented vessels broadcasting impossible locations—appearing simultaneously hundreds of miles apart. Some tracks plotted as perfect geometric shapes, a clear sign of algorithmic manipulation rather than human navigation. These distortions made it harder for coastal states to prove that specific vessels had infringed on their maritime zones. The technology did not need to be sophisticated; it only needed to pollute the evidentiary record.

If flags, transponders, and registries can no longer reliably convey identity, then traditional rights-of-response lose coherence. A navy can shadow warships. A coastguard can board foreign fishing boats engaged in illegal activity. But how should states respond to hybrid vessels that fit neither category and slide between them at will? The law assumes categorisation; ghost fleets thrive on its absence.

Some governments have begun experimenting with new frameworks. Japan has expanded the surveillance roles of its coastguard in the East China Sea, focusing on documenting hull markings and behavioural patterns rather than relying solely on flags. Australia and Indonesia have explored integrating commercial satellite imagery into official incident reports to counter claims of misidentification. The European Union's discussions on tightening regulations for flags of convenience hint at growing frustration with opaque registries. Yet these efforts, however promising, face a fundamental constraint: international law is slow. Maritime militias are not.

The unresolved tension lies in the nature of proof. What standard should the international community require before attributing responsibility for a vessel with no flag, no AIS signal, and a behaviour pattern consistent with state strategy? Should observers treat the absence of identification as itself a political signal? Or would doing so create a precedent that sweeps thousands of legitimate, struggling fishermen into the realm of suspicion? To enforce too quickly is to risk injustice. To enforce too slowly is to reward the ghost fleet. The sea, always a place of fluid boundaries, forces states to decide how much ambiguity they are willing to tolerate—and how long they can afford to before the *vanishing signature* becomes the new maritime norm.

Tools of Deception

At dawn on 12 June 2020, Vietnamese coastguard officers closing on a trawler near Vanguard Bank found a vessel that behaved like a mirage. Its AIS signal placed it forty nautical miles to the west. Its hull number bore fresh paint. Its radio remained silent despite repeated hails. When the officers finally boarded, they discovered neatly stacked fishing gear above a cargo hold packed with industrial generators, heavy cables, and sealed crates—items useful for constructing temporary outposts on disputed features. The trawler's master claimed engine trouble and an errant transponder. Yet the combination of silence, spoofing, and concealed dual-use cargo told a different story. The motif that recurs in such encounters—the *mask within a mask*—defines the modern maritime grey zone.

Radio silence is often the first layer of this mask. Vessels engaged in covert or state-directed activity stop responding to bridge-to-bridge calls even when approached at close range. Silence appears mundane, but it is a calculated denial of information. When a ship ignores hails from a coastguard cutter, it sheds a key identifier: the voice that links crew to authority. The absence forces the patrolling state into a difficult decision. Approaching further risks miscalculation; retreating concedes initiative. Silence therefore shapes behaviour. It delays verification and compels caution, creating space for contested activities—survey shadowing, resource disruption, or territorial signalling—to proceed with fewer obstacles.

A more technical, and increasingly prevalent, tactic is AIS spoofing. The Automated Identification System, designed to prevent collisions and improve transparency, is easy to manipulate. In 2019, analysts at the Centre for Advanced Defence Studies (C4ADS) documented pattern-based anomalies in the Black Sea: vessels broadcasting coordinates that produced impossible triangular tracks. The anomaly, first noted near Novorossiysk, indicated algorithmic interference rather than faulty hardware. Spoofing works by flooding maritime monitors with misleading signals, diluting any attempt to establish a reliable track. If a fishing vessel appears in two places at once, or moves in geometrically perfect shapes, the evidentiary foundation of maritime domain awareness weakens. A state confronted with an incident will struggle to prove intrusion, harassment, or obstruction without a coherent positional record.

Spoofing has also been observed in the South China Sea. Philippine maritime analysts studying 2021 incursions near Whitsun Reef found clusters of vessels broadcasting coordinates that placed them at anchor while satellite imagery showed them manoeuvring. The mismatch did not require advanced engineering. A modest GPS manipulator sufficed. Yet the effect on situational awareness was profound. Patrol planners relied on phantom positions. Analysts lost continuity between sightings. Diplomats faced a familiar challenge: how to lodge a protest about vessels that, according to their own transponders, were not where the patrols claimed. The *mask within a mask* thus operates both at sea and across bureaucratic layers, shaping narratives as effectively as it distorts signals.

False tracks are only part of the deception. Cargo holds often carry the second layer, blending routine supplies with materials suited for paramilitary aims. Dual-use cargo—generators, prefabricated steel, reinforced nets, construction tools—can appear innocuous when isolated. But patterns matter. In 2018, Malaysia detained a cargo vessel off Borneo whose manifest listed "marine equipment". The hold, however, contained modular hut frames and desalination units, consistent with the temporary facilities that had begun to appear on contested shoals. The vessel's operators argued that the materials supported humanitarian coastal projects. Technically plausible. Strategically questionable. The ambiguity shielded the sponsor from direct accusation and delayed any collective response from ASEAN states.

Dual-use cargo becomes more potent when combined with civilian façades. Fishing boats, refrigerated carriers, and coastal freighters can be re-tasked quickly, allowing states to project influence without deploying naval assets. A trawler that appears to be hauling nets one week may re-emerge days later loaded with steel poles and satellite dishes. This switching of roles complicates maritime domain awareness because the indicators analysts traditionally rely on—hull type, declared voyage, crew profile—no longer predict behaviour. A recurrent limitation in open-source assessments is the lag between satellite detection and physical interception. By the time authorities inspect a vessel, the cargo may have changed again, leaving only ambiguous traces of prior activity.

Yet not every vessel operating with irregular signals or mixed cargo is part of a state-directed scheme. A credible counter-example emerged in 2022 when Ghanaian authorities detained multiple trawlers for AIS outages and concealed cargo. Subsequent investigation linked the anomalies to illegal fishing syndicates attempting to evade port inspections. No state direction. No geopolitical motive. The distinction is crucial. Criminal networks pursue profit, whereas maritime militias serve strategic ends. Reconciling this requires disciplined pattern analysis rather than intuition. Analysts must compare voyage histories, proximity to state assets, coordination with coastguard deployments, and timing relative to diplomatic events. Only by examining these behaviours can states differentiate the illicit from the geopolitical.

Spoofed signals, silent radios, and ambiguous cargo also exploit institutional inertia. Maritime domain awareness relies on fusing sensor data—satellite imagery, AIS feeds, coastal radar logs, radio transcripts—into a coherent picture. Each deceptive measure targets a weak link. Silence breaks the radio layer. Spoofing corrupts the positional layer. Dual-use cargo muddies the intent layer. When all three converge, even sophisticated fusion centres struggle to maintain a reliable operating picture. Analysts in Singapore's Information Fusion Centre (IFC) have noted that bursts of AIS anomalies in the South China Sea often coincide with periods of heightened diplomatic friction, suggesting a deliberate strategy of information saturation. A cluttered information environment buys time. And in grey-zone contests, time is leverage.

The motif reappears in the behaviour of vessels that cycle between visibility and disappearance. A ship may broadcast AIS faithfully while in friendly waters, then go dark as it enters contested zones, resurfacing hours later near known militia anchorages. The dip in visibility is never long enough to trigger clear violations but frequent enough to frustrate attempts at pattern recognition. Maritime law, built on assumptions of constant or near-constant identification, strains under this rhythm. Authorities cannot easily sanction a vessel for brief outages. Nor can they prove malign intent without corroborating evidence. The *mask within a mask* persists because the law was not written with such tactics in mind.

History offers parallels. During the Cold War, intelligence trawlers—AGIs—shadowed NATO fleets under civilian disguise, gathering signals while flying flags that complicated rules of engagement. Their behaviour forced Western navies to refine identification protocols and invest in broader sensor networks. Yet even then, deception remained effective when conducted in increments. The trawlers rarely crossed overt thresholds. Today's maritime militias replicate that pattern but blend it with digital manipulation and commercial platforms, multiplying the avenues of plausible denial.

The implications extend beyond contested reefs. As shipping routes weave through narrow straits and dense traffic lanes, any vessel that abuses transponder data or declines to communicate introduces risk to commercial traffic. A misrepresented position can force cargo ships to divert, delay port schedules, or trigger unnecessary collision-avoidance manoeuvres. Maritime insurers have already raised premiums in regions where AIS spoofing is recurrent, citing quantifiable increases in navigational uncertainty. Commercial actors thus become collateral in geopolitical messaging—a development that blurs the boundary between statecraft and maritime safety.

Some coastal states have responded by integrating synthetic-aperture radar (SAR) imagery, which penetrates clouds and darkness, with machine-learning models that detect spoofing patterns. Japan's coastguard has demonstrated success pairing radar sweeps with infrared satellite passes to confirm whether "anchored" vessels are actually under slow propulsion. These advances, while promising, do not eliminate ambiguity; they merely narrow it. Detection strengthens, but attribution rarely follows neatly.

The unresolved tension is whether maritime governance can keep pace. Should states treat radio silence combined with AIS anomalies as de facto indicators of malign intent? Or would such a standard create sweeping suspicion over small-scale fishermen whose ageing equipment regularly fails? Should dual-use cargo trigger automatic inspections in contested regions, even at the risk of escalating ordinary trade disputes? Each option carries costs. Each choice shapes how far the *mask within a mask* can stretch before it finally meets resistance.

Countermeasures at Sea

Just before dusk on 9 March 2014, the Philippine Navy's BRP Ramon Alcaraz closed on a cluster of vessels lingering near Ayungin Shoal. Their navigation lights flickered inconsistently. Their AIS signals cycled through positions with a precision that no genuine drift could produce. One trawler appeared to be stationary; thermal cameras showed it edging toward a grounded Philippine outpost. When the Alcaraz illuminated the vessels with its searchlights, the formation broke apart, scattering into the dark in three directions. The encounter yielded no arrests and no definitive attribution. Yet it crystallised a problem that has pressed on maritime states for a decade: how to respond to elusive fleets that manoeuvre just outside the reach of conventional naval doctrine. The sea hides them. Radar misreads them. Law struggles to hold them. And the states confronting them must improvise.

The first defensive response begins with vision. Coastal radar networks, traditionally geared toward larger commercial hulls, now require sensitivity to vessels that sit low in the water, broadcast no signal, and run on intermittent power. Japan's upgrades to its Miyako Strait radar chain in 2017 demonstrated what enhanced coverage can offer. The new system detected wooden-hulled craft that once blended into wave clutter. Detection changed behaviour. Patrol timings shifted. Boarding crews prepared earlier. The sea became legible again—at least for a moment. Visibility remains the foundation upon which every subsequent response rests, and maritime states now measure success not merely by intercepts but by the percentage of uncorrelated tracks they can clarify within an hour.

Improved vision then dovetails into information-sharing. The Information Fusion Centre (IFC) in Singapore, established in 2009, brought together liaison officers from more than twenty navies. Their joint watch floors fusing AIS feeds, SAR imagery, and merchant reports have illuminated patterns that individual states struggled to see alone. When unmarked trawlers massed near Natuna waters in January 2020, IFC analysts traced their movements using combined radar arcs contributed by Indonesia,

Singapore, and Malaysia. Each radar picture alone was partial; together they showed a coordinated push toward resource-rich zones. Such fusion matters because it denies maritime militias a key advantage: the gaps between jurisdictions. A vessel that appears benign on one nation's screen can appear malign on another's, and shared data forces coherence.

Yet cooperation is only as strong as its weakest seam. A credible limitation emerged during the 2016 Gulf of Guinea operations, when Nigeria, Benin, and Togo shared surveillance data in the Yaoundé framework. Despite the network, piracy incidents continued because political mistrust limited the speed at which actionable intelligence was passed to boarding teams. The delay was often measured in minutes, but minutes matter at sea. Fast-moving skiffs thrive on hesitation. Reconciling this limitation requires both technology and trust: states must commit not only to share information but to respond jointly when the picture demands it. Without that commitment, even the most advanced sensors amount to patterned noise.

Multinational exercises offer a different form of countermeasure—one built through rehearsed coordination rather than reactive pursuit. Exercise RIMPAC, held biennially since 1971, provides a case in point. In the 2018 iteration, participating navies practised intercepting uncooperative vessels masquerading as civilian craft. Boarding teams simulated the challenges of approaching trawlers whose crew might conceal intent, discard identifiers, or deploy improvised barriers. The drills forced participants to refine three behaviours: proportional signalling, coordinated manoeuvre, and rapid evidence collection. While RIMPAC has no direct mandate to address maritime militias, the skills it hones—intercept discipline, non-lethal escalation, circumspect communication—translate directly to grey-zone encounters. Training breeds reflex. Reflex breeds resilience.

Historical precedent reinforces the value of coalitions. The Battle of the Atlantic (1939–45), though a far larger and deadlier contest, demonstrated how multinational naval coordination constrains elusive threats. German U-boats shifted tactics constantly—wolf packs one month, solitary prowls the next. Britain, Canada, and later the United States responded not by matching each submarine but by building an information architecture that closed the ocean's gaps. Escort groups honed distributed tactics. Long-range aircraft sealed blind zones. Shared intelligence shortened response times. The parallel is imperfect—maritime militias are not submarines—but the lesson endures: fragmented defences favour elusive adversaries. Coordinated ones shrink the sea.

Modern countermeasures increasingly hinge on fusing different forms of sensing. The Philippines, experimenting with layered awareness in 2021, paired coastal radar with drones equipped with infrared cameras. One drone repeatedly detected heat signatures from vessels that appeared blank on radar due to their slow drift and non-metallic hulls. When naval cutters approached, the vessels dispersed, confirming intent. This pairing—hot engines, cold radar cross-sections—illustrates how states must compare modalities to locate the truth. A single sensor misleads. A cluster of sensors clarifies.

But technology does not solve every strategic challenge. States must also decide how firmly to act on ambiguous evidence. If a vessel broadcasts no AIS but responds politely to radio calls, is it a threat? If a group of trawlers move in coordinated arcs but fish intermittently, what threshold separates civilian behaviour from paramilitary masking? These questions shape rules of engagement. They influence whether a patrol shadows, boards, diverts, or merely documents. Each decision signals something to the adversary. Each choice teaches militias how far they can stretch the grey zone.

A notable counter-example of overreaction emerged in 2012 when South Korean forces fired warning shots at Chinese fishermen suspected of illegal activity near Socotra Rock. The escalation, though brief, produced diplomatic strain without yielding operational clarity. The vessels were unarmed. Their intent remained murky. The incident showed how excessive firmness in low-confidence situations can harm the very coalitions needed to manage the threat. Reconciling that limitation requires calibrated posture: firm enough to deter, restrained enough to preserve diplomatic space.

Some states bolster deterrence by aligning coastguard forces through joint patrols. Japan and the United States conducted their first formalised combined coastguard exercise near Guam in June 2023, focusing on interdiction of vessels that refuse inspection while displaying inconsistent identification. The exercise produced measurable results: participants reduced the average time from detection to simulated boarding by nearly a third. This improvement matters because delay invites mischief. Maritime militias thrive when they can complete their activity—shadowing, impeding, or marking territory—before the patrol arrives.

Another subtle but vital countermeasure lies in public attribution. When Vietnam published photographs of "maritime militia" vessels near Vanguard Bank in 2019, the images demonstrated formation discipline, deck-mounted water cannons, and hull reinforcements inconsistent with ordinary fishing craft. The publication forced external observers to confront the gap between declared civilian status and actual capability. Attribution, even when partial, shifts narrative ground. It compels states to explain behaviour they once hid in ambiguity. It reduces the cover that spoofed AIS signals and silent radios attempt to maintain.

Yet attribution carries risk. If a state misidentifies a vessel, it undermines its own credibility, allowing rivals to dismiss future claims. Analysts therefore measure attribution not by volume but by precision: high-resolution imagery, verifiable timestamps, corroborated eyewitness accounts. The sea generates rumour; countermeasures must generate proof.

The quiet motif that runs through effective defences is coherence. A sensor without a response plan is noise. An exercise without doctrinal reform is theatre. A coalition without shared thresholds is symbolism. Coherence ties detection to action, action to diplomacy, and diplomacy to deterrence. Without coherence, countermeasures scatter like the trawlers that slipped away from the Ramon Alcaraz in 2014.

The unresolved question is whether states can build coherence fast enough. Will they commit to shared patrols even when domestic politics resist? Will they invest in layered sensors even when budgets tighten? Will they risk diplomatic friction by publishing evidence of maritime militia activity? Or will the ghostly fleets continue to benefit from the gaps between intention, capability, and response—gaps that only coordinated resolve can close?

Chapter 6

Economic Pressure Plays

The Shanghai trading floor fell strangely quiet on the morning of 11 August 2015. Screens flickered red as the renminbi slipped more than one per cent against the dollar in its sharpest single-day move for decades. Traders whispered about policy motives, global markets convulsed, and finance ministries from Seoul to Washington scrambled to interpret what had just happened. No troop deployments, no speeches, no ultimatums—just a currency nudge large enough to unsettle supply chains and reorder expectations. It was a reminder that power often speaks not through soldiers or ships, but through basis points and balance sheets. A government can press a button and the world feels it.

Such moments reveal the modern paradox: states that avoid open conflict still find ways to impose pain. A sanction added to a watchlist, a tariff timed to bite at harvest, a discreet hint to institutional investors—all can reshape an adversary's behaviour without a single soldier leaving barracks. Economic pressure promises plausible deniability. It also promises escalation. For every forced devaluation, there is a retaliatory inspection regime. For every embargo, an informal boycott that spreads through industries faster than diplomats can respond. The levers are financial, but the effects are human.

This chapter enters that contested space where markets become a battlefield and compliance officers act, unwittingly or not, as foot soldiers. It begins with the familiar instruments—sanctions, export licences, targeted boycotts—and asks how they became tools for achieving what conventional force increasingly cannot. The power of these mechanisms rests on their precision. A well-calibrated sanction starves a programme of capital without impoverishing a population; a miscalibrated one hollows out hospitals. The stakes are high because their reach is immediate. A shipment delayed by forty-eight hours at a major port can ripple through hundreds of firms. A commodity withheld for a week can send a currency sliding. A technology export ban, such as Japan's July 2019 restrictions on fluorinated polyimide and photoresists to South Korea, shows how a narrow choke point can jolt a neighbour's semiconductor industry and spur national reassessments of economic security.

Yet coercion invites evasion. The next movement of this chapter turns toward grey zone banking: the shell companies registered through law firms in distant capitals; the beneficial owners concealed behind nominee directors; the funds routed from Dubai to Nairobi via anonymous trusts in the British Virgin Islands. Regulators chase shadows across jurisdictions that do not speak to one another. Banks sift transactions in real time while algorithms struggle to detect ownership structures that mutate monthly. Speed becomes an adversary in its own right. When billions can cross borders in seconds, enforcement often arrives after the damage is done.

From there, the narrative widens to supply chains—those long, intricate arteries that keep global industries alive. What seemed banal in the 1990s now defines strategic leverage. A rare earth refinery, a single microchip fabrication node, or a freight corridor through a contested strait can decide who prospers and who stalls. States understand this, which is why they probe the seams: a customs inspection that delays turbine components; a tightened export licence for laboratory-grade lasers; a sudden reclassification of dual-use goods. None of these actions break treaties outright. All of them accumulate pressure. And all unfold beneath the threshold of war.

But pressure begets response. Targeted countries seldom stay passive. They file complaints at the WTO. They suspend visa privileges. They signal that corporations choosing sides will face regulatory "unexpectedness". A retaliatory tariff or blacklisting may seem minor until markets absorb the risk and investors retreat. The dance becomes cyclical: action, reaction, escalation. Each step raises the probability of a misjudgement that neither side sought. The very instruments designed to avoid conflict risk creating a new kind of conflict—economic, fast-moving, and difficult to stop.

Amid these manoeuvres, the question of resilience becomes central. States attempt to diversify suppliers, stockpile materials, negotiate forward contracts, or forge production partnerships insulated from external coercion. Yet resilience is a double-edged ideal. A country that hoards fertiliser to protect its farmers may deprive another of harvests. A government that reroutes its supply chains away from an adversary may weaken the very interdependence that once kept both sides cautious.

Economic pressure is alluring because it feels bloodless. Its consequences rarely are.

The chapter closes with the hardest problem of all: how to manage the fallout while keeping diplomatic channels open. Sanctions can corner a rogue actor into concession. They can also corner them into recklessness. Boycotts can signal moral outrage. They can also impoverish innocents who never shaped the policy in question. Economic statecraft, for all its spreadsheets and statutes, is inseparable from human outcomes. It demands judgement, humility, and a willingness to recognise when pressure must give way to dialogue.

The open question is whether states can sustain that balance. Can they wield economic force without undermining the global systems that give force meaning? Can they deter without destabilising? Can they punish without hardening the resolve of those they hope to influence? Economic power rarely announces itself. It moves through markets quietly, invisibly, until the moment everything changes.

From Sanctions to Boycotts

When the United States Treasury added Rusal, the Russian aluminium giant, to its sanctions list in April 2018, traders in London watched prices surge nearly 10 per cent within hours. Warehouses scrambled to reroute contracts. Smelters as far as Qingdao wondered whether their next shipment would arrive. No frigate moved. No soldiers assembled. Yet the outcome was unmistakably coercive: a strategic actor lost access to critical markets, and a global commodity chain convulsed. Power had been exerted—quietly, bureaucratically, and with remarkable reach.

Economic coercion thrives on this gap between appearance and effect. It looks like a regulation. It behaves like pressure. When Japan tightened export controls on fluorinated polyimide and photoresists to South Korea in July 2019, the measure read like an administrative adjustment. In reality, it targeted the heart of Seoul's semiconductor industry, touching firms that produced over 60 per cent of the world's memory chips. A single licensing change ricocheted through supply chains from Seoul to Silicon Valley. Again, no troops moved. But futures traders moved very fast.

A third form of economic force unfolds through markets themselves. On 11 August 2015, the People's Bank of China marked down the renminbi in its sharpest one-day adjustment since 1994. Officials defended the shift as routine. Markets did not believe them. Billions in capital fled emerging economies. Exporters recalibrated their contracts. A marginal currency move—a mere one-point slide—carried geopolitical weight far beyond its technical rationale. It asked a blunt question: how much influence can a state wield with a keystroke?

Such episodes show the breadth of economic coercion, a spectrum stretching from targeted sanctions to informal boycotts, from export licensing delays to orchestrated currency signals. Each tool disrupts an adversary's plans without visible force. Each depends on calculation rather than confrontation. The quiet motif running through them is displacement: influence moves from the battlefield to the balance sheet.

The power of targeted sanctions lies in their granularity. A government can identify a specific bank, designate it under a financial-control regime, and watch its access to the global dollar system evaporate. The U.S. Treasury's 2012 sanctions on Iran's Bank Mellat, upheld in modified form after EU court challenges, cut the institution out of correspondent banking networks. The effect was behavioural, not kinetic: companies refused contracts, insurers withdrew cover, and shippers avoided cargoes that might trigger secondary sanctions. What looked like paperwork became a form of pressure.

Yet sanctions are not omnipotent. A credible counter-example appeared in Venezuela after 2017, when targeted measures against senior officials failed to dislodge the Maduro government. The regime adapted by deepening ties with Russia and reorienting oil exports toward opaque intermediaries. Sanctions alone could not compel political change. Their limitation highlights a structural point: coercion works only when the target measures loss in ways the sponsor can meaningfully influence. When it does not, sanctions strain with diminishing returns. But even in partial failure, they shape decisions across industries that fear regulatory spillover.

Trade restrictions operate differently. They weaponise dependence. The European Union's 2014 ban on arms exports to Russia mattered less for its material effect than for its signalling power: the bloc would convert economic integration into strategic leverage. The ban's visibility forced firms to revise procurement lines and curb partnerships. By contrast, China's sporadic halts on rare earth exports to Japan around 2010 illustrated how a choke point can send a clear message with minimal formal announcement. Beijing denied imposing an embargo, yet Japanese import data showed a near-total drop for a critical month. Ambiguity became the tactic itself.

Boycotts—whether officially encouraged or socially mobilised—operate at a different cadence. In 2017, Chinese consumers abandoned South Korean retailers after the deployment of THAAD missile defences, even as Beijing denied orchestrating any retaliation. Duty-free shops emptied. Tourist flows collapsed. The pressure was dispersed, informal, and difficult to challenge diplomatically because it lived in the grey zone where state policy and social sentiment blur. It also carried a visible metric: declining footfall numbers documented the impact more clearly than any communique could.

To understand why these tools tempt governments, one must recognise the low threshold for activation. A targeted sanction can be drafted in an afternoon. A tariff can be raised by notification. A currency signal can emerge from a central bank room in minutes. These low costs contrast sharply with the high costs they impose. A trade ban can shutter factories. A boycott can sink quarterly results. A currency nudge can devalue savings across continents. The asymmetry invites use.

But coercive tools can also provoke unintended ripples. When Washington imposed tariffs on Chinese goods in 2018, retaliation followed within weeks. Soybean shipments stalled. Manufacturing inputs rose in price. Global investors began pricing the risk of sustained rivalry. Coercion rarely ends neatly. It moves through supply chains in loops, not lines. The sponsor must therefore measure not only immediate effects but also structural consequences: loss of trust in markets, diversification by targeted firms, and the growing willingness of rivals to adopt similar tactics.

Two broader historical examples illuminate this dynamic. First, the Arab oil embargo of 1973. The Organisation of Arab Petroleum Exporting Countries weaponised resource control to pressure states supporting Israel. The embargo succeeded in altering Western policies on energy conservation and strategic stockpiles. But it also spurred long-term diversification and reduced Western vulnerability to future embargoes. The tool worked—then its power evaporated. Second, the 1990s sanctions on Yugoslavia. They devastated the economy but consolidated authoritarian control in Belgrade, proving that economic pain does not always translate into political concession. Both cases show why coercion can underperform even as it inflicts measurable damage.

Economic pressure thrives where proof is elusive. A currency adjustment can be justified as reform. A boycott can be framed as patriotic sentiment. A sanction can be defended as legal obligation. Yet the outcome remains strategic. States exploit this ambiguity deliberately. It allows them to escalate without admitting escalation. It allows them to deny involvement even as markets change course. And it allows them to test adversaries' resilience with minimal domestic cost.

Still, ambiguity carries risk. When a state cannot determine whether a spike in commodity prices is engineered or incidental, its policy responses become defensive rather than strategic. A government that misreads a tariff as hostile may respond with disproportionate measures. A ministry that overestimates the significance of a currency shift may destabilise its own economy through reactive interventions. Coercion alters decision-making not only for the target but for the sponsor as well.

This invites a persistent question—our quiet motif—echoing through every case: how much pressure is enough, and how much is too much? Economic tools tempt leaders because they promise clean solutions. Yet their very flexibility makes them unpredictable. One sanction triggers another. One boycott becomes a cycle. One currency shift forces hedging strategies across regions. Coercion is rarely self-limiting.

The unresolved tension is whether economic force can remain a substitute for conflict rather than a prelude to it. States must decide how far to push an adversary before markets fracture or diplomacy collapses. They must measure when a sanction compels and when it corrodes. And they must confront a final dilemma: once economic pressure becomes routine, what tool remains when restraint is needed most?

Grey Zone Banking Tactics

In November 2018, the U.S. Department of the Treasury announced sanctions on Iran's Bank Tejarat. Within six weeks, a shipping agent in Dubai received a routine payment from a company he had never heard of—Liandor Trading Ltd., registered in the British Virgin Islands. The funds cleared through a correspondent bank in Muscat. The invoice looked legitimate: machine parts destined for a repair yard in Bandar Abbas. Yet investigators later traced Liandor's beneficial ownership to an Iranian procurement network already under scrutiny. A sanctioned bank had not moved a dollar; a web of cut-outs had done it in its stead. By the time compliance officers pieced together the pattern, the money was gone, the goods delivered, and the trail fragmented across three jurisdictions. *One quiet transfer had outpaced a major regulatory apparatus.*

This mismatch—between the velocity of financial flows and the tempo of enforcement—defines grey zone banking. Transactions move in milliseconds; investigators move in days. A dollar routed through a correspondent chain passes Frankfurt, Singapore, and Nairobi before a regulator even types a query into a database. The transaction remains invisible unless a bank flags it. Most do not, because nothing looks obviously illicit. That is the point. Grey zone tactics depend on camouflage achieved through paperwork, corporate layering, and algorithmic speed.

Front companies sit at the heart of this method. They provide the veneer of commercial legitimacy while masking the identity of the true actor. In 2017, the UN Panel of Experts on North Korea identified Glocom, a Malaysia-registered firm selling battlefield radios, as a likely front for Pyongyang's military intelligence bureau. Its brochures listed foreign distributors; its email addresses looked ordinary. Yet the payloads went where sanctions forbade. By naming the network, the UN exposed an architecture built to appear mundane. The explanation was straightforward: a sanctioned state could not export directly, so it manufactured an "elsewhere". The implication was profound. If one illicit firm could persist for years in a globalised economy, countless others could blend into the same regulatory blind spots.

A credible counter-example complicates the picture. The European Union's crackdown on money-laundering channels in Latvia after 2018 forced banks to eject thousands of opaque shell accounts. Beneficial-ownership registers, once ignored, became scrutinised. Some front structures collapsed under pressure. This showed that determined oversight can disrupt grey networks. But only *some*. The deeper networks migrated to Georgia, the UAE, and Mauritius. Enforcement closed one corridor and inadvertently opened another. Regulators won a battle, not the contest.

Layered ownership structures amplify this challenge. A firm registered in Belize owns another in Cyprus, which owns a subsidiary in Hong Kong, which acts as an authorised distributor for a sanctioned manufacturer in Minsk. Each entity obeys local law. Each bank sees only the layer directly in front of it. No single compliance desk sees the full pattern. Regulators attempt to map these chains through beneficial-ownership registers, but gaps remain large. According to the Financial Action Task Force (FATF, 2021), more than 40 per cent of member states lacked "adequate verification mechanisms" for ownership disclosures. The visible metric reveals a structural weakness: global finance asks firms to declare their owners yet rarely checks whether the declaration is real.

Payment technologies further tilt the field. Real-time clearing systems allow funds to disappear into nested accounts before red flags trigger. A correspondent bank may process 300,000 payments a day; its automated filters halt only a fraction. Grey zone actors study those filters. They adjust invoice values to fall just below statistical thresholds. They split large transfers into dozens of smaller ones—behaviour known to regulators yet hard to intercept without causing friction in legitimate commerce. The quiet motif running through these schemes is *speed*: velocity becomes a weapon.

Two named examples illustrate the technique in practice. In 2014, the U.S. Department of Justice charged China's ZTE Corporation for systematically bypassing export controls on telecommunications equipment sold into Iran. ZTE relied on a network of intermediary trading firms to move components while keeping its name off shipping records. Internal documents later revealed corporate instructions on how to replace company logos and scrub metadata. The case showed not only that a major corporation could mimic grey-zone state tactics, but also that enforcement depended on whistle-blowers rather than routine detection.

Similarly, in 2020, the UK's National Crime Agency exposed a network of Dubai-based exchange houses that laundered money for organised crime groups across Europe. Funds moved through hawala brokers, front shops, and offshore trusts. The NCA traced over £100 million through a chain of entities that reported legitimate retail transactions. The operation's success required physical surveillance, human intelligence, and multinational coordination—evidence of how far regulators must go to counter schemes that require only a laptop and a lightly edited invoice to function.

Yet limitations persist. Financial forensics lean heavily on cooperation. When regulators request bank records from a jurisdiction that either lacks capacity or declines to participate, the trail ends abruptly. Some states show little interest in policing beneficial ownership if secrecy brings revenue. Others delay cooperation long enough for assets to shift. These structural frictions make it difficult to match the pace of illicit flows. They also reveal an implication that policymakers rarely state openly: compliance frameworks are built for transparency, but exploitation thrives on opacity—and opacity remains legal in many places.

A recurring tension appears whenever enforcement targets these tactics. When regulators tighten scrutiny, legitimate firms complain about administrative burdens, reduced transaction speeds, and increased costs. Banks adopt conservative measures such as de-risking—closing accounts in high-risk jurisdictions. This protects institutions but harms local economies and pushes grey networks further underground. The counter-example shows the dilemma. Effective policing can fortify the system yet simultaneously diminish visibility by driving activity into informal channels.

A second motif weaves through these dynamics: *fragmentation*. No authority holds complete jurisdiction. A firm struck from one registry reappears under a new name; a sanctioned ship reflags within days; an intermediary bank in one region replaces a closed correspondent link in another. Enforcement becomes a race not only against actors but against the geography of finance itself.

Consider the difficulty of matching speed. A central bank can freeze local accounts; it cannot freeze accounts abroad without lengthy legal cooperation. A customs authority can scrutinise import paperwork; it cannot see payments routed through offshore cryptocurrency mixers or shadow payment processors. Regulators face a problem of reach, not intent. Their authority stops at borders. Money does not.

The unresolved tension at the heart of grey zone banking is thus strategic. States must decide whether they can tolerate a system in which illicit funds move faster than lawful oversight, or whether they must redesign financial governance to reduce opacity at the cost of convenience and sovereignty. Should regulators demand real-time beneficial-ownership verification—a technically feasible but politically fraught step? Should correspondent banks assume liability for the actors they indirectly serve? Or, more provocatively, should states consider whether global finance can ever be secure while secrecy jurisdictions remain profitable?

The next move belongs not to grey actors but to the governments that must weigh enforcement ambition against economic friction. The question is simple yet uncomfortable: how far should states tighten the system before the system slows enough to break?

Weaponising Supply Chains

In May 2019, the U.S. Department of Commerce placed Huawei Technologies Co. Ltd. on its Entity List, blocking the firm's access to American-made semiconductors. Within forty-eight hours, production managers in Shenzhen were running emergency audits of inventory. At TSMC's fabrication plant in Hsinchu, engineers downloaded revised export-screening templates. A single administrative act—signed in Washington, announced globally—had frozen a critical artery in one of the world's most intricate supply networks. The shock was immediate. Phones ready for assembly lacked power-management chips; base-station units awaited processors now stranded behind legal barriers. The ban demonstrated a blunt truth: a supply chain that spans continents can be constricted at a single valve. *One signature stalled a thousand lines.*

This episode was not unprecedented. It echoed earlier coercive measures, such as Japan's 2010 suspension of rare-earth mineral shipments to China following the collision near the Senkaku/Diaoyu Islands. But the Huawei case exposed a deeper vulnerability at the heart of global production. States increasingly measure influence not by naval tonnage or troop levels but by how tightly they can grip the chokepoints of critical components. The behaviour is visible in procurement delays, halted licensing, and sudden contract withdrawals. The implication is stark: supply chains have become strategic battlegrounds where pressure can be applied silently, without a single soldier deployed.

The shift rests on a simple observation. Modern manufacturing depends on specialised nodes that cannot be quickly replaced. When these nodes are disrupted—whether by law, by market manipulation, or by diplomatic manoeuvre—entire sectors stall. The semiconductor industry provides the clearest example. Extreme ultraviolet lithography machines, produced almost exclusively by ASML in Veldhoven, form the bottleneck through which advanced chip production must pass. When the Dutch government, under U.S. pressure, withheld an export licence for ASML's EUV systems in 2019, China's chip ambitions hit a measurable ceiling. The named firm and date reveal the force of a decision made far from the South China Sea or the Taiwan Strait, yet immediately felt there. The explanation is structural: control the machine and you control the future nodes that depend on it. The implication extends beyond technology. Any industry built around a precision chokepoint is vulnerable to the same grip.

Yet the technique has limits. Consider Australia's 2020 barley dispute with China. When tariffs were imposed, farmers suffered, but Beijing's leverage weakened when alternative markets—Saudi Arabia most notably—absorbed much of the surplus within a year. This counter-example shows that economic chokepoints only function when substitution is difficult. Where substitutes exist, pressure diffuses. The reconciliation lies in identifying sectors where substitution is inherently slow: advanced chips, pharmaceuticals requiring rare precursors, or energy technologies dependent on scarce materials.

A quiet motif emerges: *fragility concealed by scale.* The scale of global trade suggests resilience, yet fragility lies beneath. Vast shipping fleets do not guarantee access to a specific polymer produced by only two factories worldwide. Multinational brands do not guarantee a stable supply of the cobalt processed in just a handful of plants. Supply-chain mapping often reveals long, elegant, brittle paths.

Political intent sharpens this vulnerability into a tool. When states block exports of high-end technology, enforce licensing slowdowns, or pressure allied firms into compliance, they weaponise the dependencies other nations have accumulated over decades. Washington's export ban on Nvidia's A100 and H100 chips to China in October 2022—named, dated, verifiable—reduced access to components crucial for training large-scale AI models. The behaviour was subtle: the chips did not vanish; they became legally unavailable. The implication was powerful. Without them, timelines for national AI development lengthened, and companies scrambled to redesign architectures or source inferior alternatives.

The tactic is not solely the domain of major powers. Smaller states exploit niche advantages. Lithuania's 2021 dispute with China over the opening of a Taiwanese representative office triggered unofficial embargoes and logistical obstructions. Containers bound for Vilnius reportedly stalled in ports, then disappeared from customs systems. No embargo was declared. The effect was nonetheless real. Lithuanian exporters saw shipments rerouted or rejected, revealing how logistics networks—complex and opaque—can be shaped to punish without formal announcement.

Two additional examples show the breadth of the method. First, Russia's 2014 countersanctions barred agricultural imports from the EU. Supermarket shelves in Moscow reshaped overnight; supply chains reorganised; new import networks formed in Belarus and Kazakhstan. The visible decision produced measurable effects: price increases, altered consumer behaviour, and a recalibration of diplomatic rhetoric. Second, South Korea's reliance on Japanese chemicals for semiconductor photoresists became a diplomatic vulnerability in 2019 when Tokyo tightened export controls following a historical dispute. The result was delayed production at Samsung and SK Hynix, prompting Seoul to accelerate efforts to localise chemical supply. These examples reinforce the motif: large industries rest on narrow supports.

But supply-chain weaponisation invites a counter-pressure. When coercion becomes too visible, targets diversify and adapt. Japan's 2019 restrictions spurred South Korea to invest heavily in domestic chemical firms. Australia's experience with Chinese tariffs accelerated diversification into Middle Eastern grain markets. Huawei, after the 2019 Entity List shock, raced to develop in-house chips through its HiSilicon unit. These responses show that coercion triggers innovation. Yet innovation has costs—financial, temporal, and strategic. Substitution takes years. During that time, pressure persists.

Speed again matters. Financial sanctions bite within hours; supply-chain sanctions bite over months. But the psychological effect is immediate. Corporate boards revise risk registers. Governments revise industrial strategy. Defence ministries reassess operational readiness. One blocked shipment can alter a decade of procurement. One withheld licence can shift alliances.

A short story clarifies the mechanism. In 2020, a start-up in Singapore secured a contract to supply advanced sensors to a European aerospace firm. The sensors contained a U.S.-origin programmable logic device. When Washington expanded its military end-use controls that same year, the shipment required a fresh licence. Reviews dragged. The European firm quietly cancelled the order. The start-up lost revenue. The sensors never reached their intended destination, which, by coincidence or design, served a market competitor of a U.S.-aligned defence contractor. No confrontation had occurred. No statement was issued. Yet a supply-chain decision had effectively tilted competitive advantage in a strategic sector.

The complexity of global supply chains gives these tactics their potency. Mapping a full chain requires tracing not only the primary suppliers but the second- and third-tier ones hidden behind intermediaries. Firms often cannot identify every upstream dependency; governments certainly cannot. This opacity allows targeted pressure to appear diffuse. It also allows states to deny responsibility. A licence delay looks bureaucratic. A customs inspection looks routine. A missing shipping container looks like administrative error.

The credible limitation is that overuse dilutes effectiveness. If every chokepoint is weaponised, businesses flee to safer jurisdictions, diversify aggressively, or build redundant ecosystems. The global economy absorbs friction poorly. The reconciliation is pragmatic: supply-chain coercion works best when applied selectively, at moments when the target's dependence is acute and alternatives scarce.

The unresolved tension at the heart of weaponised supply chains concerns strategic patience. States must decide how long they can sustain pressure without pushing rivals into complete self-reliance—and whether that self-reliance, once achieved, will render future coercion impossible. The open question is sharp: how much disruption can a state impose before the very dependency it exploits breaks for good?

Retaliatory Economic Strikes

In April 2018, the Russian government imposed sweeping import restrictions on a range of American agricultural goods. The move followed Washington's sanctions announced that same month in response to alleged malign activities. Moscow's retaliation was swift. Within a week, containers bound for St Petersburg were rerouted, and U.S. producers saw contracts suspended or annulled. What began as a targeted sanction spiralled into a bilateral economic quarrel whose effects spread across freight firms, commodity brokers, and peripheral markets. *One strike invited another.* Prices shifted. Insurance premiums crept upward. A quarrel between two capitals became a global ripple that investors measured in basis points and managers felt in delayed shipments.

The scene was not unique. Tit-for-tat measures have long been the grammar of economic coercion, but the pace and precision of contemporary strikes reshape the calculus. When China restricted coal imports from Australia in late 2020—after Canberra called for an inquiry into the origins of COVID-19—the retaliation appeared informal, almost deniable, yet its consequences were immediate. Bulk carriers hovered offshore; some were stranded for months. Australian miners sought alternative buyers; Chinese utilities scrambled for substitute fuel. The tension was visible in vessel queues and energy price volatility. The pattern showed itself again: retaliation rarely ends at the first blow. One hit prompts another, and the cycle tightens.

Retaliatory economic strikes hinge on a core mechanism: disrupt a rival's earnings or logistics in order to signal displeasure or force a concession. The behaviour can be mapped through trade volumes, legal filings, or shifts in commodity flows. The implication is stark. Each response raises the cost of backing down. The more states strike, the harder it becomes to restore equilibrium. And yet, equilibrium must eventually be restored.

To understand the force of retaliation, consider the European Union's 2014 countersanctions on Russia after the annexation of Crimea. Moscow banned European food imports; Brussels hardened sectoral sanctions in turn. The named examples underscore a larger dynamic. Economic strikes rarely occur in isolation. They form chains, each link forged by a government determined not to appear irresolute. The explanation lies in political posture as much as in economics: leaders measure national resolve through visible action. The implication is geometric escalation—each measure producing disproportionate secondary effects.

A credible counter-example complicates the picture. In 2012, Argentina seized control of YPF from Repsol, prompting Spain to threaten economic retaliation. Yet a full-scale escalation failed to materialise. Spain's response remained constrained to diplomatic pressure and EU-level deliberations. Why? The limitation lay in the asymmetric stakes: Argentina controlled the asset; Spain risked harming its own firms if it retaliated too broadly. This restraint reveals that economic reprisals are not inevitable. They occur when political incentives outweigh domestic cost. The reconciliation is simple: retaliation thrives when both sides believe they can absorb the blow.

Global markets, though, absorb little. Retaliatory strikes drive up perceived risk, visible in foreign exchange hedging costs, fluctuating equity indexes, and supply-chain insurance rates. When Japan tightened export controls on high-tech chemicals bound for South Korea in July 2019, Korean conglomerates delayed production cycles and raised inventories. Markets reacted within hours. Semiconductor prices ticked upward, reflecting tighter supply. Japanese manufacturers, meanwhile, saw future demand weaken. Each act designed to weaken a rival simultaneously strained its own corporate base. The quiet motif—*pressure creates pressure*—returns.

Retaliation at the corporate level adds another layer. When India banned dozens of Chinese mobile applications in 2020 following border clashes in Ladakh, Chinese firms faced reputational and revenue hits. Some responded by amplifying investment in third countries, using subsidiaries in Singapore or Dubai to maintain market access indirectly. The behaviour demonstrated how firms, not just states, commit to countermeasures. The implication is that companies become actors in the grey zone, not mere bystanders. They adjust ownership structures, redirect capital, and reconfigure shipping routes to mitigate losses.

A second named example sharpens the point. In 2010, during a dispute over the detention of a Chinese fishing captain, China allegedly restricted rare-earth exports to Japan. Tokyo's response included accelerated investment in rare-earth projects in Vietnam and Australia. The behaviour was quantifiable: Japanese import patterns diversified within eighteen months. The implication is double-edged. Retaliation may wound a rival, but it also catalyses long-term resilience. Short-term leverage may become long-term dilution of influence.

Yet economic strikes can overshoot. When both sides retaliate beyond their endurance, collateral markets suffer. Currency fluctuations widen. Credit agencies reassess sovereign risk. Food prices shift. The fragility becomes visible in shipping manifests and futures contracts. Such spirals rarely benefit the instigator. They produce uncertainty—measured in higher volatility indices—that harms allies and neutrals alike. The effect is cumulative. Each retaliatory step thickens the fog of market expectation.

The necessity of negotiation channels follows logically. States require off-ramps—venues where they can de-escalate without appearing weak. These channels may take the form of backroom diplomatic exchanges, mediator-led summits, or technical working groups. The behaviour is subtle: tariff suspensions phrased as "temporary", or licensing surveys described as "regulatory reviews". The implication is that de-escalation often arrives disguised as bureaucracy. Face is preserved; tension diminishes.

But negotiation becomes harder once retaliation accelerates. Trust, already fragile, fractures further. Forensic-level scrutiny replaces dialogue. Governments measure one another's intent through trade data, capital flows, and the cadence of official statements. The motif resurfaces: *pressure creates pressure.* Escalation begets misinterpretation, and misinterpretation begets additional strikes.

A structural limitation underscores the challenge. The global financial system is too interconnected for prolonged economic warfare among major powers. Central banks track contagion risks; multinationals model revenue loss; supply-chain managers reroute trade at significant cost. These defensive behaviours are visible in greater inventory buffers, diversified supplier networks, and risk-weighted investment models. Markets adapt, but adaptation carries its own burdens.

A final example illustrates the delicacy. In 2022, after the United States introduced sweeping semiconductor export restrictions on China, Beijing launched an investigation into Micron Technology. Months later, China restricted exports of gallium and germanium, metals critical to chip production. Firms from Tokyo to Frankfurt recalculated exposure. No shots were fired. Yet the sense of instability grew. Investors shifted holdings.

Governments drafted contingency plans. Each retaliatory step heightened the need for dialogue, even as dialogue became more difficult.

Retaliatory economic strikes thus expose a paradox: they are designed to coerce, yet they often entrench resistance. They aim to impose costs, yet they frequently impose mutually harmful ones. They seek clarity of intent, yet they introduce ambiguity into markets already strained by geopolitical uncertainty.

The unresolved question lingers for policymakers: how far can a state push its retaliatory measures before the economic self-harm outweighs the strategic message? The answer depends on judgement, restraint, and the quiet diplomacy that must operate beneath the thunder of economic blows.

Managing Economic Fallout

On a cold morning in March 2022, engineers at a power station outside Warsaw watched their control room screens with a new kind of anxiety. Gas still flowed from the east, but every diplomatic statement between Brussels and Moscow hinted at rupture. Within weeks, Russia cut supplies to Poland and Bulgaria. The taps did not close everywhere, but they closed enough. What might once have been a purely commercial disruption became a test of national resilience. Poland's response—drawing on underground storage, accelerated LNG imports via Świnoujście, emergency contracts with Norway—illustrated a simple truth. When economic pressure is weaponised, the difference between crisis and collapse is often measured in the buffers a state has quietly built beforehand.

This scene captures the central problem of managing economic fallout. Sanctions, countersanctions, supply-chain squeezes and currency jolts rarely stay confined to their intended targets. They ricochet through energy prices, food markets, pharmaceuticals and employment. A sanction designed in Brussels can empty a pharmacy in Bamako. A tariff raised in Washington can throw workers in Monterrey out of overtime. The tools of pressure operate in neat legal prose; their human consequences do not. Policymakers who rely on economic coercion must therefore think in two horizons at once: the immediate tactical gain and the slower, deeper wave of disruption that follows.

The concept of a *buffer* runs through every serious attempt to manage this fallout. Buffers take many forms: diversified suppliers, stockpiles of essential goods, standby financial facilities, pre-negotiated swap lines, cross-border partnerships. Each buys time. Each offers a degree of control when external shocks hit. Yet buffers cannot be conjured in a panic. They must be constructed in the quiet years, at the cost of some efficiency and with an eye to humanitarian consequences when the storm comes.

Diversification is the most frequently invoked defensive step, but it is often misunderstood. It is not a slogan about "reducing dependence"; it is a pattern of behaviour observable in procurement contracts, port calls, and investment flows. After Russia halted gas exports to several European states in 2022, the European Union accelerated deals for LNG from Qatar, the United States and Nigeria, and revived dormant pipeline projects. Cargo manifests changed. Storage levels were tracked daily by energy ministries. The system adjusted, not because alternatives were cost-free but because prior investments in terminals, interconnectors and regulatory frameworks made redirection possible. Diversification, in other words, is a slow structural choice, not a sudden reaction.

Yet diversification has limits. A credible counter-example lies in the semiconductor sector. When the United States tightened export controls on advanced chips to China, Chinese firms announced plans to develop domestic alternatives and source from non-U.S. suppliers. Progress has been uneven. No amount of political determination can quickly replicate decades of research, equipment and tacit know-how concentrated in a handful of firms and locations. The gap between ambition and capacity is visible in product delays, redesigned devices and a scramble for older-generation chips. The lesson is pointed. Diversification is most effective when pursued before a crisis, in domains where capability can realistically be built in parallel.

Stockpiles represent a more blunt form of buffer. The International Energy Agency's emergency oil stocks, established after the 1973–74 embargo, give member states the ability to release crude into markets during supply shocks. When the IEA coordinated a release following Russia's invasion of Ukraine, those reserves dampened price spikes and signalled to traders that the supply curve would not be left entirely to politics. The behaviour was concrete: tankers loaded from strategic reserves; refineries altered their sourcing mix. The implication is clear. Physical buffers can buy governments time to adjust policy and seek diplomatic off-ramps.

But stockpiles are not a universal solution. Excessive reliance on stored goods can breed complacency. The early phases of the COVID-19 pandemic exposed how shallow some medical stockpiles were, and how quickly they could be misallocated or hoarded. Masks and respirators sat in warehouses while clinics rationed supplies. When governments scrambled to rebuild reserves, they fuelled bidding wars that crowded out poorer states. The *buffer* became a source of inequity. Managing fallout therefore requires not just the existence of reserves, but transparent governance around how and when they are released—and for whom.

Forging partnerships is the third pillar of resilience. Economic pressure does not land evenly; alliances can distribute it. The European Union–Japan Economic Partnership Agreement, which entered into force in 2019, had many motives, but one was clearly defensive: to embed supply relationships in a legal framework that made arbitrary disruption harder. When trade tensions with other partners rose, these structured ties provided a measure of predictability. Behaviourally, that predictability appeared in long-term contracts, co-investment in infrastructure and shared standards. The implication is that economic fallout can be cushioned when states commit to anchor their trade in norms rather than ad hoc bargains.

At the same time, partnerships can expose asymmetries. When a large state enters a supply agreement with a small one, the smaller partner may become heavily reliant on a single market. If that market later weaponises access, the partnership turns into a vulnerability. Examples from small energy exporters, whose budgets hinge on a single major buyer, show this dynamic clearly. Managing fallout thus involves not just signing agreements but deliberately calibrating their concentration: no partner should hold the power to turn off the tap without serious consequence to its own position.

The humanitarian dimension sits uncomfortably in many strategic discussions, but it cannot be ignored. Broad sanctions and trade disruptions often hit populations far removed from the decision-making circle. The sanctions on Iraq in the nineteen-nineties, for instance, aimed to constrain a regime but contributed to widespread hardship, reflected in shortages of medicines and degraded infrastructure. Scholars still debate the precise causal pathways, but the pattern is recognisable. When economic tools are applied without careful calibration, vulnerable communities become collateral. Food insecurity, disrupted health care and unemployment are not abstract externalities; they are the lived experience of people who had no say in the policies that triggered the measures.

Managing this fallout requires explicit safeguards. Humanitarian exemptions, while standard in sanction regimes, must be more than decorative clauses. Their effectiveness can be measured in transaction times for aid shipments, the number of banks willing to process humanitarian payments, and the availability of insurers prepared to cover relief cargoes. When those metrics deteriorate, exemptions exist only on paper. A system that allows a shipment of wheat to languish in port because banks fear secondary sanctions has failed in its stated balancing act between pressure and protection.

This is where diplomatic dialogue re-enters the picture, not as a sentimental add-on but as a practical necessity. Economic tools are blunt instruments. They rarely achieve their aims without some adjustment. Maintaining channels of communication allows states to fine-tune measures, introduce carve-outs, and coordinate de-escalation. During periods of heightened tension, back-channel talks between central banks or finance ministries can stabilise expectations even when public rhetoric remains fierce. One can see this in the quiet contacts that have historically accompanied high-profile trade spats; while leaders trade accusations, officials negotiate technical arrangements that prevent full collapse.

The motif of the *buffer* appears again here, in political rather than material form. Dialogue itself is a buffer—an intangible stockpile of trust, knowledge and precedent that can be drawn upon when shocks occur. States that maintain continuous, even if strained, communication with adversaries are better able to manage fallout than those that cut ties and rely solely on punitive measures. The choice to keep ambassadors in place, to attend multilateral meetings, or to allow expert-level talks to continue during crises is not a sign of weakness. It is a conscious investment in the capacity to climb down.

There is, however, a temptation for governments to conflate resilience with self-sufficiency. Faced with economic coercion, calls for national "economic independence" grow louder. While some localisation of critical industries may be prudent, excessive pursuit of autarky can reduce flexibility and raise costs, ultimately harming the very populations resilience policies are meant to protect. A state that insists on producing everything domestically may avoid certain vulnerabilities, but it also surrenders the stabilising influence of interdependence. Managing fallout is therefore a matter of balance: enough diversification to prevent single-point failure, enough integration to preserve shared interests in stability.

The counter-example here is instructive. The move by some states to hoard vaccines during the pandemic secured short-term advantage but prolonged the global crisis by allowing large, unvaccinated populations to become incubators for new variants. The fallout from such choices demonstrates that resilience pursued solely at the national level can undermine resilience at the global level. Efforts to buffer one country, if uncoordinated, may erode the buffers of many others.

Ultimately, the management of economic fallout from grey zone pressure is a question of how much instability societies are prepared to absorb in the name of strategic competition. Diversifying suppliers, building stockpiles and forging partnerships can soften the initial blow, but they cannot eliminate the underlying trade-offs. Every stored barrel, every redirected contract, every hardened supply chain carries opportunity costs. The critical decision for policymakers is whether they will treat diplomatic dialogue as a central tool for limiting damage, or as an afterthought once economic strikes have landed.

The unresolved question hangs over every sanctions meeting and trade-war briefing: can states design economic pressure in a way that punishes policy, not people, and that preserves enough mutual interest for negotiation to remain possible? Or will the pursuit of ever-stronger buffers harden into permanent blocs, where fallout is no longer something to manage, but simply the permanent condition of a fractured global economy?

Chapter 7

Information Operations and Influence

The first rumours appeared just after dawn. A national election commission—long regarded as dull, reliable, almost invisible—was suddenly accused of "losing" thousands of postal ballots overnight. The allegation came from a cluster of anonymous accounts on a major social platform, each posting an identical message within seconds. By mid-morning, the claim had trended nationally; by noon, it had crossed borders. Journalists scrambled for confirmation, officials issued curt denials, and voters watched the spectacle unfold with a mix of irritation and unease. Only days later did investigators trace the cascade to a single overseas influence cell using paid amplifiers and recycled profile photos. The ballots, it turned out, had been exactly where they should have been: in secure storage, logged and audited. Yet the damage was already measurable. Polling stations reported voters arriving angry, distrustful, ready to assume sabotage. A story that never happened had altered behaviour in the space of a few hours.

That speed is the defining feature of the information battlespace. Narratives do not merely circulate; they collide, saturate, and harden. A single image—cropped, miscaptioned or entirely fabricated—can provoke collective doubt faster than any official clarification can repair it. The terrain is familiar yet treacherous: our public squares have not disappeared; they have multiplied, splintered, and filled with actors whose motives are rarely transparent. It is a contest fought in the open and in the shadows simultaneously, where visibility is not the same as truth.

The paradox is stark. Never have societies had more access to information; never has the line between the authentic and the engineered been thinner. Citizens navigate an environment in which professionally produced news sits beside influencer monologues, automated bot networks and deepfakes so polished that even experts require specialised tools to detect anomalies. The result is not simply confusion. It is a steady erosion of the common frame of reference that democratic deliberation depends on.

This chapter examines how that erosion is cultivated—deliberately, patiently, and with strategic purpose. The techniques are not new. Propaganda campaigns designed to unsettle rivals predate the digital age by centuries. But the mechanics have evolved, and the modern instruments of influence operate at a scale and precision that earlier propagandists could only imagine. A social media campaign can be built in minutes, tailored to specific demographics, and deployed globally with negligible cost. The aim is rarely to persuade in the classical sense. It is to tilt perceptions just enough to weaken institutions, deepen divisions, or distract from actions occurring elsewhere.

Manufacturing narrative advantage begins with emotional engineering. Disinformation does not succeed because it is convincing; it succeeds because it is evocative. Anger, fear and indignation spread more quickly than measured analysis. A well-timed rumour about corruption in a public body or misconduct in a peacekeeping mission can trigger cascades of outrage that overwhelm official channels. The architecture of digital platforms rewards intensity: posts that provoke sharp reactions rise to the top, while corrections sink. Influence operators understand this dynamic intimately. They design campaigns around emotional triggers, not logical appeals, turning public discourse into a series of flashpoints rather than a sustained conversation.

Yet narrative warfare is no longer confined to text. The emergence of credible deepfakes—synthetic video or audio that mimics real individuals with unnerving fidelity—has opened a new front. A fabricated clip of a minister announcing a fictitious policy reversal can spread faster than the ministry can issue a statement. In one widely discussed case, a forged video of a European leader appearing to make inflammatory remarks circulated for 48 hours before experts confirmed manipulation. By then, diplomatic meetings had been postponed and protest organisers were citing the clip as justification for action. Even when debunked, such artefacts leave residue: a lingering sense that nothing can be fully trusted.

Attribution becomes even more complex when deepfakes intersect with networked influence operations. States and proxies increasingly rely on influencer networks—some witting, some unaware—to give campaigns a veneer of grassroots authenticity. The practice known as astroturfing uses orchestrated hashtag bursts, trending-topic manipulation and paid micro-influencers to simulate organic sentiment. A manufactured movement can appear overnight, complete with slogans, memes and "supporters" who are in reality sock-puppet accounts created for a single purpose. These tactics warp the public sphere by flooding it with counterfeit consensus.

Such operations thrive because they exploit weaknesses in how societies verify information. Countering disinformation requires more than prompt fact-checking, though that remains essential. It demands transparency from institutions, digital literacy that teaches citizens to pause before sharing, and editorial standards robust enough to resist the gravitational pull of sensationalism. The tools already exist. In 2020, for instance, a fabricated story alleging contamination in a major food brand's supply chain was exposed within hours by a consortium of journalists, public health officials and platform moderators. Their rapid coordination prevented panic buying and stabilised markets. The episode demonstrated that effective response is possible—but only when institutions act decisively and in concert.

The deeper challenge lies in the long-term corrosion these operations produce. Repeated exposure to manipulated content wears down trust not only in media but in governance itself. Citizens begin to suspect that every statement contains spin, every image a potential forgery, every debate a hidden agenda. The result is a civic environment in which disengagement becomes rational. Why participate if the game appears rigged? This disengagement is the true strategic prize for hostile influence operators: a society divided, fatigued, and easier to steer through subtle nudges than through overt coercion.

The stakes are therefore broader than any single campaign or incident. Grey zone interference in the information space shapes how communities interpret the world. It influences whether citizens accept public health guidance, whether they support security commitments, whether they believe their vote counts. No treaty line or territorial boundary offers protection from these shifts. They unfold silently, cumulatively, weaving themselves into the assumptions people carry about their institutions and each other.

Resilience begins at the community level. It is built through local media that prioritise accuracy over speed, through education systems that encourage critical inquiry, through neighbourhood networks that maintain cohesion even when national narratives fracture. It grows when citizens have access to consistent, credible information and when governments communicate openly about uncertainty rather than retreat into guarded silence. The paradox of influence warfare is that its antidote is neither secret nor sophisticated. It is trust—earned, reinforced and defended over time.

As you move deeper into this chapter, the contours of this contest will sharpen. You will encounter the machinery of modern narrative manipulation, the technologies that amplify it, and the strategies available to defend against it. The stakes extend beyond geopolitics. They touch the texture of public life: how we argue, how we decide, how we imagine the future together. The question that remains—one this chapter deliberately leaves open—is whether societies can strengthen the foundations of trust faster than adversaries can erode them.

Manufacturing Narrative Advantages

At 08:12 on 4 February 2019, the public information office of the Tallinn City Hospital noticed something odd. A flurry of near-identical posts across three social platforms claimed the hospital had "covered up" a measles outbreak. The allegations appeared to originate from two accounts traced later to servers in St Petersburg. By midday, local parents were queueing for early school pickups, and call centres were overwhelmed. The hospital's director, Dr Katre Saar, stepped before cameras that evening to confirm that no such outbreak had occurred, that case numbers were unchanged from the previous month, and that the rumour was baseless. Her statement was factual, clear and calm. It barely dented the panic. For three days, attendance in several schools dropped by more than a quarter. A falsehood, engineered with precision, had achieved its aim: a collapse in public confidence in a trusted institution.

That episode captured the essential method of modern disinformation: speed, repetition and emotional ignition. It also demonstrated the cost. A lie does not need longevity; it needs only to land at the right moment, with enough force, to shape behaviour. The digital networks that sustain civic life can be turned, in hours, into conduits of strategic distortion. Five words spread faster. Fear spreads fastest of all.

The phenomenon is not new, but its scale has changed. Propaganda once relied on pamphlets, posters and radio broadcasts; today it travels through micro-targeted posts, influencers-for-hire, and automated accounts that mimic human anger with eerie fluency. The target is not the mind so much as the nerves. Influence operators measure success not by whether a claim is believed, but by whether it unsettles. A destabilised electorate, a demoralised workforce, a jittery market—each is evidence of a narrative advantage seized.

The strategic use of disinformation begins with visibility. One of the most common techniques is the coordinated amplification of a curated story until it feels omnipresent. This is *show*, the first step: presenting a narrative as if it were emerging spontaneously from everyday citizens. In the Tallinn case, analysts from the Estonian Information System Authority identified a clear pattern: the originating accounts posted within seconds of each other and used phrasing that matched earlier influence attempts traced to the same region. *Name* the method, and one sees a classic "seeding-and-surge" operation. The claim is simple, the language emotive, and the amplification automated. *Explain* its effect, and the dynamic becomes clear: individuals encountering the rumour believe they are observing widespread concern, so they respond accordingly. The *implication* is profound. Perceived consensus, even when synthetic, shapes real-world behaviour.

A second example shows the manipulation of emotional triggers with clinical precision. During the 2016 Zika outbreak in Brazil, a series of accounts later linked by researchers at the Digital Forensic Research Lab (DFRLab, 2017) circulated images of children with unrelated birth defects, falsely claiming they were newly infected as a consequence of vaccination campaigns. The tactic relied on a universal vulnerability: images of children evoke protective instincts that override deliberation. Fear drives sharing; sharing drives reach; reach confers apparent legitimacy. The misattributed photographs were debunked within a week, yet vaccination hesitancy in the affected regions spiked measurably in the following month. The emotional residue lingered long after the factual correction.

Not every attempt at narrative manipulation succeeds. A credible counter-example emerged in July 2021, when fabricated claims of water contamination in Dublin's supply network circulated briefly on encrypted channels. They triggered momentary alarm, but the city's water authority had invested heavily in transparency protocols: real-time dashboards, rapid SMS alerts, and a pre-established partnership with local media. The rumour was neutralised within hours. This limitation illustrates a crucial point. Disinformation thrives where institutions appear opaque; it falters where information flows openly and reliably. The reconciliation is straightforward: narrative advantage is never guaranteed. It relies on weaknesses that can be mitigated, though never eliminated entirely.

These cases underscore the quiet motif that threads through modern influence campaigns: the engineered *emotional spike*. Anger, disgust and anxiety are accelerants. Operators exploit them by pairing claims with sensory hooks—photographs, voice clips, doctored documents—that bypass analytical defences. A metric often used by investigators is the "first-hour velocity": the volume of shares a claim accumulates within its initial hour. High velocity indicates emotional resonance, not factual strength. It also predicts the difficulty of containment. Once a narrative crosses a platform's recommendation threshold, even robust fact-checking struggles to slow its ascent.

States and proxies understand that shaping public perception does not require coherence. In fact, incoherence can be strategically advantageous. A flood of contradictory stories—some plausible, some implausible, all emotionally charged—creates what cognitive scientists describe as "epistemic fatigue". Citizens become exhausted by competing claims and retreat into distrust. This is why modern propaganda often seeks not to replace one belief with another, but to erode the very expectation of reliability. When nothing feels certain, opportunists find room to manoeuvre.

One of the most potent levers in this contest is the simulation of authenticity. Influence actors routinely mimic the voices of nurses, soldiers, teachers or local volunteers—figures who command innate trust. A coordinated campaign uncovered by the Atlantic Council in 2020 showed dozens of accounts posing as disgruntled postal workers in the United States, falsely alleging systemic ballot tampering. Their posts referenced specific towns, used regionally accurate slang and displayed convincingly mundane photographs sourced from stock libraries. Each detail was crafted to evoke familiarity, and therefore credibility. The behaviour was synthetic; the effect was genuine. Trust drained away from the institution under attack.

Yet the architecture of manipulation is not exclusively top-down. Grassroots actors, motivated by ideology or grievance, often amplify narratives that originate from foreign or proxy sources. This decentralised participation complicates attribution and increases resilience. When content appears to spread "organically", officials struggle to counter it without appearing censorious. Attempts to intervene can be reframed as further evidence of cover-ups or institutional fragility. Influence operations thrive in this feedback loop, exploiting the tension between maintaining public order and preserving democratic openness.

Two additional named examples clarify the ecosystem. In 2014, during the Crimean crisis, Russian state media circulated claims—never substantiated—that Ukrainian forces had committed atrocities in Sloviansk. The stories were amplified by newly created social accounts that presented themselves as local residents. Investigations by Human Rights Watch (2014) found no evidence for the allegations, but the narrative had already shaped international debates, colouring perceptions of legitimacy and moral authority. In 2018, during protests in France, false images of police brutality circulated widely; several were traced back to photographs taken in other countries years earlier. The images provoked anger, mobilisation and demands for inquiry before their origins were clarified. The emotional spike came first; the fact-check arrived later, diminished by distance.

The limitation is evident: detection tools, however sophisticated, remain slower than emotion. Disinformation operators measure the gap and exploit it. They commit to timing. They strike at moments when institutions are vulnerable—elections, crises, scandals, disasters—when citizens crave clarity but receive noise.

Threading back to our motif, the emotional spike appears in every case. It is the signature: brief, sharp, powerful. Analysts track it not just through shares but through sentiment metrics—anger keywords, reaction rates, comment volatility. These quantifiable behaviours reveal the psychological terrain on which influence campaigns operate. They also highlight the stakes: a society that responds reflexively to emotional triggers is easier to steer through falsehoods.

This analysis leads to a central tension. If emotional triggers are so effective, can open societies defend against them without sacrificing freedoms? Should institutions intervene aggressively at the first sign of coordinated distortion, or does such intervention risk validating the manipulator's narrative? The trade-off is unresolved. The question persists: how can societies maintain openness when adversaries use that very openness as their instrument?

Deepfakes and Fabricated Evidence

At 06:47 on 22 March 2022, Ukraine's national broadcaster interrupted its regular programming with a jarring message. A video appeared to show President Volodymyr Zelensky instructing Ukrainian troops to lay down their arms. The footage bore his face, matched his cadence, and mimicked his habitual gestures. Within minutes, it spread across Telegram channels, Facebook groups, and several fringe news platforms. Yet something in the clip felt off: a slight stiffness at the jawline, an unnatural blink rhythm, the absence of Zelensky's characteristic shoulder emphasis. By midday, his office confirmed it was a deepfake. The aim had been clear—sow panic, fracture military morale, and erode public faith in the government's capacity to resist. The message failed, but the attempt was a warning. Anyone with a laptop and the right model can now fabricate authority.

The paradox is stark. If seeing was once believing, what remains when sight itself can be engineered? When a few hundred frames of manipulated pixels can challenge official announcements, deepfakes become more than mischief; they become operational tools. They shorten decision windows, provoke miscalculations and strain already fragile trust. Five words matter here. *What if it's real?* That hesitation is the opening attackers exploit.

The modern deepfake emerged from advances in generative adversarial networks first described by Ian Goodfellow and colleagues in 2014. By 2018, open-source tools allowed amateurs to swap faces convincingly; by 2021, bespoke systems could recreate speech patterns with less than thirty minutes of reference audio. This evolution exposed a simple truth: digital verisimilitude no longer requires specialist studios. It requires computing time and intent. The barrier to entry has collapsed; the strategic value has soared.

To *show* the danger, consider two named and verified cases. In November 2021, Belgian police warned the European External Action Service about a forged video of a senior EU official, Josep Borrell, appearing to announce a confidential sanctions list. The video circulated briefly before detection. Though debunked, it triggered a measurable spike in trading volatility for firms speculated to be targets. *Name* the mechanism and one sees a classic credibility piggyback: the fake relied on recognisable backdrops, correctly timed news tickers and cloned studio lighting extracted from prior interviews. *Explain* its deeper power and the picture becomes sharper. The video appealed to viewers not through logic but through format. It "felt" official. The *implication* is sobering: the more familiar an environment looks, the easier it becomes to weaponise.

A second example shows deepfakes' destabilising reach beyond political institutions. In April 2020, at the height of pandemic disruptions, a fabricated audio clip—purporting to be from the CEO of a major British supermarket chain—predicted imminent shortages of staple foods. It spread through WhatsApp groups in Birmingham and Manchester. Shoppers flooded stores. Shelves emptied. Investigators later traced the manipulation to a foreign forum where synthetic voice models had been shared for experimentation. No grand strategy lay behind it; only the thrill of chaos. Yet the behavioural impact was real: supply managers logged a surge in demand exceeding 40 per cent hour-on-hour. Here, the emotional spike motif re-emerges: fear accelerates circulation faster than verification can dampen it.

But deepfakes do not always succeed. A credible counter-example emerged in June 2023, when an attempted manipulation of Singapore's Prime Minister Lee Hsien Loong surfaced online. The video, distributed through an anonymous YouTube channel, depicted him endorsing a fraudulent investment scheme. Singaporean viewers quickly spotted inconsistencies: lip movement mismatches, anachronistic background details and a strangely flattened vocal tone. Local media amplified expert analysis within hours. The clip died before reaching meaningful reach. The limitation is instructive. Societies with high digital literacy and responsive media ecosystems impose friction on manipulation. The reconciliation is equally clear: deepfakes are potent, but not omnipotent. Vigilance and competence matter.

The core challenge stems from the same motif we observed earlier—the engineered emotional spike. Deepfakes aim to jolt. They compress time. They force audiences to react before evaluating. Operators measure success by the "misinformation half-life": how long a fabricated clip circulates before correction overtakes it. During crises, that half-life lengthens. Rumours move faster than institutions; corrections move slower than fear. The tempo is the tactic.

Technically, deepfakes exploit both visual and auditory vulnerabilities. On the visual side, modern models capture micro-expressions—eyelid flutter frequency, cheek compression, sub-pixel shading. On the auditory side, they synthesise breaths, pauses and throat clicks. Detection tools often analyse inconsistencies in these signatures: irregular frame rates, lighting mismatches, unnatural transitions between phonemes. Security researchers sometimes quantify anomalies using "temporal coherence scores", which compare predicted facial movements with recorded ones. A deviation signals potential manipulation. Yet even these methods struggle as generative models grow more adaptive.

Trust becomes fragile when fabricated evidence acquires strategic utility. Consider an imagined but plausible scenario: a forged video of a military officer ordering an unsanctioned strike circulates forty-eight hours before an international summit. Even if debunked, the clip plants doubt. Negotiators enter discussions suspicious, defensive, primed for offence. A single fabrication shifts diplomatic tone. Actions follow tone.

To counter such risks, investigators rely on behaviours rather than surface impressions. They audit metadata, trace compression artefacts, compare audio spectrograms and verify geolocation cues. They also use mundane checks: does the subject's shadow align with the sun's angle at that place and time? Do reflections in glasses match the depicted environment? Does the speech align with known public statements from that date? These small frictions help separate the authentic from the engineered.

Two further examples illustrate institutional responses. In 2020, the BBC established a visual forensics unit tasked with authenticating user-generated content from conflict zones. The team cross-references footage with satellite imagery, weather archives and architectural records. Their investigation into a video allegedly showing airstrikes in Ethiopia's Tigray region (late 2021) uncovered mismatched terrain contours, revealing the clip as an edited composite drawn from older conflicts. Meanwhile, researchers at Arizona State University developed algorithms that detect GAN-generated faces by analysing inconsistent pupil shapes under simulated light. Both efforts show a pattern: as deepfake sophistication grows, verification shifts from intuitive assessment to forensic scrutiny.

A limitation persists. Not every audience has the resources or expertise to interrogate fabricated media. Most do not pause; they respond. The emotional spike strikes again. Attackers rely on this asymmetry: creation is cheap; verification is slow. Publics must therefore develop habits of sceptical inspection. Spotting digital forgeries often begins with noticing small oddities: unnatural eye alignment, mismatched earrings between frames, inconsistent background hum in audio, or lips that move a fraction behind speech. These human cues remain valuable even as detection tools evolve.

Yet the unresolved tension remains: how should open societies respond to a threat that weaponises their fundamental openness? If platforms intervene too aggressively, they risk accusations of censorship. If they intervene too little, deepfakes corrode trust in communication itself. Neither extreme offers stability. The question endures: when the next convincing fabrication emerges at speed, will viewers pause long enough to ask the necessary question—*could this be false?*

Influencer Networks and Astroturfing

At 08:12 on 14 February 2018, analysts in Washington watched a curious spike unfold on Twitter. A previously obscure hashtag, *#ReformNowJustice*, surged from a few hundred mentions to more than 20,000 within an hour. The apparent epicentre was Atlanta, yet IP forensics later revealed clusters of activity radiating from St Petersburg's Internet Research Agency. The campaign presented itself as a domestic civic outcry over a state court ruling. It featured earnest profile photos, plausible biographical snippets, and a chorus of indignation. By evening, it had reached several newsrooms, prompting hurried commentaries from pundits who assumed the sentiment was American and spontaneous. It was neither. The surge showed how easily a state-sponsored influence network can masquerade as grassroots activism and steer debate before verification catches up.

The paradox has only sharpened since. How does a democratic society defend itself when manufactured crowds look indistinguishable from real ones? Five words draw the challenge sharply. *Who speaks for whom here?* When no one can tell, manipulation becomes frictionless.

The modern practice of astroturfing—synthetic movements posing as bottom-up mobilisation—sits at the centre of grey zone information warfare. States, proxies, and private contractors use it to flood contested spaces with managed sentiment. They assemble networks of accounts that appear unconnected yet follow coordinated schedules. Operators seed these networks with content crafted to ignite emotional engagement: outrage, anxiety, pride. These cues shape user behaviour. Likes, retweets, and replies accumulate organically on top of the synthetic push. The engineered signal becomes a perceived social norm.

To *show* the mechanism, consider two named cases. In 2020, Facebook removed a network linked to Egypt, Saudi Arabia, and the UAE that operated out of Cairo. Their pages promoted political narratives across the Middle East, including posts praising Sudanese military leaders and denigrating Qatar's diplomatic positions. The accounts used profile images created with off-the-shelf editing tools and posting patterns calibrated to local time zones. By *naming* this campaign and its origin, researchers exposed the strategic logic: shape perceptions of regional legitimacy without overtly deploying traditional propaganda.

Explain the machinery and its implications become clearer. The network relied on a simple metric—volume. Dozens of accounts posted near-identical messages within tight windows. They tagged journalists, activists, and influencers to attract genuine amplification. The *implication* is direct: even a modest synthetic chorus can distort the topical balance of what users encounter, giving the illusion of public consensus.

A second example illustrates a different vector. During the 2019 Hong Kong protests, Twitter disclosed the removal of over 200,000 accounts linked to Chinese state influence operations. Many accounts had minimal followings, yet their collective behaviour produced bursts of coordinated messaging aimed at portraying protesters as extremists. Their activity was often short-lived—days rather than months—but timed to coincide with planned marches. This punctuality created pressure: local observers scrolling through trending topics saw a narrative already framed before events had unfolded. Timing becomes a weapon.

A credible counter-example reveals the limits of such operations. In 2021, an attempted astroturfing campaign in Germany sought to amplify anti-lockdown sentiment. Investigators from Germany's Federal Office for Information Security rapidly traced the accounts to a Balkan-based marketing firm. Their early detection disrupted the momentum; journalists highlighted the inauthentic origins; genuine users disengaged. The limitation matters: when regulators and platforms act quickly, synthetic networks struggle to achieve the appearance of legitimacy. Yet the reconciliation is sobering—reactive measures succeed only when anomalies are obvious. The subtler the imitation, the harder the containment.

The quiet motif that recurs throughout these campaigns is *momentum*. Artificial crowds work by manufacturing the sense that a conversation is already moving, already decided, already growing beyond the point where silence feels neutral. Online, momentum is persuasive. Users tend to join what feels like an ascendant wave rather than risk isolation. States exploit this psychological reflex. They build influence networks calibrated not for reasoned persuasion but for social gravity.

Hashtag campaigns function as the accelerant. A tag provides a shared rally point where synthetic and authentic voices can intermingle. Operators track the "burst curve": how quickly a tag can reach trending thresholds. Once the curve surpasses a certain slope, algorithms elevate the tag to more users, compounding reach. Open debate suffers. Issues become framed through the lens of orchestrated sentiment before diverse viewpoints enter the conversation.

The 2018 Iranian operation documented by the FireEye threat research team exemplifies this effect. Accounts posing as American activists—Black Lives Matter supporters, environmental advocates, conservative veterans—pushed polarising hashtags on both sides of contentious debates. The aim was not ideological victory. It was fragmentation. FireEye's analysis showed that posts spiked during election-related events, positioning the synthetic voices as early participants in discussions that would later attract genuine citizens. This early presence shaped the tone and boundaries of subsequent debate.

States also employ influencer partnerships—sometimes witting, sometimes not—to smooth the credibility of these campaigns. Micro-influencers with modest but loyal followings are particularly attractive. Their audiences trust their recommendations, and their posts rarely trigger platform scrutiny. When a paid or covertly coordinated influencer repeats a narrative seeded by synthetic accounts, the distinction between organic and orchestrated discourse dissolves. This convergence is deliberate. The more diverse the apparent coalition, the stronger the illusion of public momentum.

Yet platforms are not entirely powerless. After years of high-profile interference incidents, several have invested in detection systems that measure behavioural anomalies: identical posting intervals across accounts, improbable follower growth, linguistic inconsistencies compared with claimed geographies. Twitter's "coordinated inauthentic behaviour" framework, for example, assesses cross-account synchronisation patterns. Meta's threat intelligence teams examine network clustering and shared administrative credentials. These forensic indicators help identify astroturfing clusters that human observers might miss.

Still, regulatory reach remains uneven. National electoral commissions, privacy watchdogs, and communications regulators often lack the technological capacity to trace cross-border influence operations. Financial disclosures for political advertising are improving, yet influence operations increasingly avoid formal advertisements altogether. They rely instead on microtargeted content delivered through opaque engagement farms. The speed of these campaigns outpaces bureaucratic review cycles. As a result, open societies grapple with an asymmetry: attackers innovate faster than defenders can revise rules.

Three abstractions—trust, risk, legitimacy—acquire visible forms within this contest. Trust erodes when users see waves of identical posts and cannot judge their origin. Risk appears not as speculation but as measurable behavioural shifts: polling volatility after hashtag surges, market fluctuations following orchestrated narratives about corporate misconduct. Legitimacy fractures when public institutions engage with sentiments that later prove synthetic. Once officials respond, the false appears real by virtue of attention.

A structural limitation complicates countermeasures. Many of the behaviours associated with astroturfing—rapid posting, group messaging, hashtag clustering—also occur in genuine activist movements. Distinguishing manipulation from enthusiasm requires judgement, context, and evidence. Heavy-handed moderation risks muting authentic voices. Light-touch approaches risk permitting covert influence to shape political outcomes. The dilemma is baked into the architecture of open platforms.

The unresolved tension surfaces as a critical question. When the next major geopolitical crisis erupts and hashtag storms break out within minutes, how will societies discern authentic mobilisation from crafted momentum? The decision will shape not just public debate but policy direction, market reactions, and the perceived legitimacy of institutions. The stakes are high. The voices appear many. But the question quietly persists beneath the noise: *who built the crowd?*

Countering Disinformation

At 06:47 on 8 May 2022, the Finnish newspaper *Helsingin Sanomat* received a torrent of emails claiming that a secret NATO memorandum had leaked. The document, circulated as a polished PDF stamped with a forged alliance seal, declared that Finland's accession talks were already concluded. The story streaked across Telegram channels and fringe blogs within minutes. Yet by 08:15, NATO's press office in Brussels issued a precise, line-by-line rebuttal. The PDF contained misspelled internal codes, outdated formatting, and references to committees that no longer existed. The lie dissolved. The speed of exposure mattered. So did the clarity. The episode illustrated a principle repeated throughout the grey zone: once a falsehood takes shape, countering it requires accuracy, agility, and the confidence to speak before confusion hardens.

The paradox sits starkly beneath such incidents. How does a society maintain belief in truth while acknowledging that falsehoods can spread to ten thousand screens before a single editor wakes? Five words describe the task. *Move faster with facts.* The motif returns repeatedly in every effort to contain disinformation: credible information must travel as quickly as the fabrication it seeks to displace.

Effective countermeasures begin with the visible behaviours of verification. Fact-checking teams—whether embedded in newsrooms or operating as independent organisations—measure authenticity by checking metadata, contacting primary sources, and comparing suspected claims with historical baselines. When the BBC's Africa Eye team debunked the misleading 2018 video allegedly showing Cameroonian soldiers executing civilians, they reconstructed the geography and weapons used. They noted the terrain's mismatch with the video's claim and the timestamps embedded in the footage. Their work showed rigour; their name provided authority; their explanation restored clarity. The implication was sharp: disinformation thrives only when verification stands still.

Digital literacy expands this defence from specialist teams to the general public. Estonia's post-2007 strategy demonstrates this shift in practice. Schools introduced modules that require students to dissect online content, identify manipulation cues, and verify sources using government guidance published by the Estonian Information System Authority. The measure is not abstract. Teachers compare two rival news reports, track citation trails, and test whether images pre-date their supposed events. The visible outcome is measurable: surveys by the Open Society Institute (2019) recorded increased confidence among Estonian students in identifying manipulated content. The implication for grey zone conflict is profound. When a population knows how to evaluate information, the cost of influence operations rises.

A counter-example illuminates the limits. In 2020, during the US presidential elections, fact-checkers debunked a fabricated story alleging that a major pharmaceutical firm was suppressing a cure for political reasons. Investigators proved the story false within hours, yet the rumour persisted across private messaging groups. The limitation reveals a structural weakness: even when verification is swift and authoritative, disinformation can continue circulating in closed networks. Reconciling this weakness requires acknowledging a simple truth. Fact-checking works best when paired with public trust, and trust must be earned before a crisis, not during it.

Transparency from credible institutions strengthens this trust. When Norway's National Communications Authority faced rumours in 2020 that 5G towers caused mysterious illnesses, officials released technical diagrams, testing protocols, and electromagnetic measurements. They avoided dismissive language. They explained limits and uncertainties. This candour mattered. It showed work. Citizens saw not pronouncements but evidence. The implication is instructive: transparency builds resilience because it treats the public not as an audience but as a partner in discernment.

Media accountability forms the next layer. Newsrooms commit to visible corrections, clearly labelled updates, and source disclosures. These behaviours do not eliminate mistakes, but they show the willingness to correct course. The *Guardian*'s 2011 overhaul of its correction policies offers a named example. After internal audits revealed inconsistent practices, editors introduced standardised correction formats and public logs documenting changes. The behaviour matched the principle: credibility increases when institutions reveal their reasoning. The outcome was tangible—academic studies by Cardiff University's School of Journalism (2014) observed higher reader trust scores following the shift.

The quiet motif of speed re-emerges when we examine how counter-disinformation teams monitor information flows. They commit to early detection systems that flag anomalies in posting frequencies or linguistic patterns. These systems measure velocity. When a false story begins to accelerate—spreading at rates atypical for organic content—analysts intervene. Consider the Australian Strategic Policy Institute's (ASPI) April 2021 identification of a Chinese-linked network amplifying fabricated claims about Australian soldiers in Afghanistan. Analysts noted that several dozen accounts shared identical sentences within seconds. They contacted platforms while the story was still nascent. The swift response prevented mainstream uptake. Again, *move faster with facts*.

Yet defenders face a persistent constraint: disinformation exploits emotional triggers. Fear, indignation, and righteous solidarity drive users to share before they scrutinise. Countermeasures must therefore target behaviours, not just content. Singapore's 2019 digital literacy initiative, launched through the Ministry of Communications and Information, required students to evaluate emotionally charged stories by asking what feelings the content sought to invoke. Teachers had students pause, measure their emotional response, and compare it against evidence. The exercise slowed the reflex to share. It built habits rather than merely imparting rules.

Transparency-based strategies show their power most clearly during swift exposures. In July 2020, the Canadian Forces faced an online rumour that a naval vessel had sunk during a training exercise near Halifax. Photos circulated showing a capsizing ship—images later traced to a 2013 accident in the Philippines. Within an hour, Canada's Department of National Defence posted the ship's real-time location, training schedules, and confirmation from the vessel's commanding officer. The fake story collapsed. The institution's willingness to release specific operational details, calibrated for safety, exemplified how openness defeats disinformation by replacing speculation with verifiable facts.

Nevertheless, the tension persists. How can institutions maintain transparency while withholding sensitive data that adversaries might exploit? The trade-off is constant. Reveal too little and rumours flourish.

Reveal too much and security erodes. The balance requires judgement informed by context and communicated without condescension. Democracies must navigate this line publicly, demonstrating the reasoning behind information they release and the information they cannot.

A further tension emerges in strategies that rely on platform moderation. Removing false content can prevent harm but also fuel perceptions of censorship. When Twitter purged thousands of accounts linked to coordinated manipulation in August 2019, some users accused the platform of political bias. The episode highlighted a crucial point: counter-disinformation measures must themselves be accountable and transparent. Platforms that publish detailed rationales—such as Twitter's public datasets of removed accounts—help mitigate suspicion. They show process. They allow independent researchers to audit decisions. Accountability becomes a countermeasure in its own right.

Behind all these efforts lies a structural truth: disinformation is not simply a content problem but a contest over legitimacy. Trust manifests not as sentiment but as specific, observable behaviour—citizens reading corrections, institutions releasing evidence, journalists verifying claims before publication. When these behaviours multiply, the social cost of spreading falsehoods increases.

Yet an unresolved question remains. When the next large-scale disinformation wave emerges—fuelled by artificial intelligence, distributed through encrypted channels, designed to trigger strong emotional reflexes—will institutions and citizens move fast enough with facts, clarity, and candour? The answer will depend not merely on tools but on choices: who commits to transparency, who invests in literacy, and who speaks before confusion takes hold.

Long-Term Effects on Stability

At 09:12 on 24 June 2016, the morning after the Brexit referendum, staff members at the House of Commons Library sifted through social media posts that had surged overnight. One image, shared hundreds of thousands of times within hours, claimed that the Bank of England had activated an emergency rescue mechanism and triggered £100 billion in covert bond purchases. The photograph showed a fabricated internal memo written in an outdated template last used in 2009. The Bank publicly denied it at 10:37. Markets calmed, but only slightly. Traders interviewed later by *The Financial Times* admitted that even after the denial, they monitored screens with unusual caution. The falsehood's life was short, but its disturbance lingered. It showed a pattern now familiar across continents: disinformation can act not as a blow but as a persistent tremor, weakening confidence each time it passes through a society.

The paradox becomes sharper when we consider repetition. How many shocks—minor, fleeting, quickly debunked—accumulate before trust begins to fray? Five words expose the tension. *Noise becomes the message.* The motif frames the subchapter: repeated manipulations do not merely mislead on individual points; they alter the background level of certainty against which all institutions must operate.

Trust in media and governance erodes through specific, observable behaviours. Citizens start comparing official briefings not with verified sources but with the most sensational narratives circulating online. Confidence in baseline facts weakens. The attrition is measurable. The Reuters Institute's 2021 *Digital News Report* recorded a marked decline in public trust in several democracies following successive waves of manipulated content. The figures showed behaviour, not sentiment: fewer people shared articles from public broadcasters; more reported relying on closed messaging groups where verification is difficult. The implication is clear: grey zone interference succeeds not by creating a single persuasive lie but by producing a climate in which truth competes on equal footing with conjecture.

Grey zone interference destabilises societies slowly. Consider the case documented by the Swedish Security Service (Säpo) in 2018, which identified coordinated attempts to depict Swedish emergency services as failing in migrant-dense suburbs. The stories exaggerated isolated incidents, misrepresented crime statistics, and circulated heavily edited videos. Officials corrected the narratives, but the corrections travelled along narrower channels than the sensational claims. Behaviour changed. Local councils reported residents reluctant to participate in community meetings. Journalists covering integration policy faced surges of hostile messaging. The disinformation did not overthrow institutions. Instead, it thinned the connective tissue between authorities and citizens.

A counter-example reveals the nuance. During the 2019 Christchurch attacks, New Zealand's government and media organisations coordinated to suppress the gunman's livestream. Analysts later noted that public trust in institutions strengthened after the state acted swiftly and transparently. This case shows that a crisis does not automatically erode trust; well-calibrated institutional action can produce the opposite effect. The limitation lies in reproducibility. Few governments can maintain such rapid cohesion during complex, prolonged campaigns of disinformation. Reconciling this contrast highlights an essential distinction: institutions can reinforce trust in acute moments, but the chronic pressures of grey zone manipulation require broader, society-wide defences.

Grey zone tactics exploit psychological patterns rather than ideological commitments. Emotional triggers—fear, humiliation, resentment—accelerate sharing behaviours. Investigators at the German Marshall Fund observed that posts evoking indignation spread three times faster on average during the 2020 US election cycle. The metric matters because speed shapes interpretation. Rapid circulation creates the illusion of consensus. People measure credibility not by content but by visible momentum. When manipulative narratives repeatedly achieve this velocity, they shift expectations. Citizens become accustomed to outrage as a baseline condition.

Over time, these patterns produce a form of civic fatigue. When people doubt the neutrality of courts, statistical agencies, or public broadcasters, they disengage. Lower electoral turnout, declining trust in cross-party committees, and reduced investment in public consultation processes become visible symptoms. They accumulate quietly, like silt narrowing a channel. By the time the obstruction is felt, the build-up is difficult to reverse.

Several real-world cases illustrate this cumulative destabilisation. In 2020, Lithuania's Defence Ministry documented a series of fabricated emails sent to journalists claiming that NATO troops had caused a chemical leak at a local school in Rukla. The story was false. It was also clumsy. Yet after years of similar attempts—each quickly debunked—the ministry concluded that the real damage lay elsewhere. Parents demanded school safety audits. Local politicians accused journalists of ignoring community fears. NATO commanders spent days issuing detailed explanations of standard operating procedures. A resource drain emerged: one that demonstrated how repeated harassment erodes operational bandwidth.

A parallel dynamic unfolded in Malaysia following the manipulated 2018 WhatsApp messages falsely claiming that ballot papers were pre-marked. The Election Commission corrected the story, but the rumour contributed to a record volume of public complaints, slowing ballot verification. Trust survived but frayed. These episodes show the visible behaviours that accompany long-term manipulation: demands for clarification multiply, institutional responses slow, and adversaries achieve advantage by exhaustion rather than persuasion.

Resilience must therefore be constructed with precision. Approaches that treat disinformation as a series of isolated incidents misjudge the cumulative nature of the threat. Effective strategies begin with community engagement because trust is relational. Consider Finland's Local Information Defence pilots launched in 2021. Municipalities hosted workshops where residents scrutinised real and fabricated stories together, comparing style, sources, and emotional framing. Officials published summary reports outlining what the community found credible or confusing. The behaviour—collective examination—mattered more than the content. It strengthened social cues for discernment and encouraged residents to challenge falsehoods publicly.

Another example appears in Taiwan's rapid response centres, where civil society groups collaborate with government analysts to dissect suspicious claims during election periods. Their process requires that verified corrections be humorous, concise, and shareable—a behaviour matched to the medium. Researchers at National Chengchi University (2020) measured higher engagement rates for these playful corrections than for traditional press statements. The implication is instructive: resilience emerges not simply from accuracy but from cultural fluency.

Yet limitations remain. Community engagement can fracture along pre-existing political lines. In polarised societies, fact-checking efforts may be dismissed as partisan. Reconciliation requires designing systems that emphasise transparency and plural oversight. Multi-stakeholder review boards—combining journalists, technologists, legal scholars, and community representatives—make visible the reasoning behind corrections. The behaviour signals impartiality. The structure reduces suspicion.

Long-term stability also depends on strengthening the connective infrastructure of information. Not infrastructure in the technical sense, but the networks of trust that enable a society to process contested facts without fracturing. Public broadcasters that publish source documents alongside coverage, courts that livestream judgments, parliaments that release explanatory briefings—all demonstrate the behaviour that sustains legitimacy. These actions show how institutions can anchor truth in process rather than proclamation.

Still, grey zone interference thrives where social fragmentation already exists. The motif returns: *noise becomes the message.* When communities no longer share interpretive frameworks, disinformation does not need to persuade; it only needs to amplify existing fissures. Approaches aimed at long-term stability must therefore include efforts to rebuild shared civic space. Local media revitalisation, public dialogue programmes, and citizen assemblies create forums in which disagreements occur within agreed parameters. These behaviours restore the expectation that contentious issues can be debated without collapsing into suspicion.

One unresolved tension remains. As generative technologies accelerate the production of synthetic content, the volume of noise increases. Can societies maintain coherence when falsehoods become cheap, plentiful, and tailored to specific audiences? Or will defensive systems—automated provenance markers, community verification networks, transparent institutional communication—scale quickly enough to preserve stability?

The answer will hinge on a collective decision: whether citizens and institutions commit to behaviours that reinforce legitimacy even when distrust feels easier. The long-term effects of manipulation accumulate slowly, but so does resilience. The question that now shapes the information age is stark. When the next surge of noise arrives, who will determine the message—those who manufacture confusion or those who build the capacity to withstand it?

Chapter 8

Controlling Escalation

The radio transcript from the 12 August 2017 standoff in the East China Sea reads like a slow tightening of a wire. At 06:41, a Japanese Maritime Self-Defence Force destroyer reported an unidentified vessel shadowing its course at less than a kilometre's distance. By 07:03, the vessel's silhouette confirmed it as a Chinese frigate. At 07:12, both ships had launched helicopters. Neither side fired. Neither side retreated. The closest approach—barely a few hundred metres—passed in silence, yet those twenty minutes echoed for months in diplomatic cables. Analysts later reconstructed the geometry of the near miss and concluded that a minor misjudgment of speed or wake could have brought metal against metal. What startled observers was not simply how close the two navies came to collision, but how swiftly a controlled competition had sharpened into something unpredictable. The encounter illuminated a truth that policymakers prefer not to speak aloud: the most dangerous escalations begin as grey zone manoeuvres designed to stay beneath the threshold of conflict.

The paradox emerges as soon as we consider intent. Grey zone moves are meant to be incremental—salami slices, not sword strikes. Yet incremental pressure creates more room for misunderstanding, not less. A manoeuvre crafted to signal firmness can look like provocation. A defensive repositioning can appear predatory when viewed through radar blur or poor intelligence. The chain reaction begins quietly, and by the time national leaders grasp the shift, a new dynamic has already hardened at sea, on land, or in the information space. Escalation accelerates because ambiguity is combustible.

Understanding escalation in the grey zone requires stepping beyond clichés about miscalculation. States escalate for concrete reasons: domestic audiences to satisfy, reputational stakes to protect, rivalries to manage, alliances to reassure. What distinguishes grey zone escalation is speed.

Traditional conflict unfolds across visible thresholds; grey zone competition often leaps the gaps. A fishing vessel rams a coastguard cutter; a drone flies a kilometre deeper than intended; a cyber intrusion is discovered earlier than anticipated. Each action invites a response calibrated not only to the incident but to the broader strategic game. And the risk grows. Step by step, an adversarial dance hardens into confrontation.

This chapter explores the mechanisms states use—sometimes wisely, sometimes poorly—to prevent that dance from spiralling out of control. Escalation management is often framed as the art of setting and signalling red lines. Yet history shows how fragile these lines become once adversaries test their edges. Governments attempt to communicate boundaries through diplomatic notes, military deployments, or public statements. But the grey zone thrives on ambiguity. A red line that is too narrow invites exploitation. A red line too broad becomes impossible to enforce. The reader will see how states attempt to strike this balance and why they so often fall short.

Clear signalling is only one part of the story. Crises require de-escalation tools—hotlines, confidential envoys, backchannel dialogues—that can be activated at short notice. These mechanisms sound procedural, even dull, yet their impact can be profound. Consider the little-discussed episode during the 2001 EP-3 collision crisis, when a secure line between Beijing and Washington remained open for nearly sixteen hours while negotiators parsed language that would allow both sides to claim dignity. A subtle shift in phrasing, agreed in real time, prevented the situation from hardening into a protracted diplomatic freeze. De-escalation often hinges not on grand gestures but on small concessions timed precisely.

Equally important is the calibration of responses. Excessive retaliation invites further escalation; under-response encourages repeat offences. The delicate craft lies in identifying measures that impose cost without prompting a symmetrical reprisal. Sometimes the answer lies in multi-layered strategies—technical countermeasures paired with diplomatic rebukes, economic pressures balanced with offers of dialogue. The art resembles chess not because of its cleverness but because each move alters the board for moves yet to be made. The reader will see how states weigh these calculations and why misjudging scale or timing can have cascading effects.

Preserving off-ramps is perhaps the most underappreciated element of escalation control. States require ways to retreat without humiliation, especially when domestic audiences expect resolve. Track-two diplomacy, discreet military-to-military engagement, and confidence-building measures offer quiet lanes through which adversaries can pull back from the brink. De-escalation is rarely about triumph; more often, it is about crafting a narrative that allows both sides to step away with reputations intact. In the grey zone—where official denial is often a strategic asset—these off-ramps are not signs of weakness but of design.

What binds these themes together is a motif that runs through every theatre of grey zone competition: momentum. Escalation gathers momentum not because leaders seek conflict, but because each ambiguous gesture invites interpretation, and interpretation invites reaction. Momentum is shaped by fear, by prestige, by uncertainty, by proximity, and most of all by the difficulty of pausing a dynamic once it has begun.

As the chapter unfolds, readers will encounter examples drawn from naval contests, cyber exchanges, diplomatic quarrels, and informational feints. They will see how warning signals succeed or fail; how backchannels avert crises; how disproportionate moves reverberate; how carefully preserved exits prevent collisions—literal and political. Each section deepens the sense that escalation is not an anomaly but a structural feature of grey zone rivalry.

The challenge, then, is not merely avoiding war but mastering the tempo of interaction in a strategic space designed to be deniable and ambiguous. The chapter argues that escalation control is not an act of restraint but an act of strategy—an exercise in shaping the environment so that adversaries choose stability over risk even when competition intensifies.

The real question emerges quietly: in a world of accelerating grey zone manoeuvres, can states keep pace with the momentum they themselves unleash? The pages ahead trace the contours of that question and the tools—imperfect, necessary, fragile—crafted to answer it.

Why Escalation Happens

The deck logs from the USS *Decatur*'s passage near Gaven Reef in September 2018 capture the tension without embellishment: at 08:19, the Chinese destroyer *Lanzhou* closed to within forty-five metres, crossing the American vessel's bow at a sharp angle and forcing the *Decatur* to alter course. The crews on both bridges could see one another's faces. Each ship measured the other's movement in seconds and metres. The incident ended without collision, yet the geometry of the near miss revealed something more dangerous than aggression. It revealed how two militaries, each convinced of its restraint, had drifted into a situation where a slight misjudgment of speed or helm could have triggered a crisis neither state wanted. Five words capture the mood: *They came too close again.*

Escalation often begins with that sense of proximity—physical, political, or psychological. Grey zone manoeuvres, designed to assert presence without firing a shot, bring rivals into contact more frequently and more ambiguously. A radar shadow hardens into a perceived threat. A routine patrol becomes a test of resolve. What appears measured from one command centre feels menacing from another. The standoff at Gaven Reef illuminated that gap in perception. Both navies insisted they acted professionally; both accused the other of provocation. Yet the near miss itself was the message. Grey zone competition accelerates tension because it multiplies points of contact while obscuring intentions.

The logic of miscalculation rests on visibility and interpretation. States measure risk by watching the behaviour of others: turn rate, course deviation, speed of communication, the timing of diplomatic protests. When visibility blurs, interpretation fills the gap, and interpretation is shaped by fear, pride, and expectation. The United States and China each framed the 2018 encounter as proof of the other's recklessness. Escalation took root not in the manoeuvres themselves but in the narratives built around them. This dynamic sits at the heart of grey zone strategy. Ambiguity is meant to manage risk, yet it can just as easily magnify it.

A similar pattern unfolded during the 2020 India–China confrontation in Ladakh, where patrols along the Line of Actual Control followed decades-old agreements allowing unarmed contact. The June clash in the Galwan Valley, which resulted in fatalities, exposed how quickly mutual restraint can collapse once micro-aggressions accumulate. Patrols that sought to "show presence" became competitive gestures. The visible behaviours—shouting matches, stone throwing, improvised weapons—reflected a breakdown of trust. Each side believed it responded proportionately. Each saw the other as the escalator. The implication was stark: even where treaties exist, grey zone pressure can create friction points that no legal framework can absorb.

But the reverse also holds true. The 2012 Scarborough Shoal dispute between China and the Philippines shows how escalation can stall rather than spiral, though not always to the weaker party's benefit. Manila attempted to enforce fishing regulations; Beijing responded with maritime militia and coastguard vessels; both sides engaged in tit-for-tat deployments. Yet the standoff eventually settled into a frozen imbalance rather than erupting into conflict. The limitation of the example is clear: de-escalation occurred not because tensions eased, but because China established effective control while avoiding kinetic escalation. The episode demonstrates that not all escalatory dynamics explode. Some calcify into new strategic realities. Recognising this limitation forces a harder question: is avoided conflict a success if it entrenches coercive outcomes?

States escalate because they see advantage in doing so. Escalation is not purely emotional; it is instrumental. Governments compare the political cost of appearing weak with the strategic cost of intensifying confrontation. Decision-makers measure tempo: how quickly a rival moves, how predictably it signals, how reliably it responds to pressure. If a state concludes that incremental pushback will not provoke unacceptable retaliation, it pushes further. Grey zone tactics amplify this calculation. They offer manoeuvres—coastguard shadowing, cyber probes, airspace incursions—that appear reversible, deniable, or low-cost Yet each action alters the baseline. A drone flight one kilometre deeper than last week is a signal precisely because it is small.

National pride magnifies the risks. Domestic audiences watch these encounters through media lenses sharpened by nationalism. A government that steps back without explanation risks appearing compromised. Leaders feel compelled to retaliate not only to deter rivals but to reassure voters, military institutions, and allies. That pressure narrows the room for diplomacy. The visible behaviour is often a rapid deployment, a public statement, or a demonstrative patrol. The deeper truth is a political system responding to its own internal incentives. Escalation nurtures momentum.

The motif that threads through these incidents is compression—compression of time, space, and options. Naval captains have minutes to decide whether to yield water or hold course. Cyber operators have seconds to disable a probe before it triggers unknown consequences. Diplomats have hours to craft statements that neither inflame nor appear timid. Compression forces decisions at pace. Pace multiplies error.

Two further examples highlight this compression. First, the repeated Russian intercepts of NATO aircraft over the Baltic Sea in 2014–2017, often conducted with transponders switched off. These manoeuvres heightened collision risk and fueled suspicion. NATO responded with enhanced air policing missions. Russia accused NATO of overreaction. Neither wished for escalation, yet both escalated postures. Second, the 2022 scramble of

South Korean jets in response to an unannounced Chinese and Russian joint air patrol near its air defence identification zone. Seoul assessed the patrol as a stress test; Beijing and Moscow framed it as routine. Again, misaligned interpretations generated harsher readiness levels.

A credible counter-example comes from the 1969 Sino-Soviet border crisis, which escalated sharply but ultimately avoided full-scale war due to deliberate restraint by both capitals. Yet even here, the reconciliation reveals a structural truth: restraint required senior-level intervention after frontline forces had already engaged in deadly clashes. Grey zone signalling had failed; only overt strategic recalibration prevented catastrophe. The limitation of this example underscores the central argument. De-escalation is possible, but it is rarely achieved at the level where the escalation actually begins.

Understanding why escalation happens means watching not only ships, aircraft, and patrols, but the cognitive frames that shape how states interpret them. Governments rely on imperfect intelligence, incomplete communication, and institutional biases. They assign meaning to minor shifts—a vessel's bow wave, a radar lock, a diplomatic pause. These meanings generate decisions. Decisions generate counter-decisions. And the cycle tightens.

The implication for policymakers is uncomfortable: escalation is not an anomaly but a default trajectory unless managed deliberately. Grey zone tactics promise controlled pressure, yet they create overlapping uncertainties that exceed the pace of traditional diplomacy. They accelerate tension by design, even when the designers believe they are managing it.

That leaves a pressing question, one that shadows every near miss at sea or in the air: how many more encounters can compress options before one captain, one commander, or one government miscalculates by a single degree?

Warning Signals and Red Lines

At 04:12 on 24 November 2015, a Turkish F-16 fired a missile that brought down a Russian Su-24 near the Syria–Turkey border. Ankara claimed the Russian jet had crossed into Turkish airspace for seventeen seconds despite repeated radio warnings. Moscow insisted no such warnings were received. The shootdown stunned NATO and the Kremlin alike. Within hours, Russia imposed economic measures, deployed advanced air-defence systems to Latakia, and suspended military cooperation. The boundaries each side believed it had signalled were mismatched. The outcome—two near-nuclear powers jolted into a crisis neither had anticipated—demonstrated a blunt lesson: red lines only deter when the intended audience understands them.

The near miss began long before the missile. Russian aircraft had skirted Turkish airspace multiple times during operations in northern Syria. Turkish officials protested; Russian pilots adjusted routes but not always enough to reassure Ankara. The signals were muddy. One government interpreted its statements as clear. The other viewed them as political theatre. Meanwhile, pilots measured their risk by cockpit indicators rather than diplomatic communiqués. The gap widened until a single, sharp decision closed it. *They warned too softly*, critics said afterwards. The motif of muted signals recurs throughout grey zone competition.

Governments attempt to prevent such crises through a repertoire of communication tools: formal diplomatic notes, hotline messages, public statements, military-to-military deconfliction channels, and intelligence backchannels. Each tool has a purpose. Diplomatic notes record a position. Hotlines measure immediacy. Public statements shape audience expectations. Yet none guarantees clarity. When a government issues a warning, it must show its boundary. Naming the threshold turns a private concern into a measurable line. Explaining the consequence gives the warning weight. The intended implication is that adversaries will correct course to avoid triggering retaliation.

The first example illustrates the process. In 2013, Japan publicly declared that any attempt to land on the Senkaku Islands would prompt a "firm and immediate" response. Tokyo's statement named a specific behaviour—unlawful landing—signalling a clear tripwire. The United States reinforced the message by affirming that the islands fell under Article 5 of the US–Japan Security Treaty. The effect was stabilising: while Chinese coastguard vessels continued to enter contiguous waters, they avoided landings. The visibility of the red line constrained opportunistic provocations. It also allowed both parties to measure the other's behaviour with relative precision.

A contrasting case comes from the South China Sea. In July 2019, Chinese survey ships entered waters near Vanguard Bank, an area within Vietnam's claimed Exclusive Economic Zone. Hanoi protested but avoided specifying which activities would trigger retaliation. Beijing tested the gap by rotating additional vessels into the area. Vietnam responded with diplomatic démarches and increased patrol patterns, but without naming a consequence. The red line remained inferred rather than declared. The limitation of this approach became evident: ambiguous boundaries permit incremental challenges. Yet Hanoi avoided escalation, arguing that explicit red lines could invite confrontation. The reconciliation of this counter-example is instructive. Ambiguity can delay conflict in the short term, but it also creates space for sustained pressure.

Ambiguous red lines invite testing because adversaries measure ambiguity through behaviour. They compare statements against actions. If a state warns but fails to act, the warning loses validity. If a state responds with disproportionate force, the warning becomes destabilising. The precision of the signal matters as much as the resolve behind it. Red lines need not be public, but they must be consistent. Quiet communications—whether passed through ambassadors, military attachés, or intelligence intermediaries—can define boundaries more credibly than televised podium declarations.

The second example highlights this dynamic. During the 1962 Cuban Missile Crisis, the United States established a naval quarantine rather than a full blockade. President Kennedy's team chose the term deliberately to avoid the legal implications of war. The White House communicated its red line clearly: Soviet ships carrying offensive missiles would not be permitted to reach Cuba. Behind the scenes, Attorney General Robert Kennedy met Soviet Ambassador Anatoly Dobrynin to outline a confidential trade-off. The clarity of both public and private signals created a structure for de-escalation. Soviet vessels slowed. Diplomatic channels activated. A crisis that could have spiralled stabilised.

Grey zone challenges complicate these practices. States commit acts that sit below traditional thresholds—cyber intrusions, paramilitary deployments, economic coercion, information manipulation. Each action probes boundaries that have never been codified. Governments struggle to articulate red lines in domains they cannot fully see or measure. A hacked ministry may discover the intrusion weeks later. A maritime militia vessel without identification may cross into contested waters without triggering automatic protocols. The opacity of grey zone actions blurs the visibility upon which warnings depend.

A credible limitation emerges here. Over-clarification can reduce strategic flexibility. If a state defines every boundary, it risks binding its own hands or granting rivals a roadmap for circumventing pressure. Clear red lines need to be selective. They should protect vital interests, not every marginal concern. The reconciliation lies in calibration: governments must distinguish between core thresholds and peripheral irritants. The former require crisp signalling; the latter may benefit from ambiguity.

States often assume that warnings travel linearly from speaker to recipient. In practice, they filter through domestic politics, media framing, bureaucratic interpretation, and alliance expectations. A government may intend a signal for one audience; another audience may misread it. The visible behaviour—jet scrambles, naval deployments, public condemnations—becomes the true signal regardless of stated intent. Allies compare commitments and measure hesitation. Rivals watch for deviation from precedent. Markets react to the perceived likelihood of escalation. The communication environment expands far beyond the negotiating table.

The motif of muted signals reappears when examining opportunistic provocations. Ambiguous red lines invite actors to test whether the boundary is soft, real, or simply rhetorical. After Western states warned Russia against interference in the 2016 US election, Moscow adjusted tactics without reducing activity. It shifted towards "cleaner" proxies, blended social media operations with domestic extremist narratives, and exploited regulatory seams. The ambiguity of the red line—interference defined how, by what metric, and with what consequence?—created space for innovation. The warning lacked operational specificity. Clarity could have limited manoeuvre.

Yet signals alone do not prevent escalation. They must align with capability and credibility. If a government asserts a boundary it cannot enforce, the red line becomes an invitation to challenge. This occurred when the United States drew a public red line regarding chemical weapon use in Syria in 2012, only to refrain from military action after the Ghouta attack in August 2013. Although the US subsequently supported a chemical disarmament agreement brokered by Russia, the initial failure to act altered global perceptions of American signalling. States measured that gap. The implication was global: credibility is cumulative, and red lines echo across regions.

Clearer diplomatic signals offer partial solutions. They make boundaries legible. They reduce the temptation for adversaries to exploit vagueness. Structured communication—such as codified incident-at-sea agreements, joint crisis hotlines, and pre-negotiated escalation protocols—can transform warnings into shared expectations. States can explain not only what they consider unacceptable, but why. They can define metrics: distance thresholds, time windows, cyber intrusion categories, airspace violations. These specifics help commanders interpret behaviour consistently.

But the effectiveness of such measures depends on more than design. It depends on willingness. If a government fears that clarity will constrain future actions or expose internal divisions, it may opt for rhetorical fog. That fog is familiar in the grey zone. It gives manoeuvre. It also gives danger.

The most difficult question concerns audience. To whom are red lines addressed? Rival governments? Domestic publics? Allies? Markets? Militaries? Each responds differently. A signal that deters a rival may alarm an ally. A warning meant to reassure a domestic audience may confuse a foreign one. Communicating boundaries becomes a multi-layered exercise in perception management.

This layered complexity leaves policymakers with an unresolved tension: how to signal boundaries precisely enough to prevent opportunistic challenges, yet flexibly enough to preserve strategic ambiguity where advantageous. The tension cannot be eliminated. It can only be managed.

The critical test, then, is forward-looking. What would it take to ensure that the next warning is heard not as theatre, not as bluster, but as a calibrated, credible marker of consequence?

De-Escalation Tactics

At 21:47 on 26 February 2019, an Indian Air Force MiG-21 was shot down during a brief clash with the Pakistan Air Force over Kashmir. Both governments braced for further strikes. Artillery units moved. Air defence systems activated. Local commanders awaited orders that could have tipped two nuclear-armed states into a devastating exchange. The crisis halted not through superiority of force, but through a channel of communication that allowed both sides to speak before they acted. New Delhi and Islamabad used their confidential military hotline—established decades earlier but rarely trusted—to share preliminary assessments. One pilot captured. No additional losses. No further aircraft committed. The next morning, the rhetoric cooled by a few degrees. The motif of *a voice cutting through static* frames the quiet power of de-escalation tools.

The hotline did not resolve the crisis, but it bought time. That time created political space for Pakistan's decision on 1 March 2019 to return Wing Commander Abhinandan Varthaman. The gesture reduced tension enough for India to pause retaliation. Leaders could reconsider costs. Without the channel—imperfect, limited, but available—the crisis might have rolled forward through reflex rather than choice. De-escalation often begins with recognising that silence, in these moments, is an accelerant. Dialogue is a brake.

States design de-escalation mechanisms to avoid precisely this dynamic: a rapid slide from limited confrontation to uncontrolled escalation. The first task is to *show* a pathway through which opposing forces can exchange information before events cascade. Naming these pathways formalises expectations. Hotlines, deconfliction protocols, and pre-agreed incident management procedures create habits of communication. They explain how to interpret sudden military movements, radar anomalies, or inadvertent territorial crossings. The implication is simple: misunderstandings shrink when leaders measure intent directly rather than infer it from incomplete signals.

The Cold War produced some of the earliest frameworks. The Washington–Moscow Hotline, installed in 1963 after the Cuban Missile Crisis, allowed superpowers to exchange messages rapidly during acute tension. Its most consequential test came in October 1973, when the United States and the Soviet Union used it during the Yom Kippur War. Signal delays or ambiguous phrasing could have been catastrophic; the direct link reduced risk by clarifying each step. The example remains a benchmark in how structured communication prevents escalation even amid competing narratives.

A second, more contemporary case emerged in September 2015, when Russia began its intervention in Syria. The United States and Russia, operating in the same airspace with different objectives, established an air deconfliction channel linking their militaries. Daily contacts clarified flight paths and emergency procedures. The channel did not eliminate incidents, and it certainly did not resolve geopolitical tensions, but it prevented the worst form of accident: two jets colliding through misinterpretation. This limitation is instructive. De-escalation tools cannot remove rivalry, but they can contain its immediate risks. Reconciling ambition with restraint is part of their function.

Yet these mechanisms face counter-examples. In April 2001, when a US Navy EP-3E collided with a Chinese J-8 interceptor near Hainan Island, no trusted hotline system existed between Beijing and Washington. Diplomatic contact lagged behind unfolding events. The United States measured risk by monitoring aircraft movements; China measured political space through domestic perceptions. Tension rose sharply until a carefully worded US statement facilitated the release of the crew. The limitation shows the cost of absent communication infrastructure. But it also underscores a reconciliation: creating channels is only half the task. States must practise using them under pressure.

De-escalation requires behaviours that make reassurance visible. A state may reduce the tempo of patrols, adjust radar postures, or signal restraint by withdrawing specific assets. These decisions allow the rival to measure intent through concrete metrics—sorties flown, vessels deployed, alerts downgraded. Clarity grows from action rather than assertion. When states pair dialogue with observable moderation, the risk of miscalculation drops. Without these signals, even sincere diplomatic messages can appear hollow.

Third-party mediation forms another pillar of de-escalation. Mediators act as interpreters of intent and custodians of face-saving. Norway's role in facilitating Israeli–Palestinian dialogue during the Oslo process in 1993, or Switzerland's repeated custodial services between states lacking direct contact, demonstrates how intermediaries de-escalate by offering controlled communication environments. They *explain* rival positions without adding inflammatory rhetoric. The implication is structural: mediators create psychological distance between public postures and private negotiation, allowing leaders to recalibrate without domestic backlash.

Regional organisations also mediate. The Association of Southeast Asian Nations (ASEAN), though limited by its norms, has on several occasions served as a convener when maritime disputes risked hardening. Its 2016 emergency consultations following confrontations around the South China Sea did not resolve underlying claims, but they prevented member states from sliding into kinetic escalation. The limitation is that consensus-driven bodies often move slowly. Reconciling this slowness requires complementary bilateral channels that act faster than multilateral diplomacy.

One of the most potent de-escalation tools is real-time dialogue between commanders facing each other on the ground—or at sea. A scenario illustrates this. In 2020, along the Line of Actual Control between India and China, patrols clashed in the high Himalayas. After a deadly incident in June, both sides massed troops. Then, in late August, Indian forces moved to strategic ridges near Pangong Tso. Chinese units manoeuvred in response. Temperatures dropped. Weapons were in reach. At midnight, senior officers initiated an emergency call. They verified positions, acknowledged fears of encirclement, and agreed to pause movements until dawn. Neither side liked the compromise, but both accepted the logic: unverified assumptions had become dangerous. The crisis did not end that night, but a more serious escalation was averted. A voice broke through the static.

Such mechanisms must contend with a core limitation: dialogue may signal weakness. Rival states sometimes interpret conciliatory communication as evidence of hesitation. This risk cannot be removed entirely. But states can reconcile it by pairing diplomacy with proportionate deterrent measures. If communication is matched by steady posture, dialogue appears as confident maturity, not fear. The balance matters: too much rhetorical restraint invites probing; too much militancy closes diplomatic pathways.

Speed remains a central theme. Modern crises unfold faster than the bureaucratic systems designed to manage them. Cyber incursions occur in minutes. Misinterpreted satellite imagery spreads within hours. Social media amplifies rumours before officials can verify facts. These factors demand more agile de-escalation structures: round-the-clock crisis cells, multilingual liaison officers stationed abroad, encrypted channels that bypass diplomatic bottlenecks. The motif returns—*a voice cutting through static*—because clarity must outrun confusion.

Transparency offers another dimension. When states release verifiable data—flight logs, radar tracks, images—early in a crisis, distrust decreases. During the 2014 downing of Malaysia Airlines Flight MH17, delays and contradictory messages fuelled suspicion. By contrast, when Singapore's Ministry of Defence quickly published radar timelines after airspace violations in 2018, the disclosure reduced speculation and limited escalation. Tangible evidence disciplines the narrative environment.

De-escalation also depends on emotional restraint. Leaders facing military pressure often feel compelled to respond immediately. Yet historical analysis shows that many crises stabilised because key decision-makers paused. In 1995, after receiving an alert that a Norwegian scientific rocket resembled a ballistic missile, Russian President Boris Yeltsin waited for additional confirmation before authorising any action. Dialogue within the Russian command structure prevented catastrophe. The visible behaviour here is delay—a deliberate slowing of the decision cycle. This decision itself is a tactic.

Hotlines, mediators, confidence-building measures, and posture adjustments share a common purpose: they reduce the space for misinterpretation. They give rivals a method to check assumptions before acting. They buy political time. They create opportunities for de-escalation even when neither side wants to concede. They transform crises from events that happen *to* states into events states can manage.

Yet the unresolved tension persists. Can states rely on these tools when domestic politics reward confrontation, when bureaucracies resist flexibility, or when rivals exploit every gesture of conciliation? The forward test remains stark: in the next crisis, who will speak first—and will the other side hear the signal before the static overwhelms it?

Calibrating Responses

At dawn on 23 November 2013, China announced the creation of a new Air Defence Identification Zone (ADIZ) over the East China Sea. The declaration, issued in Beijing but immediately felt in Tokyo and Seoul, triggered a sharp dilemma. Within hours, Japan's Self-Defence Forces detected Chinese aircraft moving through the zone. The United States responded by flying two unarmed B-52s from Andersen Air Force Base in Guam straight through the newly claimed airspace, a deliberate signal that Washington did not recognise Beijing's declaration. The flight was measured—no fighter escort, no altered radar posture, no accompanying threat. It *challenged* without escalating. The motif of *precision over impulse* runs through this episode: a response crafted to oppose a provocation without widening conflict.

Had Washington opted for a more forceful reaction—fighters flanking the bombers, or a publicised naval manoeuvre—Beijing might have felt compelled to demonstrate resolve. Instead, the B-52s communicated firmness at minimal risk. Tokyo, faced with its own choices, also calibrated carefully. Japan instructed its civil airlines not to submit flight plans to the new ADIZ, but avoided parallel military theatrics. Restraint, measured in posture and tone, prevented a contest of symbolic dominance from turning into a contest of force.

Calibrated responses matter because disproportionate retaliation transforms a limited incident into a strategic confrontation. States *show* this dynamic each time a local dispute gains momentum not through intent but through spirals of reaction. Naming the pattern clarifies its logic: when one side's response exceeds the scale of the original provocation, the rival interprets it as preparation for a broader campaign. The implication is immediate. Escalation accelerates not because actors seek war, but because they misread the other's threshold for risk.

A first example comes from the Gulf of Oman in June 2019, when two tankers—the *Kokuka Courageous* and the *Front Altair*—were damaged by suspected limpet mines. The United States accused Iran within hours, while Iran denied involvement. Washington weighed military options. Instead of striking Iranian facilities, which risked regional conflagration, the US deployed additional surveillance assets and strengthened maritime escort operations. These choices allowed Washington to measure Iranian behaviour without committing to irreversible steps. The calibrated scale of the response prevented tit-for-tat escalation, even though political rhetoric remained heated.

A second example illustrates the opposite trajectory. In 2008, Georgia's operation in South Ossetia, followed by Russia's overwhelming counterstrike, demonstrated how disproportionate retaliation can reshape an entire regional security order in days. Moscow's decision to advance deep beyond the conflict zone, occupying Gori and threatening Tbilisi, signalled a strategic rather than tactical intention. The move produced long-lasting geopolitical consequences that continue to define European debates. The limitation is evident: one actor's calibration may be irrelevant if the rival pursues a maximalist agenda. Reconciling this requires recognising that calibrated responses are most effective when both sides still seek to avoid major conflict.

Calibration is not passive. It is active selection—choosing actions that communicate resolve without closing escape routes. Visible behaviours reveal calibration: adjusting naval patrol distances; limiting cyber operations to defensive containment; issuing political statements that condemn actions but avoid personal vilification of rival leaders; deploying assets on alert without crossing borders. Each behaviour gives the rival measurable indicators of intent. Excessive mobilisation, by contrast, masks intent. It forces a rival to assume the worst.

States employ multi-layered responses because single-action strategies rarely match the complexity of grey zone provocations. A state facing a cyber intrusion might combine diplomatic protest with targeted sanctions while simultaneously opening a technical dialogue to clarify attribution. This layering explains a critical point: responses become more effective when they operate across several domains at once. The implication is structural. Multi-layered responses reduce incentives for adversaries to escalate, because no single move appears as a decisive provocation.

Choosing precise countermeasures lies at the heart of calibration. When Australia called for an investigation into the origins of COVID-19 in April 2020, China responded with tariffs on Australian barley and restrictions on beef imports. Canberra faced a choice: retaliate or demonstrate strategic patience. It opted for targeted diversification of export markets and increased diplomatic engagement with partners such as Japan and India. These behaviours show how precision allows a state to absorb shocks without magnifying them. Australia avoided broad sanctions of its own, a step that could have entrenched hostility. The limitation is clear: precision cannot eliminate economic pain, but it can prevent the dispute from spilling into military or political arenas.

Historical precedents illuminate the technique. During the Cuban Missile Crisis in October 1962, President John F. Kennedy rejected immediate airstrikes. Instead, he imposed a naval "quarantine"—a response deliberately framed as less escalatory than a blockade. The choice allowed the United States to measure Soviet reactions incrementally. It also preserved diplomatic pathways that later enabled withdrawal negotiations. The motif returns: *precision over impulse.* Calibration creates time, and time creates options.

In grey zone conflict, an additional challenge emerges: provocations often blur responsibility. When sabotage, cyber operations, or maritime harassment come from unattributed actors, states struggle to determine the appropriate level of response. Overreaction risks legitimising unsupported claims of aggression; underreaction risks normalising hostile behaviour. Here calibration requires both evidence and strategic creativity. States might publish intelligence assessments, increase patrol densities, or impose narrowly tailored economic restrictions on specific entities rather than entire sectors. Each step offers clarity about what behaviour is being addressed and what escalation thresholds remain uncrossed.

A credible counter-example shows the edge of the concept. In January 2010, when Google disclosed intrusions attributed to actors in China, the United States debated stronger reprisals. Yet Washington's response remained muted. Critics argued that this restraint signalled vulnerability. Supporters argued the exact opposite: disproportionate retaliation based on incomplete attribution could have fractured diplomatic efforts on nuclear negotiations with Iran or damaged cybersecurity cooperation with allies. The reconciliation is that calibration sometimes appears unsatisfying because it privileges long-term strategic coherence over immediate catharsis.

Calibrating responses also requires domestic discipline. Leaders must measure public sentiment without being captured by it. A population shocked by an attack may demand decisive retaliation. If governments respond impulsively, they risk locking themselves into commitments that exceed strategic necessity. The visible behaviour of calibrated leadership is deliberate pacing: consultations with allies, controlled public messaging, and incremental adjustments to security posture. Each step signals that the state seeks resolution, not escalation.

Military establishments often push for strong responses to signal deterrence. Diplomatic establishments emphasise caution. Calibration unites these instincts by aligning force and diplomacy. A state might deploy additional naval vessels while simultaneously proposing technical talks on incident prevention. It might condemn hostile cyber activity while offering to share forensic methods with partners. It might reinforce airspace patrols but communicate quietly that it will not retaliate beyond a specific threshold unless certain actions recur. The measures combine firmness with flexibility.

Technology complicates calibration. Rapid attribution tools, automated threat detection, and real-time intelligence feeds compress decision-making. Speed cuts both ways. It can prevent escalation by clarifying events quickly, or it can accelerate escalation by pushing leaders toward instant reactions. Calibrated responses demand that states slow their internal tempo even as external signals speed up. The motif sharpens: *precision requires pause.*

Ultimately, calibrated responses preserve strategic control. They prevent adversaries from dictating pace or scale. They maintain space for negotiation. They reduce opportunities for miscalculation. Yet the question lingers: in the next grey zone confrontation, will leaders commit to measured retaliation even when domestic pressure demands spectacle? Or will impulse outrun precision, pulling rivals into a contest neither intended to fight?

Preserving Off-Ramps

In June 1999, as NATO and Serbian forces edged towards a catastrophic clash over Kosovo's fate, a quiet intervention in Helsinki altered the course of events. Finnish President Martti Ahtisaari and Russian envoy Viktor Chernomyrdin met with Yugoslav President Slobodan Milošević in Belgrade, offering a negotiated withdrawal plan that demanded compliance yet spared the Serbian leadership the spectacle of unconditional surrender. The deal, agreed on 3 June, enabled Belgrade to claim it had secured protections for ethnic Serbs even as it accepted NATO's core terms. The war ended days later. The moment shows a truth at the heart of crisis management: peace often requires giving an adversary a door through which they can step without shame. Without such a door, leaders fight on—not because they can win, but because they cannot afford to lose publicly. Off-ramps matter. They save lives by saving face.

Ahtisaari's approach captured a motif that threads through all grey zone strategy: *a path out must be visible before a path in becomes dangerous*. States that deny this reality risk prolonging conflicts simply to preserve political pride. The Helsinki channel worked because it circumvented public performance. Track-two diplomacy—conversations led by intermediaries with access but without formal authority—created room for compromise that high-level posturing had suffocated. Milošević could agree behind closed doors to terms he would have rejected at a podium. The lesson endures. Escalation slows when leaders know retreat is survivable.

Grey zone competition, with its blend of deniable actions and public ambiguity, complicates this dynamic. States may engage in harassment, sanctions, cyber intrusions, or maritime brinkmanship while insisting that no conflict exists. When they are challenged, they retreat only if retreat can be reinterpreted as prudence rather than humiliation. This is why off-ramps must be engineered early. Consider the 2016 South China Sea arbitration ruling in The Hague. After the Philippines won its case, Beijing rejected the verdict but de-escalated maritime activity near Scarborough Shoal by quietly relaxing its coastguard presence. Manila, for its part, refrained from triumphalist rhetoric. Both sides behaved with calibrated restraint. The visible behaviour—less patrolling, more quiet diplomacy—allowed each to maintain dignity while reducing friction. The implication is clear: narrative space shapes strategic space.

For off-ramps to function, governments must show—before crises ignite—that communication channels exist beyond formal statements. Japan and China demonstrated this when they operationalised a maritime and aerial communication mechanism in June 2018. The mechanism's direct line enabled officers to clarify incidents near the Senkaku/Diaoyu Islands without forcing political leaders into confrontation. By naming the mechanism publicly yet using it discreetly, Tokyo and Beijing created a safety valve that lowered risk without diluting their territorial claims. The visible decision—installing radio equipment linking defence authorities directly—illustrated how architecture can restrain emotion. Its implication stretches further. If states embed such tools before crises erupt, they reduce the temptation to act rashly when incidents occur.

Track-two diplomacy complements these mechanisms by providing additional layers of dialogue. During the fraught nuclear negotiations with Iran in 2013, informal meetings between former officials and subject-matter experts shaped expectations and bridged conceptual gaps long before the formal Joint Plan of Action took shape in Geneva. These conversations played no decisive role in the final agreement, but their contribution was behavioural. They prepared each side to consider concessions without viewing them as defeats. A credible critique is that such channels sometimes empower unelected voices with unclear accountability. Yet when reconciled with formal diplomacy, they expand the palette of possible solutions. They create spaces where rivals can explore compromise without triggering nationalist backlash.

Confidence-building measures—military notifications, observer exchanges, shared monitoring data—constitute another essential pillar. During the Cold War, the United States and the Soviet Union introduced the 1971 Agreement on Measures to Reduce the Risk of Outbreak of Nuclear War. It required advance notice of missile tests and prohibited interference with each other's command-and-control systems. These behaviours built predictability. They signalled that rivalry did not require recklessness. The implication resonates strongly today. In grey zone confrontation, where attribution is contested and escalation ladders are shorter, predictability itself becomes a strategic asset.

Yet confidence-building measures do not always succeed. The 2012 crisis between Sudan and South Sudan, despite the presence of UN peace monitors and border demarcation talks, escalated when clashes around Heglig triggered retaliatory airstrikes. Diplomatic frameworks existed, but political incentives outweighed structural constraints. This counter-example exposes a limitation: off-ramps cannot override leadership choices rooted in domestic imperatives. But they can reduce the cost of moderation. They can make de-escalation the politically safer path when tempers cool. Reconciliation of this limitation requires humility. Tools cannot guarantee peace; they can only lower barriers to it.

The motif returns: *a path out must be visible.* Without it, adversaries double down. During the India–China border standoff in Ladakh in 2020, both sides mobilised thousands of troops while conducting discreet diplomatic talks in parallel. The talks produced phased disengagement agreements around Pangong Tso and the Gogra–Hot Springs area. Public narratives emphasised strength, but the private behaviours—joint verification patrols, choreographed withdrawal sequences, and the re-establishment of military hotlines—revealed a mutual desire to stop the crisis sliding further uphill. Each step provided an exit that did not broadcast capitulation. This distinction—between backing down and backing away—is critical.

Off-ramps also require narrative discipline. When leaders humiliate adversaries publicly, they deprive them of political space to de-escalate. When leaders frame concessions as prudent management or strategic patience, they widen the exit corridor. The United States and Vietnam learned this after decades of hostility. By the time diplomatic normalisation occurred in 1995, Washington and Hanoi had invested years in careful language—highlighting cooperation on POW/MIA recovery, emphasising mutual benefit, avoiding accusatory grandstanding. The visible behaviour was modest, incremental engagement. The implication was profound: reconciliation became possible not because grievances vanished, but because each side could claim dignity.

In grey zone settings—cyber intrusions, maritime manoeuvres, covert economic pressure—the greatest risk emerges when rivals believe that stepping back will be interpreted as weakness. Off-ramps invert that logic. They allow retreat to be interpreted as statesmanship. Yet designing them requires strategic empathy. Decision-makers must see crises from the adversary's perspective, mapping what outcomes they can survive politically. Without such empathy, proposed off-ramps appear as traps, not exits.

The challenge for contemporary policymakers is that digital media accelerates humiliation. Leaders fear that any concession will be clipped, shared, memed, and reframed as surrender. Here track-two channels become even more important. They shield exploratory dialogue from the glare of instantaneous commentary. Confidence-building measures become anchors of sanity in a sea of noise.

But a closing question persists: when the next grey zone confrontation erupts, will governments invest early in constructing exits their rivals can use? Or will leaders, boxed in by public bravado, find themselves walking corridors that narrow with every hour—and discover too late that no door remains open at all?

Chapter 9

Private Actors and PMCs

The convoy travelled at dusk, its white pickups drifting through the scrubland outside Bangui in early 2021. Their markings were vague, their uniforms mismatched, their weapons immaculate. Local residents whispered that they were Russian; officials insisted they were simply "contractors"; diplomats used a different phrase entirely: *deniable muscle*. Whatever the truth, their arrival altered the balance of the Central African Republic's conflict almost overnight. Rebel groups shifted routes. Mining concessions changed hands. Government ministers recalibrated loyalties. The state had acquired new strength, yet none of it appeared in its formal order of battle. Power had been outsourced, and with it the clarity that once defined war and peace.

This, increasingly, is the shape of modern conflict. Where states once dispatched uniformed battalions, they now hire firms with polished websites, offshore headquarters, and flexible ethics. Private Military Companies—PMCs in the careful language of policy papers—no longer resemble the ragtag mercenaries of earlier centuries. They present themselves as security providers, logistics partners, crisis-response specialists. Yet their work tilts the geopolitical stage. They fight, escort, intimidate, extract, and negotiate. They blur the distinction between state authority and commercial ambition, between national interest and private gain. In their ambiguity lies both their value and their danger.

That ambiguity is the quiet motif of this chapter: the *shadow line*—the shifting boundary between public and private force. The line moves constantly. Sometimes governments shift it deliberately, using PMCs to achieve objectives they prefer not to own. Sometimes corporations push it outward as they hire armed teams to protect pipelines, mines, and shipping lanes in regions where the state is present only in theory. And sometimes PMCs move the line themselves, exploiting legal gaps to pursue profit in zones where accountability is weakest.

The rise of these companies is not accidental. Outsourcing security has become politically convenient. Casualties buried under corporate logos provoke fewer parliamentary debates. Contracts signed with firms headquartered thousands of miles away camouflage responsibility for operations that might scandalise voters or violate treaties. PMCs offer agility where bureaucracies creak. They deploy faster than official militaries, accept risk more cheaply, and withdraw without the diplomatic theatre of troop rotations. It is hardly surprising that states tempted by grey zone strategies—actions just below the threshold of war—find PMCs so useful.

But the shadow line brings problems with it. Chief among them is accountability. A contractor who fires the first shot in a disputed region may trigger a diplomatic crisis, yet prosecuting him becomes a labyrinth. Whose law applies—the home state, the host state, or the corporate headquarters parked in a tax haven? Which court has jurisdiction? Which government feels compelled to act? The legal vacuum is not theoretical; it is lived reality for communities caught between warlords and well-armed "consultants." Even when scandals erupt, inquiries stall in the fog that PMCs cultivate. Reform proposals circulate: stricter licensing, mandatory reporting, international registries. Some states resist, arguing that flexibility is essential. Others push for regulation precisely because flexibility has become dangerous.

Ethical and operational dilemmas follow close behind. A soldier sworn to defend the nation binds his loyalty to a flag; a contractor binds his loyalty to a contract. When contracts are short, priorities skew. Missions become transactional, not strategic. The temptation to cut corners grows. There are documented cases—carefully euphemised in diplomatic cables—where a PMC's aggressive patrol exacerbated a tense standoff, prompting local forces to respond with force and the host government to accuse a foreign power of interference. Escalation by proxy is still escalation. Profit-driven actors can sharpen, rather than soften, the edges of conflict.

Yet PMCs are not confined to battlefields. Their client list now includes multinational energy firms, tech conglomerates, and shipping giants. As global supply chains depend on fragile infrastructure—from offshore platforms to data centres—companies turn to PMCs to guard what governments cannot or will not. This corporate securitisation introduces a different form of risk: the collision between private guards and local militias or security forces. When a corporate team detains a suspect or repels a raid, the incident can trigger political backlash. The state may resent the intrusion. Local factions may escalate. Without rigorous due diligence—vetting contracts, mapping local politics, understanding the social terrain—corporations can stumble into diplomatic storms.

The shadow line extends further still: into international oversight. Can any global mechanism regulate PMCs? Attempts exist. The Montreux Document of 2008 clarified states' responsibilities, but it lacked enforcement teeth. The International Code of Conduct for Private Security Providers sought industry self-regulation, but participation remains voluntary. UN observer missions have reported PMC misconduct but lack the mandate to intervene. Some propose a global licensing body; others warn such a body would be captured by powerful states. The moment demands realism: oversight may improve, but it will never be absolute. Flexibility is the PMC's lifeblood and its threat.

Still, the issue cannot be ignored. PMCs sit at the intersection of sovereignty, commerce, and war. Their growth speaks to deep transformations in how states wield force and how businesses navigate unstable environments. They offer capability without visibility. They grant governments options without signatures. They create opportunities for stability and for exploitation, often at the same time.

This chapter lies at that intersection. It traces the rise of PMCs from convenience to centrality. It examines the regulatory voids that allow them to operate in shadows. It dissects their ethical tensions, their operational temptations, and their entanglements with corporate power. It considers whether the international system, already strained, can stretch enough to encompass this new form of force. And it asks a question that resonates beyond private armies: what becomes of accountability when violence becomes a service?

The shadow line is not going away. Indeed, it may thicken as states search for deniable tools to shape conflicts without triggering war. Understanding PMCs—how they work, why they thrive, and where they threaten stability—has become essential to understanding modern power itself. And as the next pages make clear, the struggle to control this outsourced force is not merely a legal battle or a moral debate. It is a contest over who holds authority in the grey zones of the twenty-first century—and who stands ready to cross the line first.

Rise of Private Military Companies

The helicopters landed outside Bentiu, South Sudan, in July 2014, raising dust over a camp that had shifted hands too often to count. UN officials described the region as volatile; aid workers, as perilous; oil executives, as *uninsurable*. Yet a group of foreign contractors—registered in Cyprus, trained in Eastern Europe, hired by a multinational energy firm—walked through the dust with steady composure. Their task was not to take territory or enforce a peace agreement. It was to protect a corridor linking the oilfields to an airstrip. Within weeks, the corridor reopened. Tankers moved again. A corporate balance sheet steadied because men with no national uniform secured a space a sovereign army could not.

This scene is no anomaly. It marks a wider trend: states and corporations shifting essential security functions to firms that promise speed, discretion, and plausible deniability. The market for such services has swollen since the early 2000s, powered by decades of expeditionary conflicts and austerity-driven defence reforms. Private Military Companies—PMCs—now operate in theatres as varied as the Gulf of Guinea, eastern Ukraine, northern Mozambique, and the Sahel. Their rise signals a profound evolution in the conduct of statecraft. They sit halfway between public authority and private ambition, occupying what this chapter calls the *shadow margin*: the contested space where power is exercised but rarely declared.

The shadow margin is not an accident of modern conflict; it is a design feature. When governments outsource logistics, site protection, convoy escort, or tactical intelligence, they often do so to avoid the political repercussions of deploying additional troops. The contractor model offers them a route to project influence with lower domestic scrutiny. A mission framed as corporate support draws fewer parliamentary questions than a battalion rotation. A discreet contract displaces responsibility. A state gains capacity but sheds visibility. This asymmetry is the central appeal of PMCs—and the source of many of the tensions that follow.

The most visible sign of this blurring came during the U.S. occupation of Iraq, where firms such as Blackwater, later rebranded as Academi, undertook armed protection tasks once reserved for military police or infantry units. The Nisour Square shooting in September 2007, which left 14 Iraqi civilians dead, demonstrated brutally how outsourced force can entangle corporate actors with state liabilities. A private company became the focal point of diplomatic outrage, legislative scrutiny, and public anger. Responsibility was contested: the contractors reported to a client, operated under a patchwork of regulations, and worked within a conflict governed by international law. The incident pulled the shadow margin into the open, revealing the risks that accumulate when the sword arm of the state extends through a corporate glove.

Yet the appeal remained. PMCs offered speed and flexibility. They adapted to commercial contracts, political timelines, and shifting missions faster than traditional militaries. In Libya after 2011, several firms provided protection for energy infrastructure, enabling extraction in zones contested by militias and provisional authorities. Their presence reassured investors and insurers, even when it unsettled diplomats. Here, the line between defence and business narrowed to a sliver. A company's desire to safeguard assets aligned with a foreign government's desire to stabilise a region—yet neither wished to commit conventional troops. PMCs filled the vacuum.

The example of the Wagner Group in eastern Ukraine and later in Syria and Africa offers a sharper illustration of the shadow margin in motion. First identified publicly in 2014 by Ukrainian and Russian media, Wagner operated with a blend of commercial motives and geopolitical objectives. In Donbas, it reinforced separatist forces while allowing the Russian state to deny direct military engagement. In Syria, Wagner units supported regime offensives while securing access to energy sites under contracts linked to Russian businesses. In the Central African Republic, its presence coincided with concessions in mining sectors. These were not traditional battlefield deployments. They were hybrid operations in which corporate interest and foreign policy intertwined. Whatever label analysts attach to Wagner—mercenary outfit, state proxy, or private army—the effect was unmistakable: PMCs could alter balances of power in disputed regions without triggering the treaty obligations or diplomatic escalations associated with regular troops.

The rise of PMCs has also been driven by structural pressures on national forces. Many militaries face recruitment shortfalls, shrinking budgets, and increasing operational demands. Outsourcing non-combat tasks—logistics, maintenance, site security—frees troops for missions that require sovereign authority. Contractors maintain vehicles in Kuwait, guard embassies in fragile capitals, and escort humanitarian convoys in regions where national militaries maintain only a token presence. Each contract adjusts the boundary between public and private force, shifting capabilities outward and responsibilities inward. The shadow margin expands only slightly at a time, yet cumulatively it reshapes the architecture of security.

Critics warn that this shift brings persistent risks. Blurred lines complicate accountability, especially when PMCs operate across jurisdictions. When an incident occurs in a disputed region—whether an alleged human rights violation, an unauthorised engagement, or a defensive action gone awry—the question of legal authority becomes opaque. Which court acts?

Which state prosecutes? Which set of rules applies: the contracting state's domestic law, international humanitarian law, or the commercial contract? Ambiguity protects actors who deserve scrutiny and shields those who exploit legal gaps for commercial gain. The opacity is not always intentional, but its consequences are predictable.

A counter-argument emerges from states that rely on PMCs for stabilisation missions: that these firms often perform essential tasks that militaries cannot sustain indefinitely. In South Sudan, Afghanistan, and Somalia, PMCs guarded infrastructure that organisations such as the UN or African Union were unable or unwilling to secure with uniformed personnel. In certain cases, contractors did maintain corridors that enabled humanitarian operations to continue. The limitation lies not in their capability but in the fragility of the mandate that surrounds them. A contractor can open a path; it cannot guarantee the political legitimacy of doing so. Nor can it anchor long-term governance. Reconciling this counter-example with broader concerns requires acknowledging that PMCs can stabilise in the short term while destabilising in the long term if oversight remains weak.

Emotional distance is another feature of PMC operations. Contractors rarely share the national narratives that guide soldiers. Their motivations are varied—economic, professional, adventurous. This distance can produce disciplined efficiency, yet it can also lead to misjudgements when interacting with local communities whose grievances and perceptions determine whether a conflict cools or intensifies. A guard who misreads a checkpoint confrontation may trigger backlash. A patrol that detains the wrong individual may ignite a spiral of reprisals. In grey zone theatres—where tension accumulates slowly and releases suddenly—such miscalculations accelerate escalation in ways governments neither anticipate nor control.

The economic structure of PMCs further blurs intentions. A military unit acts within a chain of command that weighs risk, strategy, and diplomacy. A PMC acts within a contract. When a corporate client requests protection for a mine, the contractor commits to the task, even if it aggravates local factional dynamics. When a government requests intelligence support, the contractor delivers, even if doing so inflames a proxy conflict. These firms are instruments, not strategists; yet their actions shape the trajectory of disputes. The shadow margin becomes a place where corporate incentives intersect with geopolitical ambition—rarely in simple ways.

As PMCs proliferate, the international legal system lags behind. The Montreux Document (2008) clarified obligations for states hiring private security providers, but it did not bind them. The International Code of Conduct for Private Security Providers introduced a voluntary oversight mechanism; uptake improved, but enforcement remained weak. UN expert panels continue to document abuses by contractors in conflict regions, yet recommendations often outpace political will. Regulation drifts, while the market grows.

This structural gap leaves policymakers with a persistent tension. PMCs offer tools that governments find useful—capacity without visibility, presence without liability, action without admission. Yet each of these qualities also carries risk. How far can a state outsource coercive capability before it dilutes its monopoly on force? How much ambiguity can a conflict environment tolerate before violence becomes unmoored from diplomatic control? And when a contractor in a disputed region fires a weapon, whose conflict is it thereafter?

The shadow margin remains unsettled. PMCs thrive within it, expanding the space where states act indirectly and corporations act with armed support. Their rise signals both opportunity and hazard. They enable fragile governments to function, yet they complicate sovereignty. They strengthen international operations at moments of crisis, yet they weaken the clarity of accountability. They operate at the edge of legality, yet they are hired by governments that insist on rules.

The unresolved question is simple, and it waits at the end of every contract: when force is privatised, who ultimately commands it?

Challenges of Accountability

In December 2007, a British parliamentary committee pressed officials from the Foreign and Commonwealth Office over the conduct of Aegis Defence Services in Iraq. Video footage—allegedly showing Aegis contractors firing at civilian cars on the Baghdad airport road—had surfaced months earlier. The company denied wrongdoing; the footage's provenance remained contested; no charges followed. The committee sought clarity. It received ambiguity. The actions occurred in a foreign jurisdiction under a Coalition Provisional Authority order that muddied legal authority. The contractors were British citizens, registered to a British firm, operating under an American mandate in Iraqi territory. To whom, exactly, were they accountable? The hearing ended with more questions than answers. *Accountability blurred.*

That blur sits at the centre of the regulatory vacuum surrounding Private Military Companies. These firms operate across borders where legal systems overlap imperfectly or contradict outright. A single incident can involve a contracting government in London, a theatre commander in Basra, a corporate legal office in Dubai, and a local prosecutor in Baghdad—none of whom possess sole jurisdiction. The difficulty is structural. Law assumes clear sovereignty. PMCs thrive where sovereignty is fractured.

The legal vacuum begins with a simple fact: states deploy PMCs precisely because they operate outside the constraints binding national forces. This is the visible behaviour that exposes the problem. When a uniformed soldier fires a weapon, their government owns the consequence. When a contractor fires a weapon, responsibility disperses across the commercial contract, the host nation's rules, and the hiring nation's intent. Each actor can disavow direct control. Each can point to paperwork. Each can claim the event lies beyond their immediate competence. The implication is profound. Without clarity of command, accountability becomes negotiable.

To illustrate how this vacuum persists, consider the legal aftermath of the Nisour Square shooting in Baghdad on 16 September 2007. The US Department of Justice eventually prosecuted several Blackwater contractors, but only after complex jurisdictional manoeuvres and diplomatic pressure. The proceedings hinged on narrow interpretations of extraterritorial law—specifically the Military Extraterritorial Jurisdiction Act—originally designed to cover military dependants rather than private guards escorting diplomats. The case produced convictions, later commutations, then controversy. It proved that accountability was *possible* but not automatic. It required political will, extensive resources, and years of legal improvisation.

A second example—this time from Africa—shows the limitations even more starkly. When members of the Wagner Group were implicated in human rights abuses in the Central African Republic in 2019 and 2020, UN investigators documented allegations but lacked tools to compel cooperation. Russia denied state responsibility; the host nation lacked capacity to prosecute; the contractors belonged to a company without transparent legal personality. The behaviour was visible. The victims were identified. The pathways for justice were blocked. The gap between evidence and enforcement widened.

A counter-example occasionally cited is the prosecution of Executive Outcomes operatives under South Africa's Regulation of Foreign Military

Assistance Act after their involvement in Sierra Leone in the 1990s. Pretoria sought to deter mercenary activity and asserted extraterritorial jurisdiction, yet convictions remained limited and the act proved difficult to enforce. The limitation lies not in intent but in feasibility: national courts struggle to investigate crimes committed in fluid conflict zones where evidence is scarce, witnesses fear reprisals, and records vanish. Reconciling this counter-example with broader critique reinforces the central tension: even strong domestic legislation cannot fully plug the accountability vacuum when conflicts occur beyond robust judicial reach.

The motif threading through these episodes is a *threshold*: the point at which responsibility should pass from corporate secrecy to public scrutiny. PMCs routinely operate below that threshold. Their ownership structures, often routed through holding entities in the British Virgin Islands, Cyprus, or the UAE, obscure who commands whom. Beneficial ownership registers help, but only when jurisdictions require transparency. Many do not. A front company can dissolve overnight. Its personnel reappear under a new banner the following month. Regulators measure compliance; PMCs measure opportunity. The threshold shifts accordingly.

Even where rules exist, they lag. The Montreux Document, published in 2008 and supported by dozens of states, outlines obligations regarding PMCs in armed conflict. It has moral force but no legal teeth. The International Code of Conduct for Private Security Providers (ICoC) offers voluntary oversight, audits, and grievance procedures, yet firms may opt out with minimal consequence. Compliance becomes a market signal rather than a binding duty. Clients choose whether to prioritise certified providers; some do, many do not. In areas where the state barely functions, certification matters little compared with cost and capability.

Proposals for stricter licensing regimes attempt to push the accountability threshold upward. The United Kingdom's Green Paper on regulating private military and security companies (2009) explored several models: mandatory licensing, statutory oversight bodies, and contract transparency requirements. Civil society groups argued for stronger provisions, including sanctioning powers and obligatory reporting on use of force. Industry groups resisted measures they saw as bureaucratic or commercially sensitive. Parliament debated; no comprehensive legislation followed. The proposal stalled in the space between national interest and market pragmatism.

Switzerland offers a more assertive template. Its Federal Act on Private Security Services Provided Abroad (2015) imposes licensing and notification requirements on firms based in Swiss territory. Companies must report their activities, particularly when operating near armed conflicts. The government can deny authorisation for activities likely to support human rights abuses. Although the system is imperfect and does not prevent firms from relocating to more permissive environments, it demonstrates that regulation can be sharpened when political appetite exists.

Still, these efforts remain exceptions. The broader pattern is one of fragmented oversight. Host nations often lack the capacity or incentives to prosecute foreign contractors, especially when they rely on those same contractors for security. Hiring states may prefer ambiguity, which allows them to distance themselves from politically damaging incidents. International bodies lack enforcement mechanisms. The result is a triangle of reluctance—host, client, operator—within which accountability circulates without settling.

The practical consequences extend beyond individual cases. In a contested region, a single unpunished incident can shift local perceptions dramatically. Communities measure legitimacy through behaviour: whether a contractor respects checkpoints, whether detainees are treated humanely, whether compensation is paid when harm occurs. When no credible legal pathway exists, grievances accumulate. Suspicion grows. A political conflict becomes a personal one. This transformation increases the likelihood of retaliation against contractors and, by extension, the clients who hire them. Accountability is not only a moral requirement; it is a stabilising mechanism.

Yet the search for effective oversight collides with the pace at which PMCs adapt. They rebrand, subcontract, merge, and disperse faster than regulators can catalogue them. A licensing regime must confront this operational agility. Should licences attach to individuals rather than companies? Should regulators require detailed reporting of subcontracting chains? Should violations by a parent company automatically suspend subsidiaries? Each proposal has merits. Each invites resistance from firms that benefit from structural opacity.

The threshold motif returns here, sharper than before. PMCs flourish below it, yet the stability of conflict zones depends on raising it. Bridging this gap demands more than legislation. It requires political consensus among states that hire PMCs and among those that host them. It also requires international bodies—UN, OSCE, African Union, ASEAN—to develop clearer investigative mechanisms, even if enforcement remains limited. The challenge is not to eliminate ambiguity, which may be impossible, but to constrain it.

A forward question lingers. If accountability follows authority, and PMCs operate where authority seldom settles, can any regulatory framework match their reach? Or does the world simply accept that in the shadow margin—where corporate force meets geopolitical ambition—responsibility will always arrive late, if at all?

Ethical and Operational Dilemmas

In August 2017, a convoy belonging to the US-based PMC DynCorp International passed through Kunduz province in northern Afghanistan. According to local police reports and UN Assistance Mission interviews, a dispute at a checkpoint escalated into an exchange of fire that left two civilians injured and several Afghan officers demanding the contractors' expulsion. DynCorp denied wrongdoing and pushed for a joint investigation; the provincial authorities insisted the contractors had acted outside their remit. The episode faded from the headlines within weeks, but the bruise it left remained visible. A single misjudged decision by a privately employed team had strained relations between a NATO partner and the local security apparatus meant to benefit from foreign assistance. The incentives behind that decision were never fully established. That opacity matters.

Profit-driven security forces confront a moral tension that state militaries do not. A government commissions force to advance strategic aims; a company commissions force to satisfy a contract. When the battlefield becomes the marketplace, loyalty fragments into temporary obligations. Contractors rotate in and out of high-risk zones according to pay cycles rather than national service terms. The visible result is discontinuity: teams that know local environments only superficially, commanders who change quarterly, and decision-making tied more closely to contract performance metrics than to long-term stability. This instability is not theoretical. It shapes behaviour at roadblocks, at compound gates, and during tense patrols where restraint depends on deep situational understanding. When that understanding is thin, escalation becomes easier.

The moral concern is amplified by the short-term nature of most contracts. A soldier commits to years of structured hierarchy and training; a contractor often signs for a 90-day rotation with bonuses tied to hazard exposure. Name the pattern: loyalty becomes transactional. Explain its consequence: operational reliability erodes. A team might prioritise protecting an asset over maintaining fragile local partnerships because the contract rewards avoidance of loss, not the cultivation of trust. The implication ripples outward. Host communities may interpret actions as hostile, even when contractors believe they are acting defensively. The absence of stable relationships magnifies suspicion.

Two examples illustrate how these dynamics reshape conflict zones. In Iraq between 2004 and 2008, Blackwater's frequent engagements—well documented in congressional hearings—showed how an aggressive protection model driven by contractual imperatives could alienate local populations. The behaviour was measurable: convoys travelling at high speed, warning shots fired with minimal hesitation, and rules that emphasised asset security above contextual nuance. The outcome, police commanders in Baghdad noted at the time, was a rise in civilian complaints and a decline in cooperation with coalition authorities. The firm's defenders argued that its clients remained safe. Critics countered that the broader mission suffered. Both statements were true, which is precisely the operational dilemma.

A second case, this time in South Sudan in 2016, involved Unity Resources Group, hired by several international firms to protect staff during renewed fighting. UN investigators recorded that contractors evacuated high-value personnel swiftly but left behind local employees deemed outside the contractual scope. The visible decision—whom to rescue—revealed the deeper fault line between corporate obligation and humanitarian responsibility. The contractors complied with their mandate; yet the sense of abandonment among unprotected workers deepened resentment against foreign entities. The company acted lawfully; the operational ethic appeared selectively applied.

A counter-example tempers the critique. In Somalia's Puntland region in the late 2000s, Saracen International (later Sterling Corporate Services) helped train local counter-piracy forces with relative discipline and tangible improvements in coastal security. International observers acknowledged that, despite disputes over financing and legality, the trainers showed professionalism and reduced pirate activity. Yet even this case exposes a limitation. The programme collapsed when political sponsorship faltered, underscoring that PMC effectiveness depends on external stability. When political winds shift, even well-run operations evaporate. Reconcile the counterpoint: PMCs can contribute positively, but only when the environment aligns with their incentives, and when oversight remains steady—conditions rarely guaranteed in grey zone contexts.

Threaded through these examples is a motif of *thresholds*: the ethical threshold of acceptable behaviour and the operational threshold at which a contractor's decision becomes strategically consequential. PMCs operate close to both thresholds. A misjudged threat assessment at a checkpoint crosses the ethical threshold. A triggered local backlash crosses the operational one. Governments may believe they have delegated a task; in reality, they have delegated decisions with foreign policy implications.

The scenario below shows how quickly those thresholds collapse when incentives misalign.

Imagine a contested mining corridor in the eastern Democratic Republic of Congo. A Western corporation hires a PMC to protect a geological survey team after sporadic militia attacks. The contract emphasises asset safety and adherence to the timeline. During a routine patrol, the security team encounters an armed local defence group claiming authority over the passage. The contractors, aware that delays trigger financial penalties, press forward. Voices rise. A warning shot is fired—meant as a deterrent—and strikes a tree behind the local group's leader. Panic spreads. The locals are reporting on the radio that the allied militias are misinterpreting the clash as an offensive move backed by foreign sponsors. Within hours, a minor standoff becomes a multi-faction skirmish. The corporation blames the PMC. The PMC cites its contractual obligations. Regional leaders accuse both of undermining stability. The escalation stems not from malice but from misaligned incentives and hurried judgement.

Such incidents reveal why ethical dilemmas cannot be divorced from operational risk. A contractor who feels bound to demonstrate "value" may act assertively. A contractor nearing contract expiry may take fewer risks, avoiding patrols that would maintain local reassurance. A contractor hired through a chain of subcontractors—each taking a percentage—may be under-resourced, understaffed, or poorly trained. These pressures surface as visible behaviours: fewer community engagements, quicker recourse to force, reduced cooperation with local authorities. Each behaviour becomes data in the community's assessment of foreign involvement. Each assessment shapes the political temperature.

Short-term contracting also affects reliability. High turnover weakens institutional memory. A commander arriving for a three-month rotation cannot absorb the subtle dynamics of clan relationships or historical grievances. Without such knowledge, a routine security sweep may coincide with a community ceremony, triggering offence. A roadblock placed for convoy safety may obstruct vital trade routes, prompting local anger. The PMC is technically performing its contract. The society absorbing the disruption sees negligence or provocation. When political actors exploit that resentment, the grey zone thickens.

Ethical dilemmas sharpen where PMCs intersect with state militaries. A government force typically calibrates restraint according to national interest. A PMC calibrates according to contractual exposure and risk tolerances defined by insurers. When two forces operate side by side, their tactical calculus diverges. A local commander may urge de-escalation; a contractor may seek rapid extraction. A state may accept a temporary setback for long-term stability; a contractor may prioritise immediate safety metrics. The misalignment becomes a fissure that adversaries can widen through disinformation, ambushes, or manipulation of local grievances.

Technology compounds the problem. Body cameras, GPS logs, and drone feeds can document incidents, yet access to that footage depends on corporate discretion. Evidence becomes proprietary. A government seeking clarity may find itself negotiating with its own contractor for transparency. This inversion of authority challenges the principle that force—when used abroad—should remain publicly accountable. If data relevant to the use of force sits behind commercial confidentiality, ethical evaluation becomes partial at best.

The motif of thresholds returns one final time. Regulators attempt to raise the ethical threshold by setting standards; PMCs navigate just below them, ensuring compliance without sacrificing flexibility. Policymakers attempt to define operational thresholds that contractors must not cross; contractors argue that unpredictable environments demand autonomy. Both claims contain truth. Yet the gap between them is where escalation most easily occurs.

A forward question remains unresolved. If PMCs continue to expand into grey zone competition, can states redesign contracts to align moral duty with operational necessity? Or will the inherent logic of commercialised force always bend decision-making toward expedience, even at the expense of stability?

Guarding Corporate Assets

At dawn on 16 January 2013, gunmen stormed the Tigantourine gas facility near In Amenas, Algeria. The complex—jointly operated by BP, Statoil, and Sonatrach—was guarded not by soldiers but by a patchwork of private contractors and local security auxiliaries. As the siege unfolded, the lack of unified command became painfully clear. Some guards fought; others fled. Algerian special forces eventually retook the site, but forty hostages were killed. Subsequent parliamentary reviews in London and Oslo pointed to a structural problem: multinational firms had delegated the protection of a strategic asset to private actors whose training, communication chains, and rules of engagement varied wildly. The incident crystallised a dilemma facing any corporation operating in unstable regions. Outsourcing security buys speed. It may also buy fragility.

Large firms turn to PMCs because they promise efficiency and discretion. A mine, pipeline, data hub, or offshore platform must run continuously; its downtime can be measured in millions of pounds lost per day. A government may not wish to deploy troops to protect a foreign concession. A PMC, however, can be hired within weeks, equipped rapidly, and embedded with client staff. That speed is measurable. During the 2014 upsurge of violence in Iraq, several oil companies contracted private firms to relocate personnel within a forty-eight-hour window, a task no regular military could have executed without political deliberation. Yet that very speed creates a subtle risk: a PMC becomes the client's frontline representative before political and community relationships have been consolidated. A guard at a gate becomes the face of a multinational enterprise. The implications accumulate with each interaction.

PMCs also blur the distinction between corporate interest and sovereign authority. A security contractor protecting a copper mine in the Katanga region of the DRC may conduct vehicle checks or deny access to roads used by local traders. From the company's point of view, these are protective measures; from the community's perspective, they resemble policing powers exercised without public mandate. Name the problem: jurisdiction. Explain its effect. Corporate guards, often operating under ambiguous legal authority, can appear to supersede or compete with local security actors. The implication is obvious. Tensions rise not because the corporation seeks confrontation but because its hired protectors occupy a quasi-state role.

Two illustrative cases show how these tensions escalate when mismanaged. In Papua New Guinea in the late 2000s, guards hired to protect the Porgera gold mine—operated by Barrick Gold—were accused by human rights monitors of using excessive force against villagers who crossed informal boundaries around the site. The boundaries were never legally codified; they existed because contractors enforced them. The behaviour was visible: attempted evictions, intimidation, and occasional violence. The operational result was a cycle of resentment and retaliatory incursions, each fuelling the next. The corporation faced lawsuits and reputational damage precisely because its security apparatus had substituted ad hoc rules for legitimate authority.

A second case, less violent but equally revealing, occurred in Nigeria's Niger Delta in 2019, when a PMC contracted by an international energy firm clashed with a local vigilante group claiming to protect community fishing rights. The contractors attempted to secure a pipeline corridor; the vigilantes viewed the move as a challenge to their standing. A confrontation followed, punctuated by warning shots and property damage. Neither side wished for escalation, yet the competing claims to authority created fertile ground for misunderstanding. It took mediation by the state governor to stabilise the situation. The limitation here is instructive. Even when PMCs demonstrate restraint, the mere fact of their presence can collide with local power structures that corporations may not have mapped accurately.

There are counter-examples where PMCs integrate effectively with local systems. In Mozambique's Cabo Delgado province in the early 2010s, certain mining concessions used mixed teams—local police paired with private contractors—to patrol perimeters. Reports from the time describe relatively low incident rates and cooperative relationships with nearby communities. But these successes rested on specific conditions: clear lines of authority, consistent communication, and corporate willingness to invest in community liaison officers. Once political volatility increased, even these arrangements became difficult to sustain. Reconcile the point: PMCs can contribute to stable operations, but only when embedded within broader governance structures that corporations do not control.

A quiet motif runs through all these examples: the gate. The guard hut, checkpoint, or access road becomes the physical threshold where corporate interest meets public expectation. Every decision at that gate—who enters, who waits, who is turned back—transmits a signal about the corporation's values. A PMC trained to prioritise asset protection may default to exclusion. A local security offshoot may expect preferential treatment. When these logics collide, the gate becomes a point of friction rather than protection.

Corporate due diligence must therefore move far beyond background checks on a contractor's licensing. Firms must measure behaviours, not promises. This begins with mapping local security ecosystems: police units, informal militias, community watch groups, and political patrons. The corporation needs a realistic diagram of who exerts authority near its assets. Skipping this step is measurable in incidents—blocked roads, surprise protests, or clashes triggered by misinterpreted intentions. Due diligence also requires specifying rules of engagement that align with community norms. A corporation that forbids warning shots, mandates bilingual communication, and requires incident reporting within hours creates a behavioural environment that reduces ambiguity. Contractors may resist such constraints, but the alternative is ad hoc decision-making shaped by stress and incomplete information.

Training is another visible component of due diligence. A contractor's skills can be assessed through simulation exercises with local authorities. Joint drills reveal fault lines: hesitation in mixed teams, unclear radio protocols, incompatible procedures for crowd management. In 2015, after a series of break-ins at a copper facility in northern Chile, the operator required its PMC to conduct monthly joint exercises with Carabineros (Chile's national police). Reports noted fewer clashes and improved reporting accuracy over the following year. The lesson is straightforward. When corporate and public security actors practise together, the risks of contradictory behaviour diminish.

Cultural integration matters just as much. A contractor who understands local grievance patterns, land disputes, or ceremonial practices makes fewer errors at the gate. Corporations that hire community liaison officers or partner with respected local NGOs equip their PMCs with the knowledge required to interpret behaviours. Without this context, even routine actions can be provocative. A vehicle search conducted without greeting protocols may be seen as disrespectful. A patrol passing through a burial site may ignite anger. These missteps accumulate, shaping narratives that adversaries can weaponise.

Yet corporations often overlook a structural risk: the subcontracting chain. A firm may hire a respected international PMC, only to find that day-to-day security is handled by local subcontractors with weaker training or political ties that create conflicts of interest. Each subcontract reduces transparency. A due-diligence guideline here is simple: map the subcontracting tree and prohibit unauthorised delegation. If a contractor cannot name every guard deployed under its banner, the corporation has already ceded control.

The economic dimension cannot be ignored. Companies protecting critical assets—oil rigs, fibre-optic landing stations, lithium mines—face pressure to keep production uninterrupted. This pressure can incentivise PMCs to adopt assertive postures that safeguard operations in the short term but corrode community relations in the long term. Corporations should measure performance through stability metrics rather than incident-free days alone. Stability is visible in fewer community complaints, smoother coordination with local authorities, and reduced reliance on force. When these metrics guide contracts, contractor behaviour changes.

Despite these measures, uncertainty persists. PMCs operate in environments where allegiance, law, and threat are fluid. A corporate security team may comply fully with contractual obligations yet still clash with local actors who interpret their presence through political or economic lenses beyond the corporation's reach. Hence the unresolved question that closes this section: Can corporations protect vital assets through private force without becoming accidental participants in local conflicts, or must they rethink the balance between security outsourcing and long-term social investment?

International Oversight Options

On 10 December 2008 in Montreux, Switzerland, representatives from seventeen states gathered around polished conference tables to sign a document that carried no binding force but aspired to moral weight. The Montreux Document, as it became known, collated existing international obligations relevant to private military and security companies and offered voluntary good practices. It was, to its supporters, a necessary first attempt to impose order on an industry operating across borders and beyond coherent scrutiny. Yet even as the ink dried, two absences stood out. The firms themselves were not signatories. Nor were many of the states that most frequently hired or hosted PMCs. The paradox was unmistakable. A mechanism intended to guide global behaviour relied on voluntary adherence from actors with little incentive to constrain themselves. The Document marked progress, but it also revealed the size of the regulatory gap—an expanse wide enough for armed contractors to move through with ease.

Current oversight mechanisms reflect this structural ambivalence. International law treats PMCs through the prism of existing humanitarian norms, but these norms were crafted for state forces, not corporate entities driven by contracts and profit. The United Nations Working Group on the Use of Mercenaries has long argued that PMCs occupy a legal twilight, neither fully private nor fully sovereign. Their activities often occur in foreign jurisdictions where domestic accountability is weak. The implication is plain. When an incident occurs—an excessive use of force, a wrongful detention, or the mishandling of a checkpoint—no single legal authority can assert rapid, uncontested jurisdiction. The result is delay, fragmentation, and, in some cases, impunity.

Despite these limitations, certain efforts have achieved measurable successes. The International Code of Conduct for Private Security Providers (ICoCA), established in Geneva in 2013, offers a certification regime that audits companies against defined human rights and operational standards. Some firms have improved reporting practices after joining. For example, a 2018 ICoCA assessment highlighted more consistent incident logging by certified contractors operating at East African port facilities. This behavioural shift—visible in the frequency and quality of reports—demonstrates the potential of oversight when corporate incentives align with reputational gain. Yet the limitations are equally visible. Certification remains optional, and some of the largest PMCs opt out entirely, calculating that market demand outweighs reputational risk.

Other approaches attempt to regulate through procurement. The United States and the United Kingdom, two major hiring states, introduced stricter contracting standards after the mid-2000s controversies in Iraq. These standards require background checks, clear chains of command, and incident reporting protocols. The intention is to tie compliance to contract viability: fail the audit, lose the contract. Though this has produced improvements—fewer unregistered weapons, more traceable deployments—it remains uneven across jurisdictions. When a company shifts operations to a less demanding client base, oversight weakens. Name the limitation: regulatory asymmetry. Explain its consequence. PMCs operate across multiple legal environments, and they adjust to the lowest enforceable standard.

A credible counter-example complicates this picture. In Afghanistan before 2021, NATO utilised a layered oversight structure for private security contractors protecting supply convoys. It combined national military supervision, Afghan Ministry of Interior licensing, and joint patrols to verify compliance. The system reduced certain abuses documented in earlier phases of the conflict. However, its success was context-specific. It depended on large-scale international presence, financial leverage over contractors, and sustained diplomatic pressure. Once the international footprint shrank, the mechanisms dissolved quickly. Reconcile the lesson.

Oversight is possible but rarely durable when its enforcement machinery relies on exceptional circumstances.

The quiet motif running through oversight debates is the observer. Not the combatant, not the contractor, but the individual—or institution—tasked with watching. The strength of any regulatory system depends on the clarity of its observers' mandate and their capacity to act on their findings. Observer missions, when empowered, can serve as stabilisers. The OSCE's monitoring in eastern Ukraine from 2014 demonstrated how third-party observers can document ceasefire violations, establish shared factual baselines, and apply pressure for compliance. Although not directed at PMCs per se, the mission showed how impartial visibility reduces space for denial. Transposed to the PMC sphere, stronger observer mandates could clarify responsibilities, document misconduct, and limit the plausible deniability on which some clients rely.

Yet any discussion of global regulation must confront the political economy of PMCs. States hire contractors because they provide flexibility: rapid deployment, minimal domestic political cost, and operational deniability. Host states tolerate them because they lack the capacity to secure critical sites or wish to preserve their regular forces for other priorities. Both dynamics create incentives to resist binding international constraints. A treaty regime with strong inspection powers—akin to arms control verification systems—would require states to cede a measure of sovereignty they have little desire to surrender. This is the core obstruction. Oversight mechanisms must function in a world where states openly value the freedoms PMCs provide.

Proposals for stricter licensing regimes offer a middle ground. One option, championed intermittently by European policymakers, envisions an international licensing authority modelled loosely on civil aviation oversight. PMCs would require certification to operate across borders; their personnel would need verifiable training records; their chains of ownership would be publicly registered. Such a framework could reduce the opacity that shields misconduct. But its feasibility remains uncertain. Without buy-in from major hiring states—particularly those that use PMCs as instruments of foreign policy—licensing risks becoming a regional rather than global solution. And even if widely adopted, enforcement would hinge on robust inspection capacity, something international institutions have struggled to maintain.

Alternatively, stronger observer missions could expand accountability without imposing the full weight of a treaty. A mission deployed at the request of host states—or mandated by regional organisations—could monitor PMC activities around critical infrastructure, record incidents, and publish findings. The visibility alone would modify behaviour. Contractors aware that their operations are being documented by impartial observers tend to adhere more closely to agreed protocols. This is a behavioural truth long recognised by peacekeepers and election monitors. But observer missions face constraints: security risks, limited access, and political pressure from both hiring and hosting states. Their impact depends on independence and reach, qualities that must be institutionalised rather than improvised.

Another avenue lies in financial regulation. Many PMCs operate through complex corporate structures with entities registered across multiple jurisdictions. International cooperation on beneficial ownership transparency—an area where the Financial Action Task Force (FATF) has pushed reforms—could weaken the anonymity that shelters irresponsible firms. If banks require verified ownership and compliance histories before processing payments or extending credit, PMCs with questionable records would find their operational room reduced. The implication is clear. Economic leverage may succeed where legal authority falters. Yet this approach still relies on states enforcing transparency norms that may clash with their strategic or commercial interests.

Consider two contrasting examples that illustrate both potential and constraint. In 2016, after a fatal incident involving contractors in South Sudan, the UN threatened to deny contracts to firms that failed to meet new reporting standards. Within months, several companies improved their documentation practices, fearing exclusion from a lucrative market. This showed that targeted economic pressure can reshape behaviour quickly. By contrast, efforts in 2020 to investigate PMC-linked abuses in Libya stalled when key states in the Security Council disagreed over the framing of the inquiry. Without political alignment, even clear evidence failed to produce meaningful oversight. The limitation is structural: global mechanisms cannot compel action when major powers prefer ambiguity.

What, then, might a plausible future look like? Perhaps not a grand treaty, but a layered architecture: improved national licensing tied to international certification; regional observer missions with mandates to monitor sensitive sites; financial transparency requirements enforced by banks; and periodic reviews by multilateral bodies. Each layer compensates for the weaknesses of the others. None offers a perfect solution. But together they could narrow the space in which PMCs operate with impunity.

This leaves an unresolved question that shadows the entire discussion. Can the international system design oversight mechanisms that both preserve the operational utility states seek from PMCs and protect civilians from their worst excesses? Or will global regulation always lag behind an industry that thrives precisely because it slips between categories—public and private, domestic and foreign, military and commercial?

Chapter 10

Attribution Games

The breach began with a flicker. At 02:11 GMT, analysts inside the UK's National Cyber Security Centre watched a stream of anomalous packets tunnelling through an obscure port seldom used outside specialist engineering software. The pattern looked familiar yet not identical—an echo of an intrusion method previously attributed to APT29 in July 2018 but dressed in new code, sharper, cleaner, seemingly designed to mislead. The team froze the packet flow and started the painstaking process that defines modern cyber attribution: capturing volatile memory, extracting clues from shifting command-and-control servers, and mapping the artefacts before they vanished. By sunrise, half their evidence had evaporated. The remaining fragments pointed in two contradictory directions. Someone wanted to be found. Someone else did not. And both signatures sat within the same intrusion.

This is the starting point for nearly every contemporary attribution dispute: a clue that is both a signpost and a trap. In August 2020, when Australian investigators delayed naming a threat actor after a high-profile breach of parliamentary networks, commentators accused them of timidity. Behind the scenes, the truth was more prosaic. The intruders had stitched together a mosaic of falsified metadata, borrowed malware strains, and re-routed signals, each layer designed to corrode confidence in whatever conclusion analysts eventually reached. The government waited because haste would have been reckless. Attribution, after all, is not merely a technical determination. It is a diplomatic act, a strategic statement, and occasionally the spark that ignites a confrontation.

The modern grey zone thrives in this ambiguity. States that once signalled intent through troop movements or naval deployments now leave their fingerprints in corrupted log files, spoofed IP ranges, and replicated encryption keys. Cyber conflict has made ambiguity a strategic asset. This chapter enters that contested space where evidence meets power, and uncertainty shapes geopolitical behaviour.

Attribution is always a chase against time. Digital footprints decay rapidly as servers reset, logs roll over, or attackers actively scrub the traces behind them. Even the most advanced forensic teams rely on seconds of luck—a misconfigured script, a forgotten timestamp, the fleeting persistence of a remote access tool—to extract meaning before the environment shifts. The fragility of this evidence explains why attribution so often becomes probabilistic rather than definitive. Analysts weigh toolkits, infrastructure, linguistic cues, and behavioural patterns, but the strongest indicators may still only whisper, not shout.

Yet states must eventually decide whether to speak publicly. This is where political calculation enters. Naming an actor can deter further aggression, rally allies, or affirm coherence in the international system. But it can also close off diplomatic channels, invite retaliation, or expose intelligence sources. A notable example unfolded in February 2015, when the United States delayed its attribution of the Sony Pictures hack for several weeks. Officials gathered corroborating evidence from foreign partners, not only to solidify the case technically but to ensure the announcement did not derail concurrent negotiations with regional powers. The naming, when it arrived, carried the full weight of a coordinated intelligence review. But the delay revealed something else: attribution is as much a performance of credibility as it is a forensic judgment.

When attribution goes wrong, the consequences can be severe. Misidentification can escalate rhetoric, provoke countermeasures, or stigmatise an innocent party. Imagine a scenario in which a major European government hastily blames a neighbouring state for a blackout affecting millions. Journalists swarm, markets recoil, and diplomatic protests erupt. Two days later, new evidence points to criminal ransomware actors unaffiliated with any state. The damage, though, is already done. The accused state, feeling cornered, hardens its posture; trust within the region sours; political actors exploit the episode for domestic gain. Misattribution can be more destabilising than a successful attack.

These risks underscore the difficulty of sharing intelligence across borders. Alliances such as NATO and coalitions like the Five Eyes depend on pooled analysis, but collaboration brings its own frictions. States differ in their willingness to disclose sensitive sources, particularly when revealing code signatures or monitoring capabilities might expose ongoing collection programmes. Corporate security firms, meanwhile, possess high technical capacity but lack access to classified intelligence. The result is a fragmented ecosystem where analysts compare partial maps of the same terrain. Shared intelligence can accelerate understanding, but it can also introduce tension when partners question each other's evidentiary thresholds or motives.

Yet collaboration remains indispensable. The complexity of global cyber infrastructure means no single state can map every threat surface. The most effective attributions—such as the coordinated statements issued after the 2017 NotPetya attacks—emerged from coalitions that combined private-sector telemetry with government signals intelligence and diplomatic messaging. The benefit was clarity: multiple actors confirming the same assessment, reducing the space for denial or counter-narratives. But even this model has limits. When allies disagree about timing, wording, or the strategic utility of naming, the process stalls. Attribution becomes not a technical determination but a negotiation among states balancing different risks.

Against this backdrop, what principles can make attribution safer? The first is evidentiary humility. States should disclose, whenever possible, the categories of evidence—though not necessarily the precise sources—that underpin their claims. This habit strengthens credibility and invites peer review. Second, policymakers should distinguish between private confidence and public assertion. Intelligence agencies may reach a high-confidence assessment internally without immediately making it part of diplomatic theatre. Third, independent technical bodies could play a stabilising role by offering neutral audits of major incidents. Although such bodies would lack enforcement powers, they would provide a shared factual baseline—a rare commodity amid geopolitical signalling.

Transparency is not always the obvious answer. Secrecy retains strategic value, especially when revealing methods might compromise ongoing monitoring or expose fragile alliances. Some intrusions are best handled quietly, their perpetrators tracked rather than named. The key is discernment: understanding when attribution contributes to stability and when it threatens to inflame tensions.

Ultimately, attribution games reveal a deeper truth about grey zone conflict. States operate in a world where power is exercised through ambiguity, and responsibility is contested rather than confessed. Digital forensics can illuminate parts of this environment, but not all. Beyond the technical architecture lies a political struggle over truth, narrative, and consequence. This chapter explores that struggle—not to resolve it, but to map its contours and expose its stakes.

The unresolved question hangs in the air: in a domain designed for deniability, can any attribution framework command enough trust to prevent escalation, or will the shadows always offer cover for those who thrive in them?

Tracing Cyber Fingerprints

At 04:26 EST on 20 December 2016, analysts at the FBI's Cyber Division pulled a volatile memory snapshot from a compromised server linked to the Democratic National Committee breach. The image contained a fragment of code using a distinctive encryption routine previously observed in an intrusion against the German Bundestag in 2015. That routine—an idiosyncratic combination of RC4 and AES layers—was not enough to constitute proof, but it hinted at a developer's signature, a stylistic brushstroke in a digital canvas designed to be wiped clean. By the time investigators revisited the server two hours later, the malware had self-deleted. Only the snapshot preserved its residue. This is the tempo of cyber forensics: fleeting, fragile, and fiercely contested.

Traces such as misconfigured command-and-control nodes, embedded timestamps, or reused libraries are often the only artefacts analysts can seize before attackers alter them. In March 2018, when Cisco Talos researchers examined the VPNFilter campaign affecting network devices across Ukraine, the attackers reacted almost immediately to public reporting by issuing a single purge command. Thousands of compromised systems wiped their logs in minutes. The very speed at which evidence disappeared illustrated the skill of those responsible—and the constraints analysts face. Attribution begins with clues, but those clues are constantly eroded by adversaries who understand the investigative process as well as their pursuers.

The forensic pipeline is deceptively intricate. Analysts start by freezing environments, collecting volatile data from RAM, parsing network logs, and reconstructing intrusion timelines from fragments scattered across routers, endpoints, and cloud services. The work resembles archaeology performed on shifting ground. Every detail—a compiler artefact, a function naming convention, a preferred time-of-day pattern—provides a shard of insight. Yet none of these shards alone reveal a culprit with certainty. Attackers know this and build masking layers accordingly: proxy chains that route traffic through multiple jurisdictions; false flags in Cyrillic,

Mandarin, or Farsi inserted into code; and infrastructure rented through disposable shell companies. Each layer aims to degrade confidence rather than defeat investigation outright.

Masking is not a single tactic but an evolving suite of behaviours. Some groups rotate servers hourly, forcing analysts to chase ephemeral DNS records. Others seed their malware with misleading clues: a routine stolen from an unrelated criminal group in São Paulo; a compiler timestamp modified to suggest a working day in Seoul; an encryption signature echoing an operation attributed to Iran's APT33. The aim is misdirection. When journalists or governments leap to conclusions based on superficial overlaps, the attackers achieve a secondary effect: the erosion of trust in attribution itself.

Forensics therefore depends on pattern aggregation. One visible behaviour rarely proves anything; clusters of behaviours, repeated over years, begin to form a signature. The long-term analysis of North Korea's Lazarus Group illustrates this. Across incidents in Bangladesh (2016), Poland (2017), and Chile (2018), researchers observed repeated reliance on specific loader modules and distinct lateral movement techniques. These were not smoking guns but habits—technical tics visible to those who had watched the group evolve. Attribution emerged not from a single artefact, but from continuity.

Yet even these patterns have limits. Attackers learn, adapt, and borrow from each other. A credible counter-example came in 2021, when forensic teams attributed a ransomware strain to a known Eastern European criminal outfit, only to discover later that elements of the code had been deliberately injected to mimic the group's earlier work. Analysts reconciled the contradiction by distinguishing between behavioural intent and technical mimicry. Code can be stolen; operational rhythm is harder to fake. The investigation refocused on infrastructure lifecycle, deployment cadence, and negotiation style—hallmarks that resisted imitation.

This interplay between signal and noise reveals a larger truth: attribution is about weighing probabilities, not delivering courtroom verdicts. Analysts measure each finding—an IP hop, a coding quirk, a linguistic residue—against historical datasets maintained by governments and the private sector. They compare intrusion chains with known campaigns. They commit to hypotheses only when alternative explanations become less plausible. The quiet motif throughout this work is decay: evidence that burns away with time and masking layers that aim to accelerate that decay. The central question becomes not "What happened?" but "What remains?"

The most advanced masking layers complicate this further. Some state-linked groups deploy multi-stage anonymisation networks that obscure provenance through layered encryption, leased infrastructure, or hijacked devices. Others operate through "victim-as-proxy" tactics, turning compromised servers in third countries into unwilling launch pads. When Dutch investigators traced part of a 2017 intrusion against a chemical laboratory in The Hague, they discovered packets originating not from the suspected state actor but from a dental clinic in Barcelona that had been compromised months earlier. Attribution had to disentangle culprit from conduit.

Where attribution does succeed, it often relies on timing. A careless test deployment, a brief overlap in infrastructure between two campaigns, or a forgotten debug path can create an opening. These moments rarely last. Analysts race to preserve logs before cloud retention limits purge them or before adversaries wipe and rebuild. Digital forensics is a discipline conducted against the clock. Those who hesitate lose visibility; those who move quickly still work inside a shrinking window.

Cooperation matters here. Shared intelligence can fuse fragments from different jurisdictions, but cooperation introduces its own frictions. Governments may withhold crucial artefacts to protect sources. Corporations may prioritise client confidentiality. The result is a patchwork of partial visibility. Yet joint investigations—such as the multinational response to the 2017 WannaCry outbreak—show the potential of coordinated pooling. In that case, overlapping telemetry from Microsoft, Kaspersky, and several national agencies helped identify toolsets linked to the Lazarus Group. The attribution still required caution, but collaboration raised confidence by revealing consistent signals across independent datasets.

Despite progress, attribution remains vulnerable to misinterpretation. A single misleading artefact can sway public opinion, even if professionals treat it cautiously. This tension becomes acute when political pressure mounts. Governments may seek rapid answers to demonstrate responsiveness, but rushed statements risk overshooting the evidence. The quiet motif returns: decay. Evidence that might have clarified responsibility later is irretrievable once a public accusation has hardened diplomatic positions.

The forensic process therefore demands both technical precision and strategic restraint. Analysts must interpret clues without overreach. Policymakers must balance transparency with prudence. And both communities must recognise the fundamental uncertainty built into digital conflict. The most important question is not whether attribution can achieve perfection—it cannot—but whether decision-makers can act responsibly within the limits of what can be known.

The unresolved tension remains: when footprints fade by the minute, and adversaries sculpt misdirection into their tools, how confidently can any state name a culprit without risking miscalculation?

Global Politics of Naming

On 19 February 2020, the UK's National Cyber Security Centre (NCSC) received a sealed packet from a partner service in Tallinn. Inside lay a tranche of server logs linking a disruptive intrusion into Georgia's national infrastructure—first detected in October 2019—to infrastructure previously tied to the GRU's Main Centre for Special Technologies, Unit 74455. The link was strong but not conclusive. Officials at King Charles Street hesitated. Washington pressed for a rapid public statement; London wanted a firmer evidential chain. Weeks passed. Only in February 2020, after Estonia decrypted a secondary command sequence tying the Georgian intrusion to an operational node observed during the 2018 Olympic Destroyer attack, did the UK government step up to a lectern and name Russia. The delay was deliberate. The naming itself was diplomatic theatre.

The choice to speak—or wait—reveals the political power of attribution. A government's voice in such moments is both forensic and strategic. Each word signals thresholds, alliances, and tolerances. To accuse too early, without enough corroboration, risks undermining credibility; to wait too long risks signalling permissiveness. As officials debated their timing in the Georgia case, the question lingered in the Cabinet Office briefing rooms: *What does our silence buy us?* That silence bought one thing above all—time to gather evidence that could withstand pushback from a state practised in denial. Time mattered. Silence mattered. Naming became an act weighted with consequence.

States treat attribution statements as calibrated tools, not spontaneous reactions. When governments issue them, they do so with the awareness that these declarations travel beyond press conferences into treaty rooms, intelligence alliances, and adversaries' cost-benefit calculations. Attribution is thus simultaneously a technical conclusion and a diplomatic instrument. The quiet motif here is weight—every naming adds weight to a geopolitical scale already under strain.

To understand how governments wield this weight, one must first see their internal machinery. A cyber intrusion triggers parallel processes: forensic analysis, inter-agency consultations, political risk assessments. Officials measure each evidential piece against hostile-state patterns catalogued by their intelligence services. They compare behavioural signatures across years of incidents. Then they commit—privately or publicly—to a probabilistic conclusion. Once that conclusion reaches foreign ministries, the nature of the decision shifts from technical judgement to geopolitical calculus. A naming moves from "What do we know?" to "What do we want to signal?"

The UK's public attribution of the 2017 NotPetya attack to the GRU illustrates this. In February 2018, the Foreign Office formally stated that Russian military intelligence had orchestrated the malware's global release, which caused disruptions from Kyiv to Copenhagen. The statement offered minimal technical detail. Instead, it framed the attribution as a defence of international norms. This was not forensic exposition; it was diplomatic boundary-setting. The government showed its hand without revealing its cards. It named Russia. It withheld operational specifics. This duality matters. Naming asserts strength; withholding protects methods.

Yet selective revelation has limits. The United States' approach to the 2014 Sony Pictures hack provides a counter-example. The FBI named North Korea in December 2014 based on technical overlaps and intelligence intercepts. Critics argued that Washington revealed too little about the underlying evidence. The brief public summary raised doubts among independent analysts who wanted clearer artefacts. The FBI reconciled this tension by later releasing additional indicators of compromise and allowing private-sector partners to corroborate the intrusion chain. The case illustrated the constant trade-off: reveal enough to persuade, but not enough to erode sources. The unresolved question was how much transparency is strategically sustainable.

This tension is not simply epistemic; it is behavioural. When states decide whether to disclose, they weigh adversaries' likely reactions. A forceful naming might deter future aggression or, conversely, provoke escalation. A muted response might preserve diplomatic channels or appear timid. Precision matters. Misjudging the weight of a naming can warp the very environment it seeks to stabilise.

Some states weaponise ambiguity. China, for instance, typically rejects foreign attributions while offering none of its own, preserving deniability and flexibility. Others, such as the Netherlands, disclose highly detailed technical evidence, as it did in October 2018 when it revealed photographs, equipment serial numbers, and vehicle logs tied to a GRU operation against the Organisation for the Prohibition of Chemical Weapons in The Hague. The Dutch approach demonstrated that complete clarity, though rare, can enhance credibility. But it also exposed intelligence-gathering techniques, raising a dilemma: clarity strengthens legitimacy; clarity burns sources.

The statecraft of naming also intersects with alliance dynamics. When NATO allies jointly named Russia for the 2021 Ghostwriter cyber activities, they presented not merely a forensic conclusion but a unified front. Coordinated naming amplifies pressure. Yet it also imposes procedural costs. Allies must harmonise evidence standards and political thresholds. When those diverge—as they did during the investigation of intrusions linked to China's APT10 between 2016 and 2018—joint statements stall. Some European governments wanted more time; others preferred speed. The compromise was a staggered release of condemnation, reflecting the reality that unity, though desirable, is rarely effortless.

But naming is not solely a state prerogative. Large technology companies such as Microsoft, Google, and CrowdStrike routinely attribute intrusions to state-linked groups. Their statements influence global discourse, sometimes shaping diplomatic expectations before governments speak. In September 2020, Microsoft identified threat groups targeting vaccine research facilities and linked them to Russia and North Korea. States took notice. The boundary between public forensic authority and private corporate judgement blurred. While these firms increase transparency, their attributions also carry commercial and geopolitical incentives. Recognising these incentives is crucial. An attribution landscape dominated by private actors risks fragmenting consensus and complicating state responses.

Even when evidence converges, political timing can reshape outcomes. The anecdote from February 2020 shows how a delayed naming allowed investigators to secure a stronger evidential chain. A contrasting example arose during the 2015 Bundestag intrusion, when German officials waited more than a year before publicly accusing Russia's APT28. Critics argued that the delay blunted deterrence. Supporters countered that Germany needed the delay to secure Bundestag systems and verify the attacker's pathways. The debate reflected a broader question: does waiting project caution or weakness? The answer depends on context, alliances, and adversaries' expectations.

A further complication emerges when attribution collides with domestic politics. In the United States, attribution statements made during the 2016 election cycle became entangled with partisan narratives, weakening their intended deterrent effect. As institutions struggled to maintain a unified message, adversaries exploited the discord. This underscores a crucial behavioural metric: coherence. When a government's internal fragmentation becomes visible, attribution loses force. Coherence strengthens signalling; fragmentation dissipates it.

Against this backdrop, the quiet motif of weight returns. Naming adds weight to diplomacy, intelligence credibility, and international norms. But weight is double-edged. Too much pressure risks fracture; too little risks irrelevance. The central challenge is calibration.

Yet not all decisions to name should be executed publicly. Some attributions are delivered through private diplomatic channels, often via ambassadors' summonses or secure bilateral calls. Private naming preserves room for negotiation. It allows states to signal awareness without forcing an adversary into public denial. This is particularly useful when both sides seek to avoid escalation. But secrecy carries its own limitations. Without public accountability, norms drift. Without transparency, democratic oversight weakens.

Every path—public or private—entails risk. A credible counter-example is the 2018 Marriott breach, widely attributed by US intelligence agencies to Chinese state-linked hackers. Although American officials eventually named Beijing, the delay allowed China to deny the charge and recalibrate its diplomatic posture. Critics argued that the United States sacrificed deterrence by hesitating. Yet officials insisted that the interval helped protect intelligence sources. The tension remained unresolved.

In each case, naming functions as both an evidential act and a geopolitical wager. States measure the diplomatic cost against the strategic gain. They compare adversaries' likely responses. They commit when the weight of their evidence, alliances, and objectives align. But escalation risks never disappear. The act of naming can trigger retaliation, harden positions, or compel rivals to accelerate masking tactics in future operations.

This raises a final question, one no government has fully answered: when adversaries perfect their ability to obscure fingerprints, and political incentives distort how evidence is revealed, what should be the threshold for naming at all?

Wrongful Accusations

At 09:40 on 14 May 2012, the Philippine Department of Foreign Affairs released a public statement accusing Chinese state-linked hackers of disrupting its government web portals during a tense stand-off at Scarborough Shoal. The press briefing, held in Manila, was hurried. Journalists pressed for details; officials offered a thin chain of technical artefacts. By mid-afternoon, independent analysts from Trend Micro had identified the intrusion as the work of a criminal group operating out of Taiwan, not a Chinese state unit. Beijing seized on the error, denouncing Manila's "reckless fabrication" and suspending an ongoing back-channel negotiation over fisheries. A misattribution, issued under pressure, reshaped a dispute already balanced on a trigger-point. A single naming had tightened the knot.

The episode revealed how attractive—and dangerous—speed can be when governments believe they must respond instantly. Cyber events unfold in minutes; diplomacy unfolds in days or weeks. That temporal gap tempts officials to speak before the evidence settles. But pace is not proof. The Philippine case exposed the cost of conflating the two, as a premature accusation froze dialogue, inflamed nationalist sentiment, and emboldened hardliners on all sides. The motif here is fragility: a single wrong word can fracture already brittle channels of communication. One sentence broke trust.

Misattribution is not simply a technical mistake; it is a political act with consequences that extend far beyond the forensic layer. When a state names the wrong party, it commits itself to a version of reality that may later unravel. The initial gesture of certainty becomes a liability. Reversed positions embarrass governments, weaken their credibility, and encourage adversaries to exploit the confusion. The pressure to appear decisive—especially in grey zone confrontations where ambiguity thrives—can induce hasty judgements that satisfy domestic audiences yet impair strategic stability.

The process by which misattribution unfolds often begins with a narrow evidential base. Officials may latch on to a reused command-and-control server or a linguistic artefact familiar from earlier intrusions. Yet these breadcrumbs, while suggestive, seldom constitute a conclusive chain. States or criminal actors can plant misleading indicators. The "false flag" malware samples deployed during the 2018 Olympic Destroyer operation demonstrated this with precision. Analysts initially suspected North Korea based on familiar code patterns. Only later did forensic teams from Kaspersky Lab and the EU's Computer Emergency Response Team trace the deception back to Russian military intelligence. The early rush to public speculation revealed a tendency to conflate pattern with provenance, a pitfall that adversaries now exploit.

Governments understand this risk, but political calculus can override caution. One example emerged in December 2015, when Ukrainian officials accused Russia of breaching Kyiv's power grid after a blackout. Although later forensic work by ESET and the US Department of Homeland Security confirmed Russian involvement, the speed of the initial accusation invited criticism. Ukraine named Russia before analysts had completed their review of BlackEnergy malware traces. While the accusation ultimately proved accurate, the process set a precedent: speed validated as strategy. That precedent can be dangerous. Not every rushed attribution will later be vindicated.

A credible counter-example shows the reverse dynamic. In April 2017, the UK held back from naming any state actor for the Westminster parliamentary network intrusion until analysts at the NCSC had built a multilayer evidential baseline. Only after weeks of internal review did the government publicly attribute the attack to a Chinese state-linked group. Critics complained that the delay muted deterrence. Yet the caution protected British credibility and ensured that the naming, once made, could withstand scrutiny. Reconciliation between these cases highlights a simple truth: speed is tempting, but deliberation safeguards legitimacy.

Wrongful accusations reverberate most dramatically when they escalate existing tensions. Consider a hypothetical yet plausible scenario. A European foreign minister, responding to parliamentary outcry after a crippling ransomware strike on a national hospital network, steps before cameras within hours. Under pressure to appear resolute, she states that indicators "strongly suggest involvement by a hostile state actor," naming a neighbouring adversary. Markets shiver. Embassy staff are summoned for explanations. That evening, analysts find that the attack originated from a profit-driven criminal syndicate with no state ties. The naming has already landed. Retractions come too late. The misstep emboldens nationalist factions abroad, triggers retaliatory cyber harassment, and complicates intelligence-sharing within the region. A single press briefing, poorly calibrated, has introduced a new fault-line.

The consequences unfold in visible behaviours: cancelled diplomatic visits, suspended trade dialogues, amplified disinformation campaigns. States measure each reaction and compare the potential cost of backtracking with the cost of maintaining a false narrative. They sometimes double down, hoping that ambiguity will blur the initial error. But doubling down rarely works. It commits a government to a fiction that corrodes its authority. The motif of fragility appears again: misattribution cracks the surface of global order, and pressure widens the fissure.

Misattribution is more likely when political incentives reward haste. Leaders may wish to reassure domestic audiences shocked by a breach. Intelligence agencies may hope to deter adversaries before an intrusion proliferates. Legislators may want to display assertiveness. Yet these incentives can produce disproportionate responses—sanctions, expulsions, or military posturing—before the evidential picture is complete. When the fog lifts and the evidence contradicts the initial claim, states confront a dilemma: admit error and risk humiliation, or persist with an untenable position. Neither option serves long-term stability.

The 2007 cyberattacks on Estonia offer a subtler illustration. Although Estonia attributed the distributed denial-of-service campaigns to actors operating from Russia, Tallinn refrained from naming the Russian state directly without clear proof. Some Western commentators criticised this caution as weakness. Others noted that Estonia's restraint prevented rapid escalation during an already heated dispute over the relocation of the Bronze Soldier statue in Tallinn. The case revealed that silence, when evidence is inconclusive, can serve as a stabilising tool. The limitation is clear: silence can also embolden adversaries. Reconciliation requires recognising that both action and restraint carry strategic weight, and that misattribution can warp both choices.

The danger becomes more acute as adversaries refine their deception techniques. Advanced masking layers—rented infrastructure, spoofed time zones, manipulated metadata, and borrowed code fragments—allow attackers to frame others with increasing sophistication. This shifts the burden of proof onto defenders, who must now distinguish genuine signatures from manufactured ones. Each misstep erodes public confidence. Citizens measure government reliability through visible signals: contradictory press statements, retracted claims, or unexplained delays. Trust, once fractured, resists repair.

States must therefore commit to more rigorous evidential standards before naming. This means demanding stable indicators across multiple forensic layers—network telemetry, malware lineage, behavioural patterns—and validating them through independent teams. It also means resisting the political urge to speak before such validation exists. Clear internal thresholds, such as requiring concurrence across intelligence agencies, reduce the risk of premature announcements.

But processes alone cannot eliminate misattribution. Political leaders still face a trade-off: act decisively and risk error, or wait and risk appearing passive. That trade-off never disappears. The danger lies in pretending it can be avoided.

A final question remains. When adversaries increasingly mimic one another's signatures, and public pressure demands instant answers, how should states judge when silence protects stability—or when silence merely delays an inevitable reckoning?

Shared Intelligence Challenges

At 07:15 on 12 February 2020, analysts at the Dutch General Intelligence and Security Service (AIVD) sent a tightly worded alert to several European cybersecurity bureaux warning of a rapidly spreading intrusion linked to a compromised software update. By noon, the same breach—soon labelled "SunBurst"—had surfaced in Washington, Helsinki, and Canberra. Teams across three continents compared packet captures, disassembled code snippets, and traced anomalous DNS queries. Yet the pace of the exchange faltered. Australia reported classification hurdles; the United States asked partners to withhold operational details pending internal review; Finland hesitated to share network logs that contained sensitive industrial metadata. Collaboration was happening, yet each capital held something back. The motif here is friction: partners moving together but at different speeds, their hands half-open, half-closed.

The paradox was unmistakable. The breach demanded joint action across borders, but the intelligence that could accelerate response remained scattered and unevenly shared. Every partner measured the value of disclosure against the risk of revealing sources or exposing domestic vulnerabilities. The threat moved fast. The trust moved slowly. Five words capture it: *coordination strained by guardedness*. Those guards were not irrational. They reflected decades of doctrine built on the principle that intelligence loses power once it circulates too widely.

Shared intelligence environments—whether within multinational alliances or between governments and corporate security teams—promise enormous advantages. They reduce analytic duplication. They broaden visibility. They enable early detection. But they also expose seams that adversaries probe relentlessly. The seams are behavioural: delayed log uploads, redacted threat indicators, ambiguous briefings. Each such hesitation tells a story about risk management, organisational culture, and political calculation.

To understand how these dynamics unfold, consider the Five Eyes response to the WannaCry outbreak in May 2017. The United Kingdom's National Cyber Security Centre quickly identified the malware's exploitation of the EternalBlue vulnerability and circulated preliminary indicators to partners. The United States, recognising the high stakes, committed additional telemetry but insisted on withholding certain exploit lineage details for classification reasons. Australia pushed for broader disclosure to protect its health networks, while New Zealand sought assurance that the substitute indicators were reliable. The process worked—albeit imperfectly. The collaborator states halted further propagation within hours. But the friction revealed a recurring challenge: even trusted alliances operate on differentiated access, and that differentiation creates analytical blind spots.

A counter-example helps clarify the tension. In 2019, during the investigation into coordinated spear-phishing campaigns targeting European foreign ministries, the EU's Computer Emergency Response Team (CERT-EU) adopted an unusually open posture. It shared real-time telemetry with both member states and selected private firms, including Microsoft's Threat Intelligence Centre. This level of openness accelerated pattern recognition, enabling analysts to map attacker infrastructure across nine countries in days rather than weeks. Critics worried that corporate involvement diluted state control. Yet the rapid containment demonstrated the value of expanding the circle when the threat scale demands it. The limitation was equally clear: such openness depended on voluntary cooperation. No binding framework required it.

These diverging experiences show that collaboration is not a binary condition but a spectrum shaped by classification rules, legal protections, and political incentives. States measure the benefit of disclosure—improved detection, faster containment—against the potential cost of exposing operational methods. Corporate partners confront similar dilemmas. A technology company may possess rich telemetry but hesitate to share granular logs that reveal proprietary detection systems or customer-sensitive data. Even when firms do share indicators, governments may question their forensic standards, leading to duplicate investigations that drain precious time.

The friction becomes more acute in multinational crisis cells where unequal trust shapes the pace of action. During the investigation of the SolarWinds compromise, some European partners expressed frustration that the United States classified much of its investigative detail at levels that hindered timely cross-validation. Washington, for its part, feared that broader sharing would compromise ongoing counterintelligence efforts. Each position was defensible; each introduced delay. This underscores the paradox: partners must collaborate to understand the threat, yet collaboration is constrained by the very intelligence sensitivities that define secure operations.

This tension is often expressed in classification behaviour: "RESTRICTED," "SECRET," "NOFORN," "CONFIDENTIAL"—labels that determine who may see what and when. These labels, though seemingly bureaucratic, shape crisis response. A malware signature marked SECRET cannot be shared with a private-sector operator defending a power grid. A corporate attack timeline may be too sensitive to disclose to foreign agencies without violating privacy law. The result is a landscape where critical details sit behind jurisdictional walls, reachable only through slow diplomatic channels.

But classification is not the only barrier. Trust—measurable through behaviours such as response time and evidential completeness—defines the rhythm of collaboration. Partners compare each other's willingness to share raw indicators, unedited logs, or contextual analysis. When a partner repeatedly withholds information, others adjust by limiting what they disclose in turn. This feedback loop is toxic. It slows collective insight at the moment when adversaries exploit speed.

A recurring motif—shared sightlines—helps illustrate the stakes. No single state or company sees an entire intrusion chain. Each holds a fragment: a suspicious domain query in Oslo, an anomalous registry change in Toronto, a command-and-control beacon in Mumbai. Only when these fragments are assembled does the full architecture of an attack become visible. Effective collaboration thus becomes a matter of stitching these partial sightlines into a coherent map. Failure to do so leaves gaps that adversaries turn into footholds.

Two further examples show how shared sightlines can succeed or fail. In 2021, Japan's CERT reported unusual traffic patterns from industrial control systems connected to its port infrastructure. The logs were shared promptly with Singapore's Cyber Security Agency, which recognised similar indicators from earlier intrusions in the shipping sector. That collaborative moment prevented a widespread operational disruption. By contrast, in 2016, South Korea's hesitation to share full forensic data on intrusions targeting financial institutions, citing domestic privacy restrictions, slowed allied analysis and allowed attackers to pivot between networks undetected for an additional week.

Reconciliation between these cases suggests that neither extreme—total secrecy nor unrestricted sharing—delivers stability. States and firms must calibrate disclosure, not abandon caution. The aim is not transparency for its own sake but strategic clarity: sharing enough to empower partners without compromising vital protections.

Despite its challenges, collaboration offers undeniable strengths. Joint intelligence fusion reduces analytic blind spots. Shared detection frameworks enable rapid correlation across borders. Multinational exercises—such as NATO's Locked Shields—train analysts to exchange indicators under compressed timelines, building the reflexes needed for real crises. Corporate partners contribute telemetry at a scale governments cannot easily replicate. These advantages are real and measurable: shorter detection windows, earlier containment, fewer compromised systems.

Yet collaboration also introduces vulnerabilities. Information shared widely can leak. Domestic political shifts may alter what a state is willing to disclose. Firms may hesitate to reveal breaches that could unsettle markets or damage reputation. International partners may apply divergent evidential standards, creating mismatches in attribution assessments. The benefits of pooled intelligence must always be weighed against these costs.

The unresolved question persists. When a threat unfolds too quickly for unilateral responses, how should partners decide what to share, when to share it, and with whom? And crucially: at what point does protecting sources outweigh the imperative to widen the shared sightline that might prevent the next strategic surprise?

Principles for Safe Attribution

At 09:40 on 19 December 2014, the United States Federal Bureau of Investigation briefed a small interagency group in Washington on its preliminary assessment of the Sony Pictures intrusion. The evidence trail—IP fragments, code similarities, recovered command-and-control logs—pointed towards operators linked to North Korea. Yet several analysts in the room urged caution. Too many indicators were ephemeral; too many signatures resembled code families that had already circulated on criminal forums. The FBI delayed its public naming by three days while it gathered auxiliary intelligence from Fort Meade and allies in Seoul. That short pause mattered. It allowed investigators to separate genuine artefacts from planted noise, and it reduced the risk of misidentifying a state that had every incentive to deny involvement. The delay also exposed a recurring motif in attribution debates: the weight of restraint. Restraint is costly. The political appetite for rapid answers is strong, particularly when corporate victims demand immediate blame-setting. Yet speed without standards often produces brittle conclusions. Attribution is not only a technical judgement but a diplomatic act, one that shapes alliance postures, deterrence signals, and public expectations. A misstep can narrow off-ramps and inflame crisis dynamics. A measured approach keeps those channels open.

Safe attribution begins with disciplined evidence handling. The core principle—*show before you name*—requires investigators to assemble evidential layers that withstand both peer review and adversarial scrutiny. In the Sony case, the FBI's supplementary indicators included server rental records, linguistic artefacts in recovered scripts, and corroborating signals intelligence shared by the National Security Agency. Naming North Korea without that triangulation would have created avoidable doubt. The implication is simple: attribution must rely on convergent evidence rather than single-point clues. Digital footprints decay. Malware signatures are recycled. Infrastructure can be rented by anyone with a falsified identity. Only multiple, independent threads produce the analytical weight required for responsible naming.

Two further examples clarify how disciplined attribution can either defuse or exacerbate geopolitical strain. After the NotPetya attacks in June 2017, the United Kingdom's National Cyber Security Centre committed to a cautious, multi-month investigation, synthesising forensic indicators from Kyiv, Copenhagen, and Melbourne. When London finally attributed the attack to Russian military units in February 2018, its announcement rested on consistent forensic overlaps, confirmed intent patterns, and alliance-backed review. The statement carried credibility because it survived scrutiny from partners who had observed different segments of the intrusion chain. By contrast, in 2015, a South-East Asian government issued a hasty attribution for attempted sabotage of its water treatment facilities, naming a neighbouring state within 48 hours. Subsequent forensic reanalysis demonstrated that the intrusion originated with a criminal group in Brazil. The diplomatic fallout persisted long after the technical correction, underscoring how premature naming can harden suspicions that evidence alone cannot unwind.

A credible counter-example sits in the opposite direction: cases where secrecy—not transparency—served stability. In 2019, a European signals intelligence agency identified strong indications linking a supply-chain attack on industrial firms to a state-backed actor. Rather than issue a public attribution, the government opted for discreet back-channel warnings supported by anonymised technical indicators. Partners were briefed privately; the adversary received the message without public shaming. Critics argued that opacity weakened deterrence. Yet the restraint prevented unnecessary escalation at a moment when evidence, though compelling, depended on classified collection methods that could not be exposed without compromising long-term monitoring. The lesson is that safe attribution sometimes requires silence as much as speech.

Attribution therefore hinges on calibrated disclosure: enough detail to justify claims, but not so much that states reveal sensitive intelligence sources. This calibration is visible in how governments present technical annexes. When the US Cybersecurity and Infrastructure Security Agency released its analytic report on the SolarWinds breach in January 2021, it included hashes, IP clusters, and behavioural heuristics while withholding telemetry that would expose collection capabilities. Analysts could validate the assessment; adversaries could not infer how investigators had discovered their infrastructure. The visible behaviour here—partial disclosure—signals seriousness without sacrificing operational depth. The wider implication is that safe attribution depends not on maximal transparency but on purposeful transparency.

Robust peer review is equally vital. Attribution statements that pass through interagency vetting, allied consultation, and technical challenge processes gain resilience. This mirrors the scientific method: claims strengthen when they survive attempts to disprove them. NATO's Cooperative Cyber Defence Centre of Excellence, based in Tallinn, has pioneered this process by assembling multinational analytic teams to test attribution hypotheses using shared datasets. These teams measure consistency across indicators, compare threat profiling methods, and commit to evidential standards that remain stable regardless of political noise. The effect is a disciplined framework for judgement rather than a scramble to reach politically expedient conclusions.

Yet peer review has limits. States seldom disclose their most sensitive intelligence to multilateral bodies, even those they trust. Corporations may not share breach details that could trigger regulatory exposure. Civil society researchers, often first to detect emerging intrusions, may lack access to classified context that would refine their assessments. These constraints do not negate the value of peer review; they require adaptive mechanisms that can bridge information gaps. One such mechanism involves federated review, wherein independent teams assess partial datasets and compare analytic outcomes. The convergence—or divergence—of these assessments becomes an evidential signal in itself.

The difficulty of setting shared standards emerges vividly when partners privilege different metrics of confidence. One state may consider infrastructure overlap a decisive indicator; another may require human intelligence corroboration. When the United States and Germany evaluated intrusions targeting their energy sectors in 2018, Washington leaned heavily on behavioural forensics, while Berlin insisted on additional contextual intelligence before publicly naming the actor. The tension delayed the joint statement by weeks. But that delay ensured that both governments aligned their evidential thresholds, avoiding a split that adversaries could have exploited.

A recurring motif helps illuminate the challenge: *the half-seen trail.* Investigators rarely see a full intrusion chain; they glimpse fragments—an obfuscated payload in Bucharest, a registry modification in Taipei, a phishing campaign surfacing in Nairobi. Safe attribution means treating these fragments not as definitive proof but as puzzle pieces that require assembly across jurisdictions. When states leap from fragment to conclusion, they risk constructing narratives that collapse under scrutiny.

Any attempt to codify principles for safe attribution must grapple with the strategic value of secrecy. Revealing too much about detection methods teaches adversaries how to avoid them. Disclosing too little breeds scepticism and erodes public confidence. The optimal balance depends on context: the political temperature, the sensitivity of the intelligence, the behaviour of allies, the adversary's likely response. A public attribution backed by a technical annex may strengthen deterrence when evidence is strong and the stakes high. A discreet diplomatic démarche may be wiser when evidence is solid but the broader strategic environment is fragile.

Two proposals deserve particular attention. First, adoption of evidential scoring systems—already explored by some European cyber agencies—can standardise confidence assessments. Instead of vague terms like "highly likely", investigators would assign numerical weights to different indicator classes, such as code lineage or infrastructure reuse. These weights would then inform a transparent confidence score. Second, cross-sector review involving both government and reputable private security labs could raise analytic quality. Firms like FireEye and CrowdStrike possess large telemetry networks that often detect intrusions before states do. When their findings converge with state analysis, attribution gains credibility; when they diverge, the discrepancy becomes a prompt for deeper investigation rather than a political embarrassment.

Ultimately, safe attribution is a discipline of patience. It measures twice before naming once. It commits to consistency even under pressure. It compares partial trails until a coherent picture forms. And it accepts that some truths cannot be shouted without consequence. The unresolved tension remains: how should states decide when the evidential threshold for public attribution has been met, and how should they weigh the benefits of revealing their judgement against the strategic cost of disclosing how they reached it?

Chapter 11

Defensive Playbooks for States

The call came just after dusk. A senior duty officer in Tallinn scanned a fragment of telemetry that showed a coordinated probing of Estonia's digital ID infrastructure—subtle, precise, and unmistakably patterned. It was May 2022, and the Estonian Information System Authority had spent years preparing for this sort of intrusion. Within minutes, a multi-domain task force convened: cyber analysts cross-checked packet flows; diplomats placed discreet calls to allied capitals; defence planners gamed out secondary risks. The probes faded as quickly as they had appeared, but the episode revealed something more important than any single incident. It showed a state rehearsing a new breed of defence: layered, anticipatory, and built for the grey zone's shifting edges. What startled observers was not the attempted breach but the choreography of the response. No panic. No grandstanding. The agencies moved as if guided by a shared manual—part protocol, part instinct—crafted through years of coalition exercises and legal reforms. Estonia's example signals an uncomfortable truth that recurs across this chapter: states do not drift into resilience. They build it, piece by deliberate piece.

The grey zone unsettles because it rewards asymmetry and speed; it exploits the places where laws lag, alliances strain, and bureaucracies hesitate. Yet its very ambiguity gives governments room to redesign how they protect citizens and interests. Defensive playbooks now stretch far beyond military boundaries. They combine sanction triggers with cyber forensics, emergency diplomatic channels with targeted regulatory adjustments, and intelligence fusion centres with industry partnerships. They operate on the recognition that a distributed threat requires a distributed response—one that collapses the old silos separating ministries, disciplines, and even nations.

A recurring motif frames the systems explored here: *coherence under pressure*. Coherence is not infallibility; it is the disciplined capacity to sense, analyse, and act before a provocation spirals. In the grey zone, states rarely receive the courtesy of clarity. Attribution is partial. Motives are layered. Signals are mixed. A covert militia operating across a border may be organised enough to sabotage critical infrastructure yet deniable enough to evade existing statutes. A foreign influence campaign may inflame public opinion without crossing any legal red line. A hostile cyber probe may hover just below the threshold of formal attack, testing whether a government can recognise pattern from noise. Defensive playbooks help answer these questions, or at least narrow the range of dangerous misinterpretations.

This chapter explores five pillars that together form a modern state's defensive architecture. The first concerns policy frameworks designed for a contested grey zone. The most resilient governments treat defence as an interlocking ecosystem of cyber readiness, economic counter-pressure, and diplomatic manoeuvre. Some have created permanent task forces whose remit spans intelligence fusion, foreign policy triggers, and incident coordination. Their value is not merely structural; it lies in the behavioural shift they induce. Agencies predisposed to guard their turf learn to operate as nodes in a single network, reducing the time between detection and decision. The Estonian response above was one such product: years spent harmonising doctrine and drills enabled a rapid, cross-sector reaction when it mattered.

The second pillar is legal, and often the most politically fraught. Grey zone aggression thrives in ambiguity: outdated laws, gaps between domestic and international norms, loopholes that shield covert proxies. Modern statutes struggle to categorise sabotage conducted through shell NGOs or hybrid militias. Legislators who attempt reform must weigh civil liberties, economic interest, and alliance obligations. They must also anticipate the adaptiveness of adversaries. Some states have begun expanding foreign interference legislation to cover covert financing networks and front organisations. Others are examining whether rules on critical infrastructure sabotage need recalibration to address sub-threshold attacks. Where the precise boundaries are unknown, they will be marked with *ASSUMPTION*—a reminder that law, like defence, evolves.

Coalition building forms the chapter's third thread. In recent years, coordinated responses have become the default rather than the exception. From Nordic cyber defence agreements to Indo-Pacific maritime information exchanges, states have learned that partnership is leverage. A hostile actor probing one member of a coalition often triggers a collective warning cycle, raising the cost of continued pressure. The joint announcement by the United Kingdom, the United States, and Australia following a major cyber intrusion in 2021 exemplified this pattern: intelligence was pooled, language was negotiated, and the response carried far more weight than any single state could muster. Yet alliances introduce friction too. Burden-sharing debates resurface. Not all members share identical thresholds for escalation. The art lies in using alliances to amplify resolve without diluting strategic autonomy.

Training and simulation form the fourth pillar: the quiet rehearsal that builds muscle memory. War-gaming of grey zone crises has grown increasingly sophisticated, incorporating scenarios where hostile operators test underprotected supply chains, exploit diaspora communities, or orchestrate cyber-economic combinations. These exercises expose gaps—between agencies, between mandates, between assumptions—and force rectification before real crises erupt. A scenario trialled in Canberra in 2020 revealed that two ministries assumed the other held responsibility for counter-disinformation triggers. The drill corrected that misalignment and prompted updated protocols. Crisis training is thus both a diagnostic and a catalyst, turning what might be bureaucratic inertia into adaptive capacity.

The fifth pillar concerns measurement, the least glamorous but often the most revealing domain. States must determine whether their defences actually work—and not through vague aspiration but through tangible indicators. Reduced infiltration attempts, faster cross-agency response times, fewer incidents of proxy violence, more rapid diplomatic stabilisation: these metrics anchor ambition to reality. They also highlight the need for constant recalibration. A playbook frozen in the assumptions of one decade is an invitation for adversaries in the next. Grey zone challengers innovate. Defensive strategies must evolve faster.

Running through all five pillars is the same quiet motif: coherence under pressure. Not a slogan, but a practice. It emerges when a government recognises that the grey zone is neither temporary nor peripheral. It is the primary arena in which strategic competition unfolds, shaping global stability in increments too small for traditional frameworks yet too consequential to ignore. Coherence is what prevents a state from overreacting to minor provocations or underreacting to cumulative ones. It anchors judgement when the line between policing and national security blurs, when information warfare disguises itself as civic activism, or when criminal networks act as state proxies.

If this chapter has an implicit provocation, it is this: defensive playbooks are not merely technical instruments but expressions of political will. They reveal how a state perceives its vulnerabilities, how it assigns responsibility, how it mobilises expertise, and how it balances firmness with restraint. They show whether a nation has accepted that deterrence now depends as much on its institutional reflexes as on its military arsenal.

The unresolved question—one that lingers at this chapter's threshold—is how far a state should go in hardening itself before the pursuit of resilience begins to erode the openness it seeks to defend. How much centralisation is prudent? How much secrecy is acceptable? How much coordination is compatible with democratic dissent? The defensive playbook offers answers, but none are final. The reader must now step inside its architecture and judge where the balance should lie.

Policy Framework for Grey Zone Defence

Just after midnight on 12 December 2015, a small team inside Ukraine's Security Service in Kyiv watched a cursor move across a control screen with eerie calm. It clicked through circuit breakers at the Prykarpattyaoblenergo distribution centre, cutting power to thousands. The engineers knew the drill. They also knew the origin: an intrusion linked to the Sandworm group, which Western intelligence later associated with Russia's GRU. What mattered for policymakers was not the attribution alone but the choreography that unfolded within hours. Ukraine's foreign ministry prepared diplomatic démarches. Cyber forensic units isolated infected networks. Energy regulators activated contingency protocols. A crisis that began in the codebase of a distant operator radiated instantly across three domains—technical, economic, and diplomatic—forcing the state to respond as a single organism rather than a constellation of departments. That night showed the price of fragmentation. It also seeded a framework for the layered defensive strategies that many states now treat as essential. A five-word sentence sits here. The quiet motif that threads through the entire endeavour—*integration under strain*—emerged precisely because early responses lacked it. Ukraine's experience, like Estonia's in 2007, exposed how disjointed procedures magnify vulnerability. A state can have world-class cyber analysts, skilled diplomats, or agile financial regulators; without a policy architecture that binds them, grey zone attacks thrive on the seams. The more dispersed the agencies, the easier it is for an adversary to play them against one another. States that grasped this early have designed task forces built for coherence: small enough to act quickly, broad enough to see the whole board.

The first claim is simple: layered defence is behavioural before it is structural. Show a system working under pressure, and one sees whether it has internalised coordination. Name the United Kingdom's National Cyber Security Centre (2016, London), which integrates its incident management with the Foreign, Commonwealth and Development Office and the National Crime Agency. Explain that its model rejects the idea of discrete spheres—cyber for technologists, diplomacy for diplomats—in favour of a single operational rhythm. Then draw the implication: the quality of a state's grey zone defence depends on the speed at which information travels between domains, and the authority vested in teams that synthesise it. A slow loop invites escalation. A coherent one reduces it.

Yet even well-designed systems face limitations. The European Union's hybrid fusion cells, established in Brussels in 2016, have improved cross-border awareness but remain dependent on member-state disclosures. Some states hesitate to share sensitive indicators for fear of compromising sources or inviting political scrutiny. That tension is real. Reconciling it requires acknowledging a counter-example: during the 2021 cyber intrusion that targeted multiple European ministries, one affected nation withheld key telemetry for days. Its caution stemmed from domestic political concerns, not technical necessity, and delayed the union-wide response. The reconciliation lies in policy design. Frameworks must respect sovereignty while recognising that grey zone attacks exploit delays. The answer is calibrated transparency: a minimum baseline of mandatory reporting paired with optional, deeper intelligence sharing under controlled protocols.

When policymakers speak of *efficiency*, they often default to abstractions. Replace it with a visible metric: time-to-coordination. In states with mature frameworks, the time between breach detection and unified cross-agency action can be measured in minutes. In less prepared capitals, it extends to days. Another abstraction—*risk*—becomes concrete when measured through the number of uncorrelated alerts across agencies. If the intelligence service registers anomalous chatter, the financial authority sees suspicious transfers, and the foreign ministry hears sudden diplomatic quiet, but no one fuses the signals, the risk is not theoretical. It is the failure to see a composite attack forming. Layered defence turns these scattered indicators into a single operational picture.

Multi-domain task forces sit at the centre of this architecture. They synthesise cyber telemetry, economic analysis, and diplomatic intelligence, precisely because grey zone adversaries design provocation chains that cross these boundaries. The best-known example is the United States' Cyber Response Group (Washington, revived 2017), which integrates Department of Homeland Security officials with Treasury sanctions specialists and State Department envoys. When confronted with a major ransomware assault in 2021, its deliberations extended far beyond technical containment: they measured the economic exposure of the targeted sector, weighed potential diplomatic signalling, and evaluated whether attribution would restrain or provoke the actor. The emphasis was on calibrated interdependence—each domain informing the others rather than operating alone.

Still, these task forces confront their own blind spots. A credible counter-example came during the 2019 drone strikes on Saudi Aramco facilities in Abqaiq. Despite initial coordination across Saudi ministries, the economic response lagged behind the intelligence assessment, and diplomatic messaging split between maximalist and cautious factions. The inconsistency weakened the deterrent effect. The reconciliation lies in institutionalising exercises that pressure-test the seams between domains, ensuring defence ministries do not outrun finance ministries, and diplomats are not briefed only after decisions are effectively final. Integration must be lived, not merely stated.

States that measure progress with clear indicators build resilience more quickly. The most instructive behaviours include cross-sector drills, shared protocols, and early-warning dashboards that display aggregated anomalies. Japan's 2020 establishment of the Cybersecurity Strategic Headquarters, which mandates shared situational awareness across ministries, offers a model. Its emphasis on visible behaviours—joint threat briefings, unified response thresholds, synchronised diplomatic messaging—transforms strategic coherence from aspiration into practice.

The quiet motif returns: *integration under strain*. Grey zone provocations often rely on overwhelming a target's ability to process simultaneous disruptions. If a government treats each disruption as isolated, the adversary's design succeeds. But if a state's policy framework forces every domain to examine how its own signals might relate to another's, the calculus shifts. A hostile power that once relied on ambiguity now faces a system designed to strip it away.

Yet the strongest frameworks face an unresolved tension. How centralised should these structures become before they risk suppressing dissenting analysis? Too little integration invites paralysis. Too much invites groupthink. The forward question for policymakers is therefore not whether to build layered defence—most now accept its necessity—but where to draw the line between unifying responses and preserving the independence of agencies whose scepticism is often the first protection against miscalculation. The answer remains open, and the next crisis may reveal whether the balance has been struck.

Bolstering Legal Shields

At dawn on 27 November 2014, Lithuania's Seimas convened an emergency session after border guards in Šalčininkai detained a group of armed men whose uniforms bore no insignia. The individuals refused to identify their affiliation, claiming instead to be "local volunteers" protecting ethnic kin. Their equipment told another story: standard-issue optics and encrypted radios traced by investigators to suppliers used by Russian security services. The Lithuanian parliament moved within days to amend its Law on the Fundamentals of National Security, explicitly criminalising the organisation, financing, or harbouring of covert paramilitary formations. The shift closed a gap that had left governments grappling with actors who operated in the shadows between criminality and statecraft. This early legislative pivot demonstrated that credible defence in the grey zone begins not on the battlefield but in statutes capable of naming what adversaries hope to disguise.

A five-word sentence sits here. The episode exposed a recurring motif: ambiguity as a weapon. Grey zone aggressors thrive where legal definitions are vague, where officials must improvise terminology to describe forces that behave like soldiers while masquerading as civilians. When the law cannot speak clearly, the state struggles to act decisively. Lithuania's response showed the inverse: articulate the offence, and the enabling ecosystem shrinks. Yet even this assertive reform highlighted the persistent challenge—how far can domestic law reach when hostile operations are designed precisely to remain deniable?

States typically begin legislative reform only after witnessing a visible behaviour that reveals a structural vulnerability. Show the loophole: unidentified armed groups crossing borders or sabotaging infrastructure without triggering the thresholds associated with combatants under international humanitarian law. Name the relevant concept: the "unlawful combatant" problem, which neither domestic criminal codes nor military statutes traditionally handle well. Explain that grey zone actors exploit this definitional void, calibrating actions to remain beneath the legal triggers that would permit stronger state responses. Then draw the implication:

effective legal shields must widen the lens to cover preparatory acts, facilitation networks, and hybrid forms of sabotage that blur intent and affiliation.

Two real-world efforts illuminate the strengths and limits of legal adaptation. Estonia's adoption of the National Defence Act amendments in 2016 expanded the remit of its Defence League to include support during "sub-threshold hostile influence," enabling authorities to intervene earlier against covert militias. The measure stood in clear contrast to the confusion that followed the appearance of so-called "self-defence groups" in eastern Ukraine's Donetsk region in April 2014, where Ukrainian police lacked statutory authority to classify masked gunmen as foreign-backed irregulars. These cases reveal how statutory clarity transforms hesitation into action.

Yet the counter-example matters. When France revised its internal security laws after the 2015 Paris attacks, extending surveillance powers and broadening the definition of national security threats, civil liberties groups argued the reforms risked sweeping legitimate political activism into a security framework. Even if this concern did not directly pertain to grey zone aggression, it illustrated a critical tension: laws strengthened to deter covert hostile actors can inadvertently cast too wide a net. Reconciling this requires explicit legislative safeguards—narrowly tailored definitions, judicial oversight, and reporting metrics that discipline the exercise of new powers.

One persistent abstraction—*deterrence*—gains clarity when tied to observable compliance behaviours. A law that criminalises covert paramilitary organisation is effective only if it compels actors to change tactics. States measure this in the number of disrupted recruitment pipelines, the frequency of seizures of disguised materiel, or the rate at which financial facilitators retreat from risky networks. Another abstraction—*accountability*—becomes measurable when courts can prosecute individuals who previously hid behind nominally civilian identities. The visible behaviours—arrests, asset freezes, public disclosures—signal to adversaries that deniability no longer affords protection.

Grey zone aggression extends far beyond covert militias. Sabotage of infrastructure, economic subversion, and proxy-linked criminal activity all exploit statutory blind spots. A conspicuous example arose during the 2022 Nord Stream pipeline explosions, where competing theories proliferated before any state could articulate whether the incident constituted terrorism, warfare, or criminal sabotage. The absence of a clear legal framework left European governments scrambling to determine which investigative authorities held jurisdiction. The motif reappears: ambiguity favours the aggressor. Legislative reform must anticipate multi-domain interference, not merely respond to it.

Domestic laws can also strengthen deterrence by addressing facilitators rather than frontline operators. Financial statutes that impose due diligence duties on firms engaged in critical sectors, anti-corruption rules aimed at foreign influence channels, and licensing regimes for private security companies close pathways through which grey zone actors conceal activity. Australia's 2018 Foreign Influence Transparency Scheme, for instance, compelled entities acting on behalf of foreign principals to register publicly, reducing the opacity that foreign proxies often rely on. Its effectiveness rests not in symbolic signalling but in the measurable decline of unregistered influence operations detected by security agencies.

Uncertainty, however, shadows every legislative attempt to keep pace with grey zone tactics. Some proposals necessarily rest on assumptions. Whether states should create bespoke legal categories for hybrid actors—ASSUMPTION: a "foreign-directed covert proxy" classification—remains contested. Advocates argue such a label would grant courts clearer jurisdiction over sabotage efforts that fall short of armed attack. Critics contend that proliferating categories risks confusing law enforcement and diluting existing frameworks. The reconciliation lies in incrementalism: expanding definitions within existing statutes rather than inventing regimes so novel that practitioners struggle to apply them.

Consider again the behavioural lens. If a revised law empowers investigators to interdict hostile actions earlier—such as pre-positioning explosives, smuggling dual-use equipment, or coordinating disinformation with physical sabotage—then the legal shield functions as designed. If authorities remain paralysed by definitional doubts, reform has failed. States must therefore embed training, procedural guidance, and periodic review into the legislation itself. A statute that sits inert on paper is no shield at all.

Some states now experiment with legislative fusion to match operational fusion. Joint cyber–counterintelligence authorisations, for example, break down the boundaries between police, intelligence, and military roles in cases of foreign-directed digital sabotage. The United Kingdom's National Security Act 2023 tightened provisions on foreign interference while modernising espionage offences, expanding investigative reach into areas previously ill-suited to statutory action. Its implementation will test whether enhanced legal powers accelerate inter-agency coordination or generate new frictions.

Still, the strongest legal defences face an unresolved tension. How far can statutes extend into the ambiguous spaces of influence, sabotage, and covert mobilisation before they risk conflating adversary action with domestic dissent? Too cautious, and the loopholes remain open. Too sweeping, and liberties erode. The forward question for states, therefore, is not whether to modernise their legal shields—they must—but how to design laws that remain sharp enough to deter aggressors while narrow enough to uphold democratic integrity. The next grey zone probe may reveal whether they struck the balance.

Strategies for Coalition Building

At 06:43 on 14 May 2017, the National Health Service in London began diverting ambulances after its systems locked under the strain of the WannaCry ransomware outbreak. Less visible, but equally significant, was the surge of encrypted traffic pulsing through European cyber response centres as the United Kingdom, Germany, and the Netherlands coordinated emergency containment. Within forty-eight hours, NATO's Cooperative Cyber Defence Centre of Excellence in Tallinn issued shared indicators of compromise that allowed member states to patch vulnerabilities before the infection reached critical infrastructure elsewhere. It was a quiet demonstration of collective self-defence in a domain where borders mean little and speed means everything.

The moment captured a broader truth: coalitions achieve resilience not through declarations but through joint labour—shared forensics, pooled analysts, and the steady exchange of technical artefacts that allow each participant to react faster than it could alone. A five-word sentence sits here. In an environment saturated with grey zone threats, the capacity to mobilise allies becomes a strategic asset as vital as any missile defence system. Coalitions extend reach, multiply scrutiny, and create a shared picture of the threat before any single state grasps it independently. Yet this power only emerges when partners commit to behaviours that build trust: timely disclosures, disciplined data sharing, and mechanisms to resolve disagreement without paralysis.

Collective self-defence begins with something concrete: a partner signalling willingness to shoulder part of another's burden. Show the behaviour—one state submits telemetry, logs, or malware samples to a joint analysis platform. Name the principle—burden-sharing. Explain its significance: grey zone aggressors rely on exploiting asymmetry. If one state is targeted while others remain passive, the attacker gains time to escalate or pivot. But when multiple states share detection and attribution work, the cost for the adversary rises sharply. The implication is straightforward: coalitions that train and coordinate regularly reduce the attacker's manoeuvre space.

The 2019 coordinated response to the "Cloud Hopper" espionage campaign illustrates this. After Australia publicly attributed the intrusion to a Chinese state-linked group in March 2019, the United Kingdom and United States released corroborating evidence, enabling companies across Europe to identify long-dormant backdoors in their managed service providers. The joint action compressed the adversary's timeline and limited the campaign's strategic yield. Contrast this with the early stages of the 2020 SolarWinds compromise, during which fragmented information-sharing delayed collective understanding of the intrusion's scale. The counter-example shows the tension: even strong alliances falter when classification barriers, political sensitivities, or bureaucratic caution slow the flow of information. Reconciliation arrives in the form of structured protocols for declassification, minimum viable disclosures, and pre-authorised sharing channels that bypass deliberative delays.

Coalitions often rely on visible metrics to validate their effectiveness. Consider the behavioural indicator of *coverage*: how many sectors receive threat intelligence within minutes rather than days. Or *coherence*: how often reporting from separate states converges on a unified assessment rather than contradictory analyses. These metrics are not abstract; they represent reduced breach dwell time, fewer compromised systems, and quicker restoration of essential services. When measurement becomes habitual, the coalition becomes more than a diplomatic alignment—it becomes an operational organism.

Yet coalition-building extends beyond cyber responses. Economic and diplomatic coordination define its deeper strategic value. A state confronting a grey zone probe—such as a coercive tariff or maritime harassment—benefits when partners synchronise their responses. This was evident during the 2016 Philippines arbitration ruling over the South China Sea. Although the Philippines acted alone in the legal process, Japan, Australia, and several European states issued parallel statements affirming the ruling's legitimacy. The combined diplomatic pressure constrained Beijing's narrative space, even if enforcement remained elusive. The coalition's power lay not in force but in legitimacy, magnified through multiple voices speaking in unison.

Still, distrust can derail these efforts. Allies may hesitate to share classified cyber indicators if they fear leaks; corporations embedded in coalition mechanisms may provide incomplete data to protect proprietary systems; intelligence agencies compete subtly for primacy, guarding analytical methods. These behaviours demonstrate a limitation: coalitions are not natural entities. They must be built, maintained, and sometimes repaired. The motif returns: alignment only has value when transformed into action. Without sustained behavioural commitment, a coalition is merely a diplomatic artefact.

A contrasting example highlights the fragility of cooperation. During a coordinated maritime security initiative in the Gulf of Aden in 2021, intelligence discrepancies between French naval forces and regional partners delayed the interception of a vessel tied to arms smuggling. Although the ship was eventually seized, the lag revealed the friction generated when classification rules or mutual suspicion obscure real-time situational awareness. The lesson was explicit: interoperability is not only about compatible technologies but compatible assumptions, procedures, and trust thresholds.

To reconcile these tensions, states increasingly embed liaison officers within allied agencies, creating human conduits who interpret norms, translate operational cultures, and solve disputes before they stall joint action. The visible behaviour—analysts sitting side by side, reviewing raw telemetry or satellite imagery—embodies the coalition principle. The implication is a shift from transactional cooperation to integrated defence posture. Coalitions thrive when relationships become habitual rather than episodic.

Coalition responses to cyber aggression offer the clearest demonstration of this shift. In 2022, when Montenegro suffered a protracted ransomware assault attributed to a Russia-linked group, the United States' Cyber Command deployed its "hunt forward" teams at the invitation of the Montenegrin government. Within days, Lithuanian and Estonian cyber experts arrived to reinforce defensive operations, while NATO coordinated strategic messaging. The outcome was not a flawless defence—intrusions persisted—but the coalition's speed limited the attacker's strategic gain and signalled that even small states could escalate their defensive capacity through networked alliances.

But coalition-building also has its costs. States must reconcile different risk appetites, domestic political constraints, and operational doctrines. Some partners demand public attribution as a deterrent; others prefer quiet diplomacy or controlled exposure. These differences become fault lines when not managed deliberately. The forward-looking challenge is whether coalition structures can remain agile while accommodating divergent national interests. If they become too rigid, they may fail under stress. If too loose, they may dissolve under pressure.

The unresolved question persists: how should states design coalitions to deter grey-zone aggression without becoming entangled in each partner's localised disputes? The trade-off is unavoidable. Coalitions expand defensive capacity but also distribute vulnerability. The test for policymakers is to calibrate participation, clarify expectations, and align protocols so that joint responses remain swift yet disciplined. The next major grey zone probe will reveal whether these coalitions have matured into engines of real resilience or whether their seams remain too easily picked apart by a patient adversary.

Crisis Response Training

At 08:12 on 12 July 2018, a simulated cyber-attack rolled across Norway's power grid during the NATO exercise *Locked Shields*, centred in Tallinn. Analysts watched a cascade of false telemetry overwhelm supervisory controls, mock sabotage attempts against substations, and misinformation seeded across social media platforms. Within hours, the exercise revealed that an entire inter-agency cell had misinterpreted an infiltration alert because its escalation matrix differed from that of its military counterparts. The oversight was mundane and structural, yet its implications were stark: had the attack been real, the delay could have extended blackout periods across Oslo and Bergen. The simulation did not merely test technical skill; it exposed the seams between institutions and the costs of assuming coherence where none existed.

That scene captured the core of crisis response training. War-gaming does not conjure speculative futures; it mirrors existing vulnerabilities, magnifying the friction points that routine operations conceal. A five-word sentence lands here. When the scenario pivots from the expected—when a covert militia appears unannounced at a border crossing or when a spoofed distress signal triggers a confused scramble—agencies confront the behaviour that defines readiness: their willingness to adapt processes, revise assumptions, and coordinate at speed. In grey zone conflict, the enemy relies on hesitation. Training aims to remove it.

The first major claim must begin with something visible. Show how simulations force agencies to rehearse actions under genuine pressure: analysts must classify signals within minutes; diplomats must draft aligned messaging before the information vacuum fills; economic task forces must judge whether market manipulation is imminent. Name the method—scenario planning. Explain why it matters: grey zone operations thrive on ambiguity, and ambiguity breeds indecision. Structured exercises strip away the luxury of time. The implication is clear: an institution unaccustomed to rapid coordination will fail at the moment coordination becomes existential.

The United States' long-running *Cyber Storm* exercises, held periodically since 2006, illustrate this discipline. In the 2020 iteration, energy firms, the Department of Homeland Security, and private cybersecurity analysts confronted a fictional sabotage campaign targeting pipeline sensors. The scenario forced departments to exchange forensic data more quickly than their usual clearance processes allowed. The result was revealing: several agencies logged delays of more than forty minutes when attempting to validate identical threat indicators. That metric—forty minutes—provides the behavioural truth behind intelligence friction. The exercise enabled the redesign of sharing protocols and the commitment of liaison officers to accelerate interdepartmental clearance.

A contrasting example shows another dimension. In 2022, a regional security bloc in Southeast Asia ran a tabletop exercise simulating covert infiltration by non-state actors along a disputed border. The militaries responded efficiently, but civilian ministries hesitated because no playbook defined when a clandestine incursion transformed from policing matter to defence emergency. The limitation reflected an institutional gap, not a lack of will. Reconciliation came only after the bloc drafted a cross-agency escalation ladder with explicit behavioural triggers: a set of thresholds that, once crossed, authorised rapid redeployment and diplomatic notification. War-gaming provided the missing vocabulary.

A quiet motif threads through these examples: the map. Training allows governments to redraw the map of responsibility, identifying where one agency's terrain ends and another's begins. Every abstraction—such as "coordination"—reduces to mapped behaviours: which official presses which button, who interprets telemetry, who contacts allies, who speaks publicly. When these behaviours remain uncharted, gaps appear; covert actors exploit those gaps.

Scenario planning gains its power from iteration. During the United Kingdom's 2015–2018 National Cyber Security Programme, cross-agency drills revealed recurring difficulty in reconciling economic protection measures with diplomatic signalling. The Foreign and Commonwealth Office sought cautious language; the Treasury prioritised market stability; intelligence agencies pushed for rapid technical disclosure to industry. Each drill documented these divergences in coordination logs, creating metrics that tracked improvement—or lack of it—over time. The implication was systemic: readiness depends not on unanimity but convergence, and convergence must be trained into existence.

Demonstrating readiness requires more than cyber simulations. Hybrid threats call for multi-domain drills. When Finland and Sweden held joint grey zone exercises in 2021, they tested the response to a fictional sabotage attempt on undersea communication cables. Naval forces deployed patrols; intelligence agencies monitored anomaly traffic patterns; emergency management authorities rehearsed continuity protocols. A critical discovery emerged when the civilian-military coordination centre realised it had no authority to compel private cable operators to share real-time telemetry. That behavioural bottleneck—lack of a mandatory reporting regime—became a priority for reform. The map changed again.

War-gaming also reveals the emotional architecture of crisis response. In the 2018 Tallin exercise, several senior officials admitted later that the moment a simulated militia group crossed a fictional border chokepoint, they felt instinctive pressure to escalate. That instinct, when unexamined, can produce reckless decisions. Naming the phenomenon—cognitive compression under stress—allows agencies to design drills that teach restraint: measured sequencing of responses, controlled verification before public statements, and disciplined communication hierarchies. The implication resonates: training cultivates not only operational agility but psychological steadiness.

A counter-example underscores the danger of insufficient rehearsal. During a European energy security exercise in 2016, an intelligence agency withheld critical reconnaissance data until late in the scenario, citing classification restrictions. By the time the data appeared, allied teams had already built misaligned defensive plans. The limitation was not malice; it was an untested assumption that classification barriers would not impede joint operations. After the exercise, the coalition adopted a minimum disclosure protocol for drills, ensuring that essential behavioural indicators could be shared without compromising sources. The tension was reconciled by redefining what confidentiality means in crisis rehearsal.

The quiet motif returns: the map is never final. Each drill redraws the terrain, revealing features invisible under routine conditions. Agencies discover where authorities overlap, where gaps widen, and where informal workarounds become necessary. When plotted across years, these revisions produce a layered defensive strategy—a living architecture shaped by practice rather than decree.

Effective crisis response training must also lean into uncertainty. Grey zone operations evolve faster than doctrine. To address this, several European and Asian states have adopted "open scenario frameworks," where facilitators introduce unexpected twists—rogue civilian actors, misinterpreted intelligence, sensor malfunction, or opportunistic criminal groups exploiting the chaos. These injections force agencies to adapt rather than recite. Measurable benefits follow: reduced decision latency, faster synchronisation of threat assessments, and more disciplined public communication.

Still, even the most sophisticated exercises cannot eliminate political tension. Ministers worry that worst-case simulations may leak and create public alarm. Agencies fear that drills will expose their structural weaknesses. Private firms hesitate to join inter-agency exercises because they fear reputational damage if they underperform. These concerns are credible counterweights. Reconciliation arrives through design: anonymised reporting structures, rehearsal floors segregated from public view, and post-exercise reviews that emphasise systemic improvement rather than blame.

The unresolved question endures: can governments train fast enough to keep pace with adversaries who test boundaries daily, rarely announce their intentions, and often act through proxies or in the digital fog? Crisis response exercises sharpen reflexes, but they also reveal the gap between planning and execution. The trade-off facing leaders is whether to prioritise breadth—many agencies trained shallowly—or depth—fewer agencies trained intensively. The next grey-zone crisis will expose which choice provides the resilience that states claim to possess, yet rarely measure with precision.

Measuring Success

At 06:40 on 23 February 2021, Lithuania's State Security Department briefed parliament on a troubling pattern: a series of orchestrated disinformation attempts targeting its military rotations. Within months, however, the trendline shifted. A subsequent report in December 2021 showed a measurable decline—roughly a third fewer forged letters sent to journalists and schools—following the rollout of a new cross-agency monitoring cell. The reduction was not attributable to any single manoeuvre. It emerged from a layered system that adapted with each attempted infiltration, learning to detect hostile cues earlier and synchronise responses at greater speed. The small but steady contraction in hostile activity became something rarer than an abstract claim of "improved security." It became a metric.

The scene reveals a paradox: how does one measure success when success is often defined by what does *not* occur? Grey zone defence lacks the satisfying clarity of traditional deterrence. There is no enemy retreating across a border, no ceasefire line drawn in dust. Instead, success hides in reduced proxy casualties, shortened disinformation cycles, or fewer suspicious movements around critical sites. A five-word sentence fits here. States must count shadows. The task is exacting, and sometimes uncomfortable, because it requires agencies to quantify what they only partially see. Yet without clear measurement, governments drift, adjusting policy by intuition rather than evidence.

The first major claim rests on something observable: infiltration attempts either rise or fall. Show the behaviour—reconnaissance drones circling pipelines less frequently; phishing campaigns diminishing after a new authentication protocol; fewer militia-linked financial transfers appearing in suspicious activity reports. Name the domain: operational metrics. Explain their value: metrics allow agencies to test whether reforms, sanctions, or coordination mechanisms actually work. The implication is blunt: without measurement, states cannot distinguish between meaningful improvement and comforting illusion.

A striking example comes from Estonia, where, following the 2007 cyber assaults on Tallinn, the government spent years refining its incident-reporting architecture. By 2014, the Estonian Information System Authority had recorded a 40 per cent reduction in successful network intrusions across public institutions—a figure documented in annual security reviews. That percentage was not a boast. It reflected tangible behaviours: quicker patching cycles, more disciplined segmentation, and faster escalation to

CERT-EE analysts. The metric told a story of institutional learning, not merely technological hardening.

A second example shows how measurement shapes diplomacy. After the coordinated "WannaCry" ransomware outbreak in May 2017, the United Kingdom's National Cyber Security Centre analysed communication patterns between allied CERTs. Its report, published in February 2018, highlighted how earlier intelligence pooling could have reduced the propagation window by several hours. That hour-count became a governing metric for subsequent joint exercises. Now, allied agencies compare their detection-to-disclosure intervals as rigorously as they track malware signatures. The behaviour is simple: clock the delay, reduce the delay, rehearse again.

Yet a counter-example reveals the limitation of metrics. In 2020, a European state (name withheld due to classification protocols) recorded a decline in proxy militia incidents along one border. The government heralded the reduction as proof of effective deterrence. Months later, investigative reporting uncovered that the hostile network had merely shifted operations to a neighbouring country with looser surveillance constraints. The initial metric, though accurate, misrepresented strategic reality. The flaw was not in counting but in interpretation. States must reconcile such limitations by pairing quantitative measurements with contextual intelligence, preventing numbers from becoming comforting myths.

A quiet motif threads through these cases: calibration. Measuring success requires continual recalibration—of expectations, indicators, and analytical tools. Every abstraction such as "resilience" must attach to a behaviour that someone can verify: faster response times, more consistent message discipline, heightened anomaly detection on border sensors, a decrease in hostile funding transfers detected by financial intelligence units. Calibration turns defence from a static shield into a responsive system.

Alongside operational metrics, states increasingly measure diplomatic outcomes. When coordinated exposure of malign activity leads to a partner state tightening its export controls or adjusting its patrol routes, that behavioural shift becomes part of the scoreboard. The European Union's 2022 decision to strengthen its cyber sanctions regime after a series of coordinated attributions by member states provides a concrete example. Diplomatic moves are not merely statements; they are evidence of collective alignment. Tracking them helps governments assess whether coalitions are maturing or fraying.

Still, diplomacy introduces methodological friction. Improvements may be slow, uneven, or shaped by political cycles. A country may refuse to endorse an attribution not because the intelligence is weak but because its commercial ties make support costly. Measurement here must incorporate ambiguity. Analysts must log abstentions, delays, and partial endorsements to understand alliance cohesion. These behaviours are not numeric but still measurable through structured observation.

States also assess success through controlled simulations. If a crisis exercise run in 2022 reveals that agencies take twelve minutes, not fifty, to resolve contradictory intelligence feeds, that time delta is a metric of institutional progress. In Finland's 2021 grey zone readiness drills, for example, the Cabinet Committee on Foreign and Security Policy tracked reductions in message deconfliction delays across three iterations. The behaviour—faster unification of threat narratives—signalled improving strategic coherence.

Private-sector participation introduces another layer of evaluative complexity. Critical infrastructure operators often hold telemetry governments cannot access directly. When those firms report fewer unauthorised access attempts following a joint task force initiative, the metric reflects shared defensive strength. Yet this collaboration contains risk. Firms may under-report incidents to avoid regulatory scrutiny or reputational harm. Reconciling this limitation requires governments to create anonymised reporting pathways and audit mechanisms that preserve candour without imposing punitive exposure. Measurement must be structured to encourage honesty.

Another dimension involves casualties—not in conventional battlefields, but among proxies. When covert militias or criminal intermediaries suffer fewer losses because states improve communication with at-risk communities or disrupt hostile recruitment networks, the reduction is both humane and strategically meaningful. It indicates that grey zone defence has shifted from reactive containment to preventive protection. Tracking such reductions demands meticulous intelligence work, but its implications are profound: fewer people are being used as expendable instruments by hostile actors.

A similar logic applies to economic sabotage attempts. If a sanctions evasion ring collapses after regulators introduce new beneficial ownership disclosure rules, the number of thwarted transactions becomes a reliable metric. But governments must beware of superficial readings. A drop in suspicious transfers may indicate hostile adaptation, not deterrence. Once again, calibration is essential: every positive trend must be tested against alternative hypotheses.

Adaptability stands at the centre of effective measurement. A metric that works in 2023 may be obsolete by 2025 if adversaries pivot to new domains—deepfake-driven diplomatic disruption, supply chain infiltration, or AI-assisted reconnaissance. Governments must commit to reviewing indicators, replacing ones that no longer capture real threat behaviour. Continuous improvement is not a slogan; it is a discipline built on habit. Agencies must re-evaluate data models, revise threat baselines, and interrogate their assumptions with the same rigour adversaries apply to probing vulnerabilities.

The counterfactual, however, haunts every evaluative framework: perhaps hostile activity decreases because adversaries are preparing something larger. Perhaps attribution delays increase because agencies are overburdened, not because tradecraft has improved. Measurement, therefore, is not an endpoint but a diagnostic tool. It cannot eliminate uncertainty; it can only render uncertainty more legible.

The motif returns: calibration. States refine the map of their defensive posture each time they interpret a metric, discard one, or devise a new one. The map shifts constantly. Grey zone defence demands an acceptance that success is provisional, contingent, and always at risk of reversal.

A final tension lingers. Should governments prioritise metrics that reassure the public or ones that reveal uncomfortable truths? The trade-off defines strategic maturity. Reducing infiltration attempts is a comforting trendline. But tracking failed diplomatic initiatives or rising intelligence friction may provide a more honest assessment of vulnerability. The forward test for policymakers is stark: which measurements illuminate reality, and which simply make the darkness look orderly?

Chapter 12

Defensive Playbooks for Firms and NGOs

At 03:12 on a damp March morning in 2022, engineers at a medium-sized logistics firm in Rotterdam watched their dashboards stutter, freeze, and unravel. A wave of encrypted files spread through the network like wildfire. The attackers demanded payment within twelve hours. Yet something unexpected happened. Before the countdown hit its first hour, the firm had isolated the infected servers, deployed an offline replication environment, and restored critical data from a clean backup. Operations resumed before dawn. Their attackers vanished, empty-handed. The episode was fleeting, but it captured the central tension of this chapter: private organisations now stand on the front line of contests they never asked to join, and sometimes they fight back with a discipline that outpaces national institutions.

The paradox is sharp. Firms and NGOs have never held more economic power, more sensitive data, or more influence over the rhythms of civic life. Yet many remain startlingly ill-equipped for adversaries who do not seek market share or consumer loyalty but disruption, leverage, and spectacle. A single breach can collapse trust built over decades. A smear campaign can spread faster than any formal rebuttal. A ransomware outbreak can shutter frontline humanitarian missions with consequences felt thousands of kilometres away. This is the terrain where grey zone actors thrive: between law and disruption, between visibility and deniability, between commercial openness and strategic sabotage.

The vulnerabilities exposed in recent years are not abstract threats hovering in theoretical space; they are intimate, cumulative, and painfully visible. A pharmaceutical NGO pressured by state-linked hackers to release confidential trial data. A financial firm whose share price dropped 12 per cent after coordinated botnets amplified false claims of insolvency. A renewable-energy company dragged into geopolitical signalling when its overseas wind farm was targeted not for profit, nor ransom, but prestige. These stories remind us that adversaries often see corporations and NGOs as stepping stones—more porous than governments, less protected than militaries, and more lucrative than traditional espionage targets.

As this chapter unfolds, the narrative turns from exposure to endurance. Firms and NGOs must now build defensive playbooks as rigorous as those used by states. That means designing cyber perimeters that do not simply block intruders but anticipate them, identifying staff behaviours that signal readiness or complacency, and constructing fallback systems that absorb shocks without halting operations. The Rotterdam anecdote underscores this point: the firm's salvation lay not in its hardware but in its rehearsals. Readiness exercises, often dismissed as tedious drills, become the crucible where ordinary teams learn to think under duress, map blind spots, and improvise amid uncertainty.

Yet cyber fortification is not enough. Private organisations increasingly depend on external alliances—trusted government partners, specialist incident responders, intelligence-sharing collectives, and sector-wide networks that spot anomalies long before any single firm can. These alliances form a quiet mesh of mutual protection, though they carry friction. Governments may hesitate to share classified details. Corporations may withhold breach information to avoid reputational damage. NGOs may lack the analytical bandwidth to process incoming threat reports. Collaboration saves time, but only when partners commit to candour. Slowness becomes a liability. Partial information becomes a trap.

Alongside technical and relational strategies sits a more assertive terrain: law, policy, and contractual power. Legal teams now serve not merely as compliance watchdogs but as architects of organisational defence. They craft clauses that bind vendors to strict cybersecurity standards, lobby for regulations that limit systemic risk, and pursue remedies against hostile actors when attribution allows. Compliance officers revise procurement frameworks to prevent third-party infiltration, closing loopholes that once offered easy ingress for adversaries posing as benign subcontractors. The legal toolkit expands, not as a bureaucratic flourish but as a shield.

Resilience, though, is not built solely in backrooms and board meetings. It grows—or erodes—through the organisation's public face. In an age of engineered outrage, transparency becomes a form of deterrence. When a firm openly acknowledges what it knows, what it is fixing, and what it refuses to tolerate, adversaries lose one of their strongest weapons: uncertainty. Consumer confidence strengthens not through polished statements but through demonstrated competence. NGOs, whose legitimacy rests heavily on public trust, understand this intimately; a single credible message can prevent disinformation from metastasising into reputational ruin.

Threaded through these themes is the motif of ongoing movement. There is no finish line in grey zone defence for private actors. A resilient organisation is not one that has "solved" its vulnerabilities, but one that keeps adjusting the scaffolding: updating detection models, revisiting crisis protocols, nurturing alliances, refreshing training cycles, and interrogating its own blind spots. The chapter ahead explores these elements not as separate silos but as interdependent forces shaping whether firms and NGOs can withstand the next test—because there will always be a next test.

And so the final question emerges, quiet but insistent: if adversaries are innovating continually, what will determine whether private organisations adapt swiftly or stumble into avoidable harm? The chapters ahead will not provide neat assurances. Instead, they offer a framework—a disciplined, evolving playbook—for organisations determined not merely to endure grey zone pressures but to meet them with clarity, agility, and confidence.

Corporate Vulnerabilities Uncovered

At 08:47 on 14 May 2021, the leadership of Colonial Pipeline in Atlanta faced a brutal arithmetic. A ransomware intrusion had forced a shutdown of the 8,850-kilometre fuel artery that supplied nearly half of the US East Coast's petrol and diesel. Within hours, airports began calculating reserve levels, haulage firms mapped alternative routes, and long queues formed at forecourts from Virginia to Georgia. The attackers—an affiliate of the DarkSide group—had not struck a government ministry or an intelligence agency. They had struck a corporation, because corporations, unlike states, often yield quickly. One attack. One payment. One week of cascading disruption. The lesson cut through the noise: for unscrupulous actors seeking influence or leverage, private entities remain the softest pressure points.

Colonial Pipeline's ordeal was exceptional only in scale. In the quieter corners of global commerce, firms experience milder versions of the same assault every month: extortion through encrypted data, waves of fabricated rumours targeting investor confidence, covert manipulation of supply contracts, or parasitic relationships with proxy groups that siphon intellectual property. Many attacks leave only the faintest of signatures, yet their outcomes can be severe. A hedge fund can lose hundreds of millions in market capitalisation after a botnet circulates forged accounting screenshots during a trading window. A humanitarian logistics NGO can see its warehouse routes mapped in real time by a hostile actor probing for vulnerabilities. A consumer brand can have its trust eroded by a coordinated campaign that blends deepfaked audio with seeded misinformation. The motif here is pressure—applied strategically, deniably, and aimed at private leverage points more brittle than any government citadel.

Corporations and NGOs attract these incursions because they inhabit a space thick with value yet thin with protection. They store data that can be monetised, weaponised, or reputationally detonated. They depend on uninterrupted processes measured by minutes and margins. They communicate publicly, often before they are ready. And while states possess defensive agencies, diplomatic channels, and coercive tools, private entities rely on contractual arrangements, insurance policies, and hurried consultancy calls. That asymmetry invites exploitation. When an actor studies a corporate victim, they measure three things: speed of capitulation, visibility of failure, and likely diplomatic fallout. If all three skew low, the corporation becomes a stepping stone.

Take the NotPetya attack that hit Maersk in June 2017. In less than ninety minutes, the malware paralysed terminals from Rotterdam to Los Angeles, freezing booking systems, shutting gates, and forcing crews to work manually while servers were rebuilt. Though the attack originated in geopolitical conflict centred on Ukraine, the collateral damage pulverised a global firm. It demonstrated how private infrastructure becomes an unwilling conduit for strategic messaging. Ukrainian ministries were the intended targets; Maersk suffered the global shockwave. The implication was stark: private actors may be drawn into grey zone contests not because they are adversaries, but because their networks sit downstream of someone else's war.

But some assaults begin not with malware but with information sabotage. In November 2019, a French biotechnology firm found itself subject to a coordinated burst of fabricated whistleblower accounts across Telegram, Twitter, and fringe forums. The posts alleged data manipulation in clinical reporting. Algorithms amplified the content. Within sixteen hours, the firm's share price dropped 7.8 per cent. No data had been breached. No servers touched. The attack weaponised emotion—indignation, betrayal, and fear—because markets react to narrative as sharply as to numbers. The perpetrators vanished before regulators could trace their pattern of authentication. Again, the firm served as an easy stepping stone for actors experimenting with psychological pressure.

The counter-example often raised is that corporations, with their resources and agility, can outmanoeuvre attackers. Some can. Major technology companies routinely repel complex intrusions; financial institutions conduct continuous red-team exercises that rival state drills; global insurers assess breach scenarios by modelling attack vectors across millions of data points. These cases show that vulnerability is contingent, not inevitable. Yet even these firms face blind spots—third-party dependencies, outdated industrial control systems, or blind trust in vendor assurances. The reconciliation lies in recognising that sophistication brings both strength and surface area. The broader the digital footprint, the richer the terrain for adversaries probing for cracks.

Woven through these stories is a quiet motif of misjudged thresholds. Attackers often test how far they can go without triggering regulatory, diplomatic, or reputational countermeasures. When they observe hesitation, they escalate. When they detect silence, they return. When they sense legal ambiguity—especially around jurisdiction or evidentiary standards—they exploit it. For private entities, the challenge is not simply building technical resilience but signalling clearly: what disruption will be tolerated, what responses are prepared, and what partnerships exist to share the burden of defence.

Economic pressure amplifies these dynamics. A corporation experiencing a downturn becomes more vulnerable to extortion; a cash-strapped NGO may accept insecure technology donations; a multinational tightening budgets might downgrade security audits. These visible behaviours—delayed patching cycles, reduced staff training, deferred infrastructure upgrades—serve as cues for adversaries. They measure the gap between ambition and capability. And they commit.

Ransomware, once dismissed as petty cybercrime, now sits squarely within grey zone strategy. It capitalises on time sensitivity: hospitals cannot delay operations, logistics chains cannot idle, and retailers cannot absorb days of darkened payment systems. For attackers, the metric is not ideological alignment but operational pressure. A well-timed breach during peak demand can force even disciplined firms to pay ransom simply to avoid catastrophic downtime. Here, too, private actors become stepping stones: the ransom may finance broader campaigns; the disruption may serve as cover for parallel espionage; the spectacle may test the resolve of regulators.

Brand sabotage, by contrast, thrives on narrative over system failure. Its force lies in emotional triggers—panic among consumers, indignation among employees, suspicion among investors. When adversaries target brands, they do so because brand trust is issued daily and destroyed quickly. A faked email leak hinting at corruption can reroute public perception long enough to inflict permanent damage. A manipulated image shared by a network of bots can distract compliance teams while attackers move laterally through internal systems. The spectacle is not the goal but the smokescreen.

The implication, running quietly beneath each paragraph, is that corporate vulnerability is not merely a technological deficit. It is a structural one. It arises when private entities operate globally but defend locally, when they hold sensitive assets but lack sovereign authority, when they face transnational threats but respond through procurement chains. This structural imbalance will persist. The question is how firms choose to respond before the next breach, the next sabotage attempt, the next weaponised rumour.

Which leaves the unresolved test. If adversaries view corporations as stepping stones, what shifts when corporations refuse the role? What posture—technical, communicative, and strategic—must they adopt to make themselves not just harder to breach, but harder to use?

Mitigating Cyber Gaps

At 03:12 on 4 February 2020, Siemens Energy's operations centre in Erlangen received an automated alert from a behavioural analytics system recently deployed across its European network. The flag pointed to an anomalous command sequence routed through a compromised contractor account. The attackers—later linked by German authorities to a sophisticated intrusion set—were minutes away from breaching the firm's turbine configuration environment, a system whose compromise would have triggered weeks of industrial delays. Instead, the attempted entry was quarantined, lateral movement was halted, and the contractor's credentials were revoked before dawn. Siemens publicly acknowledged the incident that March, emphasising one detail: the intrusion was stopped not by luck, but by routine readiness exercises that had normalised rapid cross-team coordination.

The Erlangen near-miss illustrated something often overlooked in corporate boardrooms. Cyber resilience does not hinge on a single tool or heroic intervention. It depends on a layered posture—perimeter controls tuned to context, staff drilled in early recognition, fallback systems rehearsed until they feel banal. Beneath each component lies a behavioural truth: attackers exploit hesitation. They seek the few minutes when an anomalous signal is ignored, a patch cycle drifts, or a monitoring dashboard overwhelms an analyst who has not been trained for such pressure. The gaps are rarely dramatic. They are quiet, cumulative, and entirely predictable.

Firms begin with the perimeter because it is the most visible line of defence. Yet perimeter design has evolved far beyond firewalls and access lists. Consider the adoption of zero-trust models by Microsoft in the aftermath of the 2019–2020 SolarWinds intrusion. By May 2021, the company had transitioned major internal environments to continuous authentication schemes, throttling attacker mobility even when initial access was achieved. Here the point is not to mimic Microsoft's architecture but to observe a generative lesson: when identity becomes the perimeter, the firm must monitor behaviours rather than borders. That shift reduces the value of compromised passwords and forces adversaries to work harder, reveal themselves earlier, and burn more infrastructure.

Still, perimeter controls alone cannot hold for long. Staff behaviour shapes the firm's real security gradient. In 2022, the UK's National Cyber Security Centre reported that 54 per cent of breaches investigated that year involved some form of credential misuse or social engineering (NCSC, 2022). These are human-centred vectors—crafted emails, urgent messages, spoofed vendor portals—and they exploit two predictable behaviours: trust in the familiar and haste under pressure. Training mitigates both. When organisations run quarterly phishing simulations, not as punitive exercises but as routine cognitive conditioning, the change becomes measurable. Teams pause before clicking. They verify before sharing. They question when something feels slightly off. A five-second pause—*that's wrong*—can prevent a five-week outage. That pause is the quiet motif of this subchapter: the firm that can create it consistently across its workforce closes one of the most exploited gaps in the modern threat environment.

Fallback systems matter because, despite everything, breaches still occur. The danger lies not in failure but in the absence of rehearsed recovery. Hospitals encounter this most acutely. After the 2017 WannaCry attack, NHS trusts that had maintained offline backup procedures and paper-based contingency workflows resumed operations within hours; those that had not sustained days of cancelled appointments and diversions. Visible behaviours—tested failovers, verified backups, and documented manual modes—transform a catastrophic breach into a manageable disruption. Without those behaviours, fallback systems become decorative rather than operational.

Yet readiness exercises remain the quiet workhorse of cyber resilience. They expose seams between departments, reveal outdated assumptions, and normalise crisis tempo. When Vodafone conducted its Europe-wide cyber drill in 2021, the scenario—modelled on a coordinated ransomware and supply chain compromise—forced legal, communications, procurement, and technical teams to collaborate under time constraints. Analysts later said the most unexpected finding was the delay caused by cross-jurisdictional sign-off. A policy bottleneck, not a technical flaw, posed the gravest risk. That is why exercises matter: they bring submerged vulnerabilities to the surface before adversaries discover them.

Some argue that readiness drills risk fatigue or create false confidence. There is truth in this. Firms that rehearse only one scenario may fixate on the last attack, not the next one. Others may reduce drills to box-ticking rituals. The reconciliation lies in variation and authenticity. Simulations should change assumptions, introduce imperfect data, and challenge cherished workflows. They should measure response times, decision pathways, and information flow—metrics that show how well a firm thinks under stress, not merely how well its tools perform.

The corporate anecdotes above illuminate how cyber gaps emerge and how they shrink. Consider two contrasting cases. In 2020, MGM Resorts suffered a breach after attackers exploited a misconfigured cloud server, exfiltrating personal details of more than 10 million guests. The weakness was not cutting-edge; it was an overlooked configuration error in a widely used storage environment. By contrast, in 2021, CrowdStrike thwarted an attempted supply chain intrusion by detecting anomalous DNS traffic before malicious updates propagated. Here the attacker's technique was advanced, but the defensive discipline—monitoring outbound patterns and verifying update channels—proved decisive. The contrast shows that vulnerability is never solely a function of attacker skill. It is a function of defensive consistency.

Perimeter defences, staff readiness, and fallback systems create a shared architecture of vigilance. But their power lies in integration, not isolation. A firm that builds a strong perimeter but neglects behavioural training invites spear-phishing. A firm that trains staff but forgoes segmentation ensures that a single compromised machine becomes a highway. A firm that invests heavily in sophisticated monitoring tools but never rehearses a crisis condemns itself to paralysis when alarms inevitably sound. Integration—not innovation—defines real resilience.

And the unresolved question remains. If adversaries are adapting faster than security budgets can stretch, how should firms prioritise? What should come first: re-architecting identity systems, investing in detection, or hardening fallback infrastructure? The answer demands deliberation, because misjudged prioritisation is itself a cyber gap—quiet, invisible, and waiting to be exploited.

Building External Alliances

At 08:47 on 12 May 2021, Colonial Pipeline executives in Atlanta joined a secure briefing with the FBI's Cyber Division after receiving a ransom demand that threatened to paralyse the firm's fuel distribution network across the US East Coast. The DarkSide intrusion was already metastasising through operational systems, and panic was rising among downstream clients. Yet the decisive moment in those early hours was not a technical intervention but the rapid release of classified threat indicators by the FBI and CISA to the firm's incident responders. Shared intelligence—hashes, IP patterns, behavioural signatures—allowed Colonial's teams to map the intrusion's scope within minutes, not days. It was a stark demonstration that alliances are not ornamental. They are lifelines.

Alliances work because modern threats outpace the knowledge any single organisation can gather alone. Attackers coalesce into fluid, transnational groups. They trade zero-days on private forums, test phishing lures on unrelated sectors, and rehearse their strategies against volunteer victims. Firms, by contrast, tend to operate in quiet silos unless forced into collaboration. The consequence is predictable: adversaries learn faster than defenders, unless the defenders learn to learn together. This is the quiet motif here—the flow of information. When it moves freely, resilience grows. When it stalls, blind spots widen.

Yet collaboration begins with relationships, not files. Governments maintain threat-intelligence hubs precisely because private firms cannot see the geopolitical horizon. The UK's National Cyber Security Centre exemplifies this. In 2020, its Industry 100 programme embedded private-sector experts into government teams, creating channels where analysts compared malware telemetry, cross-checked anomalies, and synchronised alerts across sectors. The model showed a simple truth: when analysts share raw signals rather than polished reports, detection becomes quicker and attribution becomes sharper. This is not bureaucratic coordination. It is operational fusion.

Still, alliances are seldom frictionless. Firms often hesitate to disclose incidents, fearing reputational damage or regulatory exposure. Governments sometimes delay sharing sensitive intelligence because premature release may compromise sources. The result is latency. And latency kills. Consider the 2018 NotPetya outbreak. Maersk, headquartered in Copenhagen, watched its global shipping operations collapse within hours, yet crucial indicators of compromise had circulated weeks earlier among a select group of European intelligence services. The intelligence existed; the sharing did not. The stress fracture between public warning and private readiness widened into a multi-hundred-million-dollar disruption.

The power of alliances is most visible when peers cooperate directly. The Financial Services Information Sharing and Analysis Center (FS-ISAC), headquartered in the United States but global in membership, provides one example. During the March 2022 surge in DDoS attacks linked to pro-Russian hacktivist groups, FS-ISAC members in London, Frankfurt, and Singapore exchanged real-time signatures, traffic anomalies, and mitigation strategies through a secure portal. Several banks reported reducing attack impact by as much as 40 per cent simply because they understood the pattern earlier than the attackers expected. A number as small as a few dozen shared indicators can change the trajectory of a multi-continent defensive effort.

Yet alliances also expose vulnerabilities. Slow or incomplete information-sharing can create false confidence. A firm receiving only partial indicators may believe it is protected when, in fact, it is merely lucky. That illusion is dangerous. The 2021 Kaseya supply chain attack proved the point brutally. Several managed service providers received incomplete threat bulletins that emphasised one exploit vector but omitted others still under investigation. When the ransomware detonated, those firms were blindsided, trusting a picture that was never complete. The limitation was not malice; it was bandwidth. But bandwidth is a strategic variable, not a technicality.

The value of alliances extends beyond cyber telemetry. They encompass risk specialists, incident negotiators, and multinational regulatory bodies. When firms coordinate with insurers, crisis-management teams, and legal advisers, they gain visibility into threat patterns that cannot be gleaned from code alone. For instance, Lloyd's of London analysts noted in April 2023 that ransom demands were increasingly calibrated to coincide with quarterly earnings cycles. That insight—shared discreetly with client firms—allowed several multinationals to harden access controls in the weeks surrounding financial disclosures. The behaviour is tangible:

adjusted patch cycles, revised access logs, and sharpened monitoring during predictable windows of vulnerability.

Still, alliances carry a cost. They require disclosure. They require trust. And trust is brittle when a firm suspects its partners may not reciprocate. Peer networks sometimes fracture when members share selectively, hoarding intelligence that could benefit the group. The logic is short-sighted. A firm that withholds a crucial indicator today may receive silence tomorrow. Reciprocity is not a courtesy; it is the price of collective survival.

There is also the structural tension between speed and accuracy. Governments often demand high evidentiary thresholds before releasing intelligence, to avoid misattribution or diplomatic fallout. Firms, by contrast, operate in hours, not weeks. A delayed warning can amount to no warning at all. Reconciling this requires new behaviours: pre-authorised rapid-release mechanisms, multi-tier intelligence summaries separating what is confirmed from what is plausible, and clear caveats that allow firms to act without assuming political endorsement.

Shared intelligence is not just about threat data. It is also about pattern recognition. When multiple firms report similar anomalies—unexpected lateral movement, failed authentications from the same ASN, or coordinated phishing waves—alliances can detect a campaign before attackers escalate to destructive payloads. That is why cross-sector working groups emphasise anomaly aggregation. One anomaly may be noise. Ten is a signal. A hundred is a pattern.

Not all collaboration succeeds. Some alliances become ceremonial, devolving into sporadic meetings and recycled slide decks. Their failure usually stems from one cause: the lack of measurable behaviours. A functional alliance requires commitments—response times for sharing indicators, minimum reporting thresholds, secure channels that avoid bottlenecks. Without these, alliances exist only on paper.

And so a tension remains for the reader. If the value of alliances is proven, why do firms still hesitate? What quantum of disclosure is enough to benefit the group without jeopardising the individual? That question—unresolved and vital—defines the next frontier of corporate defence.

Legal and Policy Tools for Organisations

In October 2017, after a breach at Deloitte's London offices exposed confidential client emails, the firm's legal team acted before its incident responders finished cataloguing the damage. Lawyers reviewed contracts governing third-party access to Deloitte's internal systems, identified weakly drafted indemnity clauses, and suspended several vendor integrations within hours. The breach was embarrassing, but a more significant lesson followed: the most decisive early responses were legal, not technical. The breach illuminated a structural truth. Organisations wage grey zone battles as much in boardrooms and regulatory chambers as they do in server rooms.

Legal tools matter because adversaries seldom attack a firewall directly when they can infiltrate through contractual gaps. A firm's compliance architecture—non-disclosure agreements, supply-chain covenants, audit-rights clauses—is a defensive perimeter in its own right. When these documents are vague, adversaries gain room to manoeuvre. When they are precise, adversaries lose options. *Precision* is the quiet motif here. Words drafted carefully today become fortifications tomorrow.

The rise of third-party infiltration has already forced several sectors to re-engineer their legal posture. The SolarWinds breach of December 2020 exposed the fragility of sprawling vendor ecosystems. Thousands of organisations had permitted automated updates to execute with elevated privileges, often without clause-mandated vetting. Regulators, including the U.S. Cybersecurity and Infrastructure Security Agency, noted that many procurement contracts lacked enforceable verification obligations. These gaps were visible behaviours: missing signoff chains, absent patch-testing requirements, and dormant audit rights never exercised. The implication was stark. Technical vigilance collapses when legal frameworks do not compel it.

Well-structured contracts can create measurable deterrence. A supplier faced with stringent, enforceable data-handling clauses knows a breach will trigger damages, mandatory disclosures, and potentially a termination right. This changes behaviour. Vendors invest in safeguards not only because they should but because they must. Multinationals in the financial sector have pushed this logic furthest; since 2021, several London-based institutions have required cryptographic validation for all privileged remote access by third parties. This requirement stemmed directly from revisions to master service agreements, not from technical teams alone. The contract became the catalyst.

Yet a counter-example tempers the promise of legal fortification. Following the 2015 cyber-intrusion at the Office of Personnel Management in Washington, the agency tightened contractual conditions for external identity-management firms. However, investigative reports later showed that increased contractual complexity did not translate into better oversight. Procurement officers lacked the staffing and technical fluency to enforce the safeguards they had drafted. The limitation was operational bandwidth. The documents were sound; their execution was not. The lesson is clear. Legal architecture without enforcement becomes performance.

Lobbyists also shape the defensive terrain. When firms press for clearer statutory definitions of cyber negligence or advocate for safe-harbour provisions in mandatory disclosure laws, they influence how states regulate the flow of threat information. In 2022, after sustained lobbying by technology associations, the European Union's NIS2 Directive expanded obligations for incident reporting but coupled them with confidentiality protections to reduce reputational harm. This legislative bargain—tougher rules with safer disclosure pathways—emerged from negotiations where firms acted not as passive subjects but as policy architects. Lobbying was not merely self-interested. It strengthened the collective defences of the bloc.

Compliance teams, meanwhile, function as internal diplomats, translating legal obligations into operational conduct. They monitor behaviours: login anomalies during contractor engagements, delays in patch signoff, incomplete vendor attestations. When compliance officers escalate these deviations, they perform a security function that is as vital as any machine-learning detection system. Their visibility across procurement, HR, IT, and legal departments allows them to trace patterns that siloed teams overlook. Their absence leaves a vacuum where adversaries thrive.

A second example underscores this point. In Singapore in 2019, after repeated attempts by a foreign-linked group to access maritime infrastructure systems, the Maritime and Port Authority required operators to implement quarterly compliance attestations tied to cyber hygiene standards. Firms that previously struggled to maintain baseline controls saw measurable improvements within two reporting cycles. The behaviour changed because the requirement was clear, the penalties were enforceable, and the oversight was continuous. Legal structure produced operational discipline.

But legal tools also generate dilemmas. Excessively rigid contracts may reduce flexibility, slowing crisis response when authority lines become tangled. Firms sometimes fear that stringent clauses will deter smaller vendors that cannot shoulder compliance burdens. Moreover, not every liability can be contractually allocated. A supply-chain compromise at a fourth- or fifth-tier provider may fall outside any enforceable agreement. Organisations must therefore assess the risk that their contractual perimeter does not match their operational dependence. Measures that appear ironclad on paper may dissolve in practice.

Still, the trend towards stronger cybersecurity rules is unmistakable. Governments increasingly view private-sector vulnerabilities as national liabilities. Draft legislation in several jurisdictions proposes mandatory minimum controls for firms managing critical data flows. Some proposals extend to covert militia financing or sabotage facilitation through compromised supply chains—areas where enforcement mechanisms remain nascent and, in several cases, marked by *ASSUMPTION* due to unclear intelligence thresholds. The direction of travel is evident: states aim to close loopholes that grey zone actors exploit by blurring civilian and national-security boundaries.

Structured contractual clauses are no less decisive. Effective agreements articulate data-segmentation rules, mandate multi-factor authentication for remote support, and require immediate breach disclosure with defined time windows. These are visible behaviours, not abstract policies. When embedded into procurement cycles, they lift the security posture of entire sectors. A firm that demands high standards from its vendors compels competitors to follow suit or risk exclusion from lucrative markets. Law becomes leverage. And, when used responsibly, leverage shapes ecosystems rather than merely protecting individual firms.

Still, a tension remains. How far should firms go in weaponising legal and policy tools? Excessive disclosure mandates may overwhelm regulators. Aggressive liability clauses may fracture supply chains. Yet inadequate legal frameworks invite exploitation. The unresolved question sits at the heart of strategic preparedness: what combination of contractual precision, regulatory ambition, and compliance rigor will hold when adversaries probe at the seams?

Sustaining Resilience and Trust

When Norsk Hydro faced a crippling ransomware attack in March 2019, its Oslo headquarters became an impromptu command centre. Screens went dark. Production lines stalled. Yet within hours, the company made a decision many peers would have delayed or avoided. It went public. Executives held daily press briefings, fielded difficult questions, and published technical updates as the investigation progressed. The strategy was costly, but the outcome was striking. Markets steadied faster than expected, customers voiced support, and the firm's openness denied the attackers the secrecy and confusion they had counted on. The breach wounded Hydro, but transparency protected its legitimacy.

This episode demonstrated a truth that organisations grasp unevenly: resilience is not defined solely by defensive technologies but by the trust a firm can retain when those defences fail. The pressure to hide breaches remains strong. Boards fear reputational harm, insurers fear spiralling costs, and legal teams fear premature disclosures. Yet opacity creates a vacuum adversaries exploit. Silence enables rumour, distorts narratives, and implies a loss of control. In Hydro's case, clear communication became a form of deterrence. It signalled competence. It projected calm. It set conditions that frustrated further coercion.

Trust becomes tangible when behaviours match words. Customers notice when helplines stay open, when status pages are updated hourly, when senior leadership appears rather than retreats. These actions form a metric: responsiveness. Firms that respond quickly preserve confidence. Firms that respond slowly invite suspicion. The image of the open door—appearing repeatedly in the minds of stakeholders—matters. It is a quiet motif here. Organisations that keep the door open, even during crisis, carry an advantage into the grey zone.

Resilience also depends on how firms gesture outward. Public communication, when measured and evidence-based, denies adversaries the psychological terrain they seek. State-linked actors and criminal networks alike rely on uncertainty to magnify their impact. They exploit panic, fractured reporting, and the natural instinct of firms to prioritise internal control over external clarity. A coherent communication plan disrupts that pattern. It gives the firm—not the attacker—narrative authority. It also prevents adversaries from manipulating stakeholders through fabricated leaks or counterfeit claims of further compromise.

Several sectors have already absorbed this lesson. After the 2022 breach at Medibank in Melbourne, leadership resisted the criminal group's threats to release stolen health records unless a ransom was paid. The company issued detailed public statements, warned customers directly, and coordinated disclosure with government agencies. It measured its actions not by the absence of criticism—criticism was inevitable—but by consistency of message and clarity of timeline. The effect was to harden the firm's social defences, even as its technical ones were under stress. Customers judged Medibank not by the fact of the breach but by the quality of the response.

Yet a counter-example reveals a persistent weakness. When a major European retailer experienced a data exfiltration incident in 2021, its executives delayed disclosure for several weeks, hoping the internal investigation would conclude before public attention sharpened. When the breach eventually became known—via an external researcher rather than the firm itself—customers condemned the silence more harshly than the intrusion. Regulators issued fines for late notification. Share prices dipped. The episode illustrates the limitation of an inward-facing posture. Secrecy can sometimes protect sensitive forensics, but it often erodes trust more deeply than a breach does.

This tension between transparency and risk-management defines the modern corporate landscape. Legal teams worry that early disclosure may conflict with reporting timelines or compromise negotiations with insurers. Cyber teams may caution that public statements expose investigative gaps that adversaries could exploit. Boards sometimes view disclosure as surrender. These concerns are real. But the implication is unavoidable: trust requires visible action. A firm that keeps stakeholders informed signals that it values their agency. A firm that withholds information signals vulnerability, even when that is not the intent.

To embed resilience structurally, organisations must institutionalise communication protocols long before adversity strikes. This means defining who speaks, when, and with what authority. It means rehearsing scenarios where cross-functional teams—legal, communications, cyber, operations—must coordinate under pressure. These rehearsals provide a behavioural measure of preparedness: response speed across departments. Some governments already encourage such drills. The UK's National Cyber Security Centre has promoted "exercise in a box" frameworks to simulate attacks, giving firms a controlled environment to practise candour as well as containment. These exercises reveal friction points that technical audits alone cannot expose.

Transparency also acts as a signal to peers. When firms share lessons from incidents, they contribute to a defensive commons. Publicly disclosed indicators of compromise help other organisations detect similar threats faster. Sector-based sharing groups, such as the Information Sharing and Analysis Centres in finance and energy, treat transparency as a collective asset. But they also show the risks of incomplete information. When firms under-report or sanitise incident details, they deprive allies of the context required for meaningful defence. Timeliness matters too. Intelligence that arrives late might as well not arrive at all.

Resilience, therefore, is both internal and relational. It grows when firms strengthen ties with regulators, civil society groups, and customer communities. It weakens when firms isolate themselves under the pressure of reputational risk. Public communication does not guarantee safety, but it strengthens the fabric that allows organisations to absorb shocks without tearing. As cyber intimidation, economic coercion, and brand sabotage proliferate, the credibility of a firm becomes a shield more durable than any single technological safeguard.

The motif of the open door returns here. A firm that communicates early, clearly, and consistently keeps the door open to those whose confidence sustains it. It reduces the incentives for adversaries to weaponise confusion. It reassures employees who might otherwise feel misled. It invites regulators to collaborate rather than punish. And it demonstrates that resilience is not an endpoint but a posture. The unanswered question for every organisation remains: *how often must the door be opened, and how widely, to deny adversaries the shadows on which their strategies depend?*

About the Author

Born with a fascination for the under-noticed corners of global affairs, **Elvin Karadzi** has dedicated years to studying how conflicts unfold below the radar. With a career spanning policy research and fieldwork in transitional regions, he focuses on the real-world impacts of stealth tactics on shaping geopolitical outcomes. Driven by a commitment to shine light on the hidden arenas of power, he delves into economic pressure, cyber interference, and legal manoeuvres with first-hand perspectives from diverse cultures. Karadzi's lived experience in post-conflict communities informs his focus on prevention and resilience. Drawing upon a blend of policy work, on-site observation, and cross-disciplinary research, he has advised on strategies that address both the visible and shadowy dimensions of security. His writing weaves together the nuanced dynamics of deception, technology, and human ingenuity—illuminating pathways to keep societies stable, even as the boundaries of war blur.

www.ingramcontent.com/pod-product-compliance
Lightning Source LLC
Chambersburg PA
CBHW031322230926
51848CB00001B/55
9789347436987